the thing is...

DAVE FANNING

the thing is...

with Ian Gittins

Collins

First published in 2010 by Collins

HarperCollins*Publishers*
77–85 Fulham Palace Road
London W6 8JB

www.harpercollins.co.uk

13 12 11 10
9 8 7 6 5 4 3 2 1

Ian Gittins is a music journalist for the *Guardian* who has written for a raft of newspapers and magazines, including the *New York Times*, *Independent*, *Q* and *Melody Maker*. He is the co-author, with Mötley Crüe's Nikki Sixx, of *The Heroin Diaries: A Year in the Life of a Shattered Rock Star*. Ian lives in London.

All photographs courtesy of the author with the exception of the following:
Picture section 1: p4, bottom, © Colm Henry
Picture section 2: p2, middle, © Amelia Stein; p6, top,
© Edmund Ross Studios; p7, bottom right, © Mark O'Sullivan

A catalogue record for this book is
available from the British Library

ISBN: 978-0-00-731076-0

Printed and bound in Great Britain by
Clays Ltd, St Ives plc

Mixed Sources
Product group from well-managed
forests and other controlled sources
www.fsc.org Cert no. SW-COC-001806
© 1996 Forest Stewardship Council

FSC is a non-profit international organisation established to promote the responsible management of the world's forests. Products carrying the FSC label are independently certified to assure consumers that they come from forests that are managed to meet the social, economic and ecological needs of present and future generations.

Find out more about HarperCollins and the environment at
www.harpercollins.co.uk/green

For Annie and Barney

ACKNOWLEDGEMENTS

Thanks to everyone I've met and am still meeting along the way. To John Masterson for getting the ball rolling, to Niamh Kirwan for keeping it rolling, to Jenny Heller for her enthusiasm, to super cook Karen Coyle for looking after us all, to Grace O'Connor for her support, encouragement and silly laugh, to Candida Bottaci for being so helpful, to Bono for his groove and all of U2 for being the most approachable band I've ever met. To Rosie Wall, Anita Notaro and Martha McCarron for their friendship along the way, to Mona Maloney for putting up with the noise, to Christine Bowers for typing up indecipherable scribbling, to Gerry and Morah Ryan for a million laughs along the road, to Ian Gittins for being cool, to Ian Wilson, Jim Lockhart, Jack Murphy and everyone at 2FM, to all the listeners down through the years, to all the producers, directors, researchers, camera crews, sound crews etc. that I've had the good fortune to work with both on radio and TV here, Virgin and Channel 4 in London, Rave TV in New York ...

And to all my family and friends.

Thanks to Noel Kelly for making the book happen.

Thanks to the four most fab people ever – no, not the Beatles – Hayley, Robert, Jack and Ursula.

FOREWORD

BY BONO

When you are 17 and in a band, you don't wear stage gear. You want the off-stage look to be the same as on stage. Our band nearly broke up in its first year because Larry Mullen turned up wearing flares for the first photo session and refused to change. This was the post-punk New Wave scene. There were very strict rules about what you could and couldn't do – like have a beard, for instance. Dave Fanning had a beard. And kind of curly corkscrew hair. In this very tome, he admits – for a period – to looking like Catweazle. We were too young and naive to realise that playing punk rock music and looking like Catweazle was a very punk rock thing to do. In '77/'78, you could count the people in this new scene in the hundreds, not the thousands. We had a sign up to announce ourselves. Dave Fanning didn't bother.

From the very beginning, Dave Fanning was always going his own way, a stubborn river appearing to meander, when in fact he was really just finding the most efficient way around the mountain. He is not serene, our Dave. His conversation is more white-water rafting … ideas percolate … he tests them out on you, wondering who will capsize first … It's a furtive intelligence; a very fast and furious brain, given to a boy and a character with impeccable manners and grace. His nervous laugh is for you, not him, filling in the spaces where the interviewee can die. The thing is, he gets to the point. He does not waste your time. And when it comes to music, he embodies the difference between wisdom and knowledge. It's not just that he knows a lot. It's more that he *understands* what's beneath the surface of the song and can see it more clearly. I'd say his greatest joy – apart from sitting at the feet of the masters (in his case, Bob Dylan and Joni Mitchell) – is the joy of discovery … watching a new talent surface. He sees the silverfish under the water, pulls them out, interviews them, and puts them back, their direction more sure after meeting him.

He is a mysterious figure, and has metamorphosed over the years. His 'expose the process' shtick – and candour on the radio – meant everyone else looked manufactured and crowd-pleasing. Dave was crowd pleasing too. But it was his crowd. And they spoke a different language. They demanded no crap. And when they stopped demanding that he shave his beard, Dave Fanning shaved his beard. Read here about his transformation from the phenomenon that was pirate radio in the early Eighties to launching the first Dave Fanning show on the national airwaves. It felt like revolution because it *was* a revolution. Ireland was about to crawl out of the primordial mud of its history, and specifically the torpor of depression that was Dublin in the Seventies. Music was an alarm clock for a lot of us. Do-it-yourself bands/radio stations suddenly became do-it-yourself businessmen, economists … a do-it-yourself country emerged. This was not all great, but it was a lot better than we had ever known. Every song released in this time became like a national anthem. When Thin Lizzy played hard rock on *Top of the Pops*, when the Boomtown Rats got to No. 1 in the UK charts ... it was like the Battle of Britain had been won by Ireland.

For a lot of us this was zero hour, when the clock started ticking. And it didn't really slow down until very recently. Dave's mate, Gerry Ryan, was the nation's therapist ... through the good times and into the bad times. For a lot of people, Dave Fanning was the Samaritans, the quiet voice, who alone could understand the pain you were in ... at having to listen to chart music.

Radio is a not well-understood medium. Its power is its ubiquity; its currency is intimacy. Dave Fanning whispers louder than most men shout. He is all over this island of Ireland and listened to in the furthest corners of the world. The size of his reach is extraordinary, but what's more extraordinary is his very intimate relationship with people who love music on the radio.

When he chose to move to television, he chose a whole new world – stealing away from the mysteries of radio. This world requires a certain humility – one that's easily lost in a world where you can see the wires, where you know how the sausages are made, how the figs get into the fig roll. Dave Fanning knows the magician has put the rabbit in his top hat before he walks out on stage – he was standing beside him as he did it. But Dave is still enraptured as the rabbit is revealed. Suspension of disbelief is the key component in the appreciation of all art, high or low.

The Muse often prefers a fresh face, as gauche as a confirmation suit or a pretend safety pin through the nose of a 17-year-old boy. Sometimes the Muse gets bored with the worldly wise and lets curious youth in her window. When our band was 17 and 18, it must have been a source of fascination for Dave, watching the Muse hang out with our band. Is She Really Going Out With Him? But he delighted over it and magnified it to a wider world, as he did with the Undertones and so many others who were just getting started.

INTRODUCTION

The Thing Is ... you should always get to the point. If there is one thing I have learned in more than thirty years of broadcasting, it is that. People may listen to me on the radio or watch me on TV but it is not because they love the sound of my voice; far from it. They tune in because they want to be entertained.

The Thing Is ... you should get to the point, because the many thousands of radio shows I have presented, and articles I have written, and interviews I have conducted have never been about me. They are about the great bands, and unbelievable singers, and fantastic actors that I am lucky enough to get to talk to.

The Thing Is ... I used to get to the Point a lot, when it existed, and one particular evening, 1 March 2004, I got there and had one of the best nights of my life – an evening that was so full of surprises, that it is as good a place as any to begin my story.

The Thing Is ... I got to the Point that evening when it was still called the Point, before Dublin's long-time prime music venue succumbed to a major concrete-and-glass overhaul and facelift and became the O2. I was there for the Meteor Awards, which as everyone knows are Ireland's prestigious main rock and pop awards, dished out annually in front of a live TV audience.

I had been to the Meteors a lot over the years. My job had often taken me there. Two or three times, I had been lucky enough to be voted Best DJ, and I had shovelled out countless gongs as a presenter in the past. This year was different. In 2004, I was being given the Industry Award.

The Industry Award is like any of those Lifetime Achievement Awards that get dished out at such ceremonies. Basically they reward longevity and hanging on in there: they acknowledge that you have done what you do for more years than you care to remember. They are prizes for being a survivor; a recognition that you are still in the game, still doing it and, if you are lucky, you've still got all your own teeth.

I'm being flippant here but it was great that the Meteors had chosen to bestow this award on me, and so many highlights from my career were running through my mind as I stood at the side of the stage. Where to begin? There was the rock magazine I had edited on a shoestring ... my strange all-night sessions on pirate radio ... my twenty-five years on Ireland's main radio network ... my countless trips to London, New York and Los Angeles ... hundreds of encounters with all my heroes and the great and the good of the music and movie worlds ... Jaysus, I had been lucky, I reflected ...

As the awards host, Dara Ó Briain, ran through his slick patter, I self-consciously mentally rehearsed a few words that would thank those kind souls who had helped my career, and my loved ones, while hopefully not boring everybody else to tears. 'The Thing Is ...' I told myself, '... get to the point. Keep it simple.'

Then Dara introduced a film clip. It was new to me. I had never seen it before; did not even know it existed. It was U2, the band whose career I have been inextricably linked to more than any other. They were in the studio to record *How to Dismantle an Atomic Bomb*, but the song they were singing now would *not* be going on the album.

U2 were serenading the Meteor Awards with a song called 'David Watts'. Originally written by Ray Davies for The Kinks, it is probably better known for the cover version by the Jam. The actual track begins 'I am a dull and simple lad/Cannot tell water from champagne', before reaching the chorus of 'Wish I could be like David Watts', but those were not the words that Bono was singing that March evening. He had made a few crucial adjustments ...

Fa fa fa fa fa Fanning
Fa fa fa fa fa Fanning
Fa fa fa fa fa Fanning
He was a pirate on the radio ...

Now this was quite something. This I hadn't expected. U2, the biggest band in the world, had recorded a video tribute to me. That would be quite mind-boggling enough in itself. But they had gone one step further – they had done it in song.

On a four-man couch, Adam was on the right crooning smartly tuneful harmonies with Larry, who was drumming along. Edge sat at the other end and yer man Bono was exactly where he is always is, hogging the camera, giving out, singing ...

... He played our songs on every show ...

Dave Fanning

Ha! That was true! Or, at least, sometimes it must have seemed like it to the listeners. I probably had played more tracks by U2 than any other artist in my quarter-century on the radio. Our careers had always been closely intertwined. We hadn't planned it that way – we had just emerged at the same time, in the same city, with the same drive and the same love of music.

... He was a punk but he kept his beard ...

A punk? Was I? Well, I guess I must have been, back in the dog-day end of the Seventies, when I was fresh out of college, desperate to avoid the nine-to-five grind, and filling my nights playing new music on an obscure, long-forgotten pirate radio station called the Big D.

As for the beard ... well, it had made sense at the time. We all have these skeletons in our closet, don't we? I mean, didn't Bono used to have a mullet and wave a white flag?

... People think he's straight but we know he's weird ...

I had to smile at that. Straight? Well, I had never been a drug addict or an alcoholic, sure, but I had spent twenty years living and breathing rock 'n' roll, totally oblivious to the things that concerned most people, such as relationships or children or a lovely home. I had criss-crossed the globe; I had done five or six jobs at once; and all for the love of music. Yeah, I guess some people might think of that as weird ...

... Wish I could be like Dave Fanning
Wish I could be like Dave Fanning
Wish I could be like Dave Fanning ...

Now (as is still there for all to see on YouTube) Edge was joining in, and Larry and Adam, chiming their voices into the chorus. The Point was in hysterics; everybody in the audience was falling about. Bono was giving it his best rock-star face ... How on earth was I to follow this?

He was the first man in our audience ...

Ah, now this was an interesting one. Had I been the first person in U2's audience? I had certainly been to enough shows, back in those super-early days, when there were two men and a dog there. But I think they were thinking more of the days on the pirate radio stations. The days when four young Irish kids without even a single to their name had come on to my show, and their lippy singer had talked long and hard into the night about their hopes, and dreams, and how they could maybe even cleave a path to world success like no Irish band had ever done before them.

Chances are U2 were thinking of the days before I transferred to RTÉ and Ireland's first legal music station, Radio 2, where I interviewed them on five consecutive nights as we let our listeners choose their first single. Well, the connection was made – so much so that their manager, Paul McGuinness, now made sure that every U2 single was played on the Dave Fanning show on 2FM before anywhere else in the world.

Dave Fanning

... He never finished a sentence ...

Were they saying I have a motormouth style? Yeah, probably guilty as charged, to be honest. Let's face it, there is so much to be said, and only so much time to say it in.

... He mumbled along about Slaughter and the Dogs ...

I had; it was true. And about Irish bands like the Vipers and the Outcasts and the Blades and a thousand other bands that were emerging from Ireland's towns and cities in those exciting post-punk days when it seemed as if the world was changing and everything was possible. See, mythology has it that I loved U2 from the second I first heard them and made it my mission to lift them to the top, but it wasn't like that at all. When I had first heard them, I thought they were OK; no more. I liked them as people but the music didn't blow me away. Truth be told, I was more interested in the Undertones (they had an album!) or the second Boomtown Rats record.

... But he kept his hat for when he kicked his clogs ...

A long way off. No towel was about to be thrown in, no bucket about to be kicked ... we've only just begun.

... Wish I could be like Dave Fanning
Wish I could be like Dave Fanning
Fa fa fa fa fa fa Fanning
Fa fa fa fa fa fa fa fa ...

The song faded out and the Edge, always a law unto himself, bizarrely began to strum the chords to 'Stairway to Heaven' as Bono stared deep into the camera and delivered his valedictory message with apparent sincerity:

> *Dave, it's impossible to describe what you mean to this group and impossible to forget what you did for us. Incredible things like ... incredible stuff like ... I remember when there was that time ... er ...*

Ah, well, Bono had always been a grade-one piss-taker – why should he change now? But it had been a grand message that I knew I would never forget, and as I stepped up to receive my Industry Award from Larry Mullen my mind was in a whirl, the notion of a carefully prepared acceptance speech long gone.

U2 were right. I was having a mad buzz being Dave Fanning and the madness and the adventures were showing no sign of abating. I had been insanely lucky but, yeah, *'Wish I could be like Dave Fanning'*? It was true: I certainly couldn't think of many ways in which my life could be improved. So, how had I come from the Dublin suburbs and being a somewhat impecunious punk-era music fan to this? As Talking Heads once asked, how did I get here?

Well, it had been a long story – and unlike many rock 'n' roll memoirs, it had started with a blissfully happy childhood.

1

Many people who sell their souls to rock 'n' roll hate their upbringings. They endure their childhoods, hightail it out of the family home as soon as they are able and set about reinventing themselves as rebels without a cause. I may have lived my life for music – and just how much will become clear as you read this memoir – but I was never anybody's idea of a rock 'n' roll rebel.

How happy were my early years? Maybe this will give you an idea: I loved my family home so much that I lived there for twenty-eight years.

I was born in mid-winter in the mid-Fifties, the youngest of six children. Or, strictly, of seven: my parents' second-born son, Brian, had died at the age of six months. It must have been hard on them but it had not put them off having a typical big Irish family and so my oldest brother John, Peter, my sister Miriam and the two brothers nearest to me in age, Dermot and Gerard, all knocked around together in the house that was to be my home for close on three decades.

The house was No. 54 Foster Avenue in Mount Merrion, right next to University College Dublin, and my parents bought it in

1943 for less than a thousand pounds. Foster Avenue links the Stillorgan Road, the main drive route south out of Dublin, with places like Dundrum. It was about five miles from the city centre, which was considered such a long way out that when my parents bought it, all their friends asked why they wanted to live in the countryside.

My father, Barney, was originally from Drogheda but moved the thirty miles south to Dublin when he met my mum, Annie. When they met she was working as a teacher in Clontarf in the north of the city. My folks weren't the sort of parents who'd regale us with soppy tales of how they met, but I know my dad proposed in Sneem, a lovely little place in County Kerry. I'm guessing their courtship would have been more like the nineteenth century than the 1940s.

With me being the youngest of six, my parents were oldish when I was born. My dad was 46, and my mum 44. I guess some kids might have found this age gap a problem but I hardly ever had a cross word with my family. I remember lots of playing with my brothers and sister around the house and in the big garden at the back with its apple, pear and plum trees.

My dad worked for the Board of Works in their office on Stephen's Green for forty-seven years. He was a senior civil servant and he was involved with the preservation of state buildings and monuments around Ireland. Once he had to organise the unveiling of a statue of Thomas Davis, the legendary Irish freedom fighter, at Trinity College. The Irish president was to unveil it and our family joke was that if the president keeled over with a heart attack on the day, it would be Dad whipping the cloth off.

I guess my dad was pretty old school, as you'd expect from a man born at the start of the century. He liked – although he never demanded – his tea on the table every night and he never boiled an egg in his life, but he was so laid-back that you could only have a good relationship with him. We all called him Barney, and his easygoing nature was one reason I was able to live at home for so long.

He had an old white Ford car with Al Capone-style boards at either door. There were many cold mornings that it wouldn't start and my dad would take the gas heater from the kitchen, stick it by the front grille and try to start the engine by cranking it up with one of those Victorian-looking iron-bar contraptions. As I recall it, he usually gave up and took the 64 or 46A bus into town, then walked through Stephen's Green.

I don't remember my dad ever missing a day's work – a trait I have inherited, as I've never had one day sick in my thirty years at RTÉ. Every evening he would bring home reports and memos and read weighty Dáil parliamentary reports as we shared a table. He would help me out as I struggled with my homework. This was a good system, as Maths was his forte and, quite frankly, it never was mine and never will be.

On Sundays my dad would often take me up to Phoenix Park. He knew the caretaker there, a man called Mr Barry, who lived in a gorgeous house that always had a big roaring log fire going. Mr Barry was a happy-go-lucky guy who looked like Santa Claus, and we'd collect chestnuts from the park. They came in handy for conkers at school. Not that I played it much. I always thought it was a daft game and preferred marbles.

Nothing ever fazed my dad and I don't think I ever argued with him about anything – except for Christmas Day *Top of the Pops*, but we'll come to that later. But if he was at heart a quiet and retiring soul, my mum, Annie, was anything but. She was everything in our house, the matriarch and the patriarch, and I can safely say that she was the most inspiring person that I have met in my entire life.

Everything in the house went through my mum. She was just an astonishing woman. She loved being at the heart of the hustle and bustle of a big family and always welcomed any friends we brought round, whatever time of the day or night it was. She was tall and slim and beautiful and somehow always well-turned-out. I've no idea how she found the time.

Annie was fun and she was gregarious. She'd have these phone conversations that lasted for hours, and then whenever people called round, she would sit in the kitchen holding court. Locally, she was well known for doing that – and for her home-made biscuits that she dispensed to all-comers. There are probably still people in Dublin who drool like Pavlov's dogs at the phrase 'Annie's cookies'.

For my family, money was fairly tight, but my mum was so skilled at budgeting and making do that I don't remember ever having to really go without. Annie cut our cloth well and knew how to count pennies without making a meal of it. She would do her weekly grocery shop in one supermarket, then think nothing of crossing a busy road to go to a different store a few hundred yards down the road just because the butter was five pence cheaper there.

My mum was a voracious reader. She belonged to two libraries, the Royal Dublin Society and the Pembroke, and I am certain she was the best customer in both of them. She always had three or four books on the go at once – I can still picture them now, stacked up in a little pile on top of the radiator. Each of them invariably had one page with the top right-hand corner turned down, to remind her how far she'd got.

When she wasn't reading, Annie was usually writing. She would sit down at her desk, take out her pad of Basildon Bond and compose these twenty-page letters to her friends. She had a lot of correspondents, but top of the list was Mrs Rohan, her lifelong friend who owned a chemist shop in Cork.

A lady called Mrs Mooney, known to me as Moo, came and helped my mum out a few times a week with whatever needed doing around the house. Because I was the youngest, she also looked after me and sometimes took me to her house, a lovely flower-covered cottage straight out of Beatrix Potter, opposite the Terisian school on the Stillorgan Road that is now the site of RTÉ's admin building.

Moo's husband, Mick, was the chief groundsman there. RTÉ – there was actually no 'T' in it at the time, as Ireland still didn't have television – was moving from Henry Street in the centre of Dublin to its current location and the masts were going up ready for the launch of TV. It's ironic that I spent so much time there when I was young, given how interwoven my life has since been with RTÉ.

My mum was a very religious woman. While, like most others, I was a good little Catholic boy, by the time I reached my later teens I had actively decided against the Church, but she never made it an issue between us. She just followed her own lights, which in her case meant walking to Mass every single morning for thirty-seven years. I guess it must have rubbed off on me a little in my impressionable early youth, because I spent a number of years as an altar boy in Mount Merrion Church.

I will never forget the trauma of my first day at school. It was such an intimidating experience. I remember standing inside the door of Mount Merrion National School, holding my mother's hand, and staring in horror at scenes of bedlam. There were so many kids running around and screaming and throwing things, and I just wanted to turn around and run away back home.

Your first school day is extraordinary. I don't remember one thing about being in the classroom, but I will never forget the chaos of the playground and cloakroom, with all the coats chucked on top of each other. I grew to not mind the school but it's all a bit of a blur now, except for a couple of the teachers: Mrs O'Callaghan, who lived on our road, and Mrs Hughes. She was all about joined-up writing and I never took to her: she just seemed so very, very old and, more pertinently, old-fashioned.

I rubbed along OK at Mount Merrion School until the age of seven, then the next year it became girls-only, so I had to move on to Kilmacud National School, which was a mile further down the road. Again, what I remember most was the first day – or rather the first week, which must have been once of the worst weeks of my life.

After Mount Merrion, Kilmacud seemed pretty rough. It also looked it. As we waited for a new school to be built at the corner of the Upper and Lower Kilmacud Roads, the classes were held in makeshift prefabs where the Stillorgan Bowling Alley now stands. Soon after they built a shopping centre across the road from it, the first mall in Ireland, and it was considered such a big deal that we were all given a day off to celebrate.

I had thought break times at Mount Merrion School were mad; at Kilmacud it was Armageddon. At lunch break there would be hundreds of kids charging around the yard playing football, smashing into walls or lamping the ball as hard as they could and not caring who it hit or who *they* hit. Or there would be piggyback fights where you threw punches and tried to push the other guy off his mate's back. This all happened on concrete: Health & Safety wasn't such a major concern in those days.

There would always be two teachers patrolling the ground with their hands behind their backs, talking to each other, and every now and then shouting someone's surname to make it look as if they were in charge. I don't think I was a particularly delicate child but I really wasn't into the massive rough-and-tumble and horseplay, so mainly I just tried to stay out of the way.

After the first week, as I grew used to the daily casual violence of the playground, I did OK at Kilmacud. That was the story of my whole academic career: OK. I wasn't particularly good, bad or indifferent. The only subject I really did well in was English. A typical exercise came when our English teacher asked us to write a four-page essay and I wrote nine pages, which I ended up reading in front of the class. I was mad for James Bond, so my story was all about me being a spy and escaping the enemy by having a bomb hidden in a button in my coat, and pulling it off and throwing it at them. Stupid stuff, really, but it's still amazing to me how, two generations on, 9-year-old boys still love James Bond.

In terms of discipline, I was fine in school: I never gave teachers a hard time and I always did my homework. This didn't always protect you though. There was a definite downside to being in school in Ireland in the 1960s and 70s; while I didn't suffer anything like the horrors of the poor kids who got abused or beaten in Church and industrial schools, there were some bad moments. Children being hit and caned in class was accepted – that was just how it was back then.

As I said, I was never great at Maths but I always did my best. In one lesson though, I dropped a howler. The teacher – and I don't think I'll shame him by saying his name, although it's a close decision – had given us all a textbook with about a hundred pages in it, and on every page there were ten or twenty mental arithmetic questions. Every day he would give us a page of the book as homework, then the next day we had to tell him the answers we had worked out.

One day in class, the teacher started examining us on the sums we should have done the night before and said, 'OK, let's hear your answers to page 78.' Disaster! I had done page 79. I must have had a brainstorm and written down the wrong page number. I thought I might as well come clean so I put my hand up and said, 'Sorry, sir, but I did the wrong page.'

The teacher just lost it. He went absolutely mad. He pulled me out of my seat and got physical with me, shoving me around the room and screaming in my face, 'Fanning! I TOLD you it was page bloody 78!' Everybody in the class went quiet, because they knew it could just as easily be them the next time – this probably happened about three times per week.

Even today, thinking back, I'm staggered at the madness and inhumanity of it all. This grown man, a trained professional, was belittling and ridiculing me, psychologically and physically bullying me for no reason at all other than I had made an innocent mistake! How could a teacher think it was OK to treat a basically blameless child in this way, and did he really think it was educative?

For weeks afterwards, I relived that scene in my mind and fantasised over what I would have liked to do to him. In my imagination, I answered him with a string of cutting, Oscar Wilde-style *bon mots* and told him to take out his frustrations on some other poor victim, not on me. I picked up his cane, snapped it over my knee, told him, 'If you need this to be a teacher, then get another job,' picked up my bag, and strode manfully out of the classroom. Of course, the reality was I did what any other terrified 10-year-old would have done: cowered, stayed silent and then slunk back to my seat.

Another time, I was caned for mixing up two words when I recited the Catechism – a question-and-answer book with simple illustrations that we had to learn off by heart. There were no ambiguities, no grey areas: you either knew the answers word-perfect or you were in big trouble. The Catechism started off:

Who made the world?
God made the world.
Who is God?
God is our Father in Heaven, the creator of all things.

Then there was some pretty odd stuff about God the Father, God the Son and the third member of the Holy Trinity, God the Holy Ghost, at which point it got *really* weird. When I accidentally said two words the wrong way round, the meaning of what I had said was 100 per cent the same, yet still I was caned for my mistake.

I never told my mum and dad about incidents like these, and to be honest, although they were loving parents, I think they would have just shrugged if I had. That was how things were back then. You had no choice but to deal with it.

Television had launched in Ireland in the early 1960s and one of the big programmes was *Tolka Row*, our weekly soap opera. An early series ended with a cliff-hanger as Sean, the decent but rebellious son played by Jim Bartley, crashed his car and sat motionless in the driver's seat as the credits rolled. They filmed the scene at the top of Foster Avenue, about a hundred yards from my house, and hordes of us excited kids swarmed over the set all day.

On another occasion, they filmed an ad for crisps at the 64A bus stop by our house. A man crunched into a crisp and suddenly a bowler hat-wearing, brolly-carrying businessman who had been walking past him was clinging to the top of the bus stop. The idea was that the crisps were *that* crispy the noise had frightened the guy and propelled him skywards, but nobody making the ad seemed to be having fun and the actor spat the crisps out as soon as he heard the word 'Cut!' I saw the ad on TV months later. It looked really stupid.

When I turned 11, it came time to leave Kilmacud and start secondary school. John, Peter and Dermot had gone to Oatlands

School, which was run by the Christian Brothers, but my mum had decided the education there was barbaric so Gerard and I were packed off to Blackrock College, another mile down the road from Kilmacud.

That was typical of Annie. She was absolutely determined that all of her children would get a good education, and it is to her credit that nearly all of us eventually went on to get a college degree. John and Peter were the first to head off to University College Dublin. John later went to London to work in advertising, then came back to McConnell's, which became Ireland's largest marketing communications business. In later years, he became chairman of McConnell's Advertising, adjunct professor of marketing at Trinity College, a non-executive director of the *Irish Times* and, for a while, a board member of the Abbey Theatre. He's an expert on branding and in 2006 wrote a very well-received book, *The Importance of Being Branded.* Having also written a doctoral thesis, he is now Dr Fanning.

Peter and I had occasional rows as boys but mostly got on just fine. He now lives in Canada, where he has taught English in Vancouver for the last twenty-five years. My next brother, Gerard, has always been huge into literature and has published four books of poetry to date. There was sometimes a degree of one-upmanship between him and John. One family Christmas, Gerard proudly produced a not-yet-published anthology of new Seamus Heaney poems – then John trumped him by flourishing a signed version of the same book!

As for me, I have never bought into the cliché that your schooldays are the best days of your life but I had a fantastic time at Blackrock. It is the best-known rugby school in Ireland, with alumni including Brian O'Driscoll, Luke Fitzgerald, Leo Cullen and Bob Casey, but neither Gerard nor I ever played rugby or were put under any pressure to do so, for which I remain hugely grateful.

Gerard was two years ahead of me at Blackrock and spent five years in the same class as a lanky kid called Bob Geldof with a mass of bouffant hair and an intense manner. Geldof always stood out a little: he just looked different from everybody else, and was the first boy around our way to ride a BMX bike. He and Gerard were mates and one year they went off to England together to do a summer holiday job shelling peas at a factory in Peterborough.

Academically, I again did OK at Blackrock while never setting the world alight. There were five graded classes, from A to E, and I was happy to be in B for a few but mostly in C, which was where I felt I belonged. I didn't struggle but nor was I in the academic A-league.

Actually, this may be just my self-serving twist on things, but I'm glad that I was middling as a student. There are definitely downsides to being an academic over-achiever. Just last year I watched a documentary about prodigies who went on *University Challenge* years ago, and most of them seem to be fucked-up and crazy nowadays. You wouldn't want to be one of them: the cleverest of all was drinking nine pints every day. At least that is one life I managed to escape by not being too brainy.

I was even happier in Class C because my two best friends were also there, middle-achievers like me. They were called Jerry Coyle and Mel Reilly, and throughout our teenage years at

Blackrock, and beyond, the three of us were inseparable. We hung out together every day, and, remarkable as it may seem, forty years on Jerry and Mel remain my two best friends in the world.

I met Jerry on my very first day in Blackrock. He told me he lived in Mount Merrion at 42 Wilson Road, right round the corner from my house in Foster Avenue. I scornfully took him to task and explained he was mistaken: 'That's ridiculous, I know everybody on Wilson Road, and I don't know you!' I even reeled off a list of people I knew on the street, but he stuck to his story.

After school we walked home together and I still thought he was having me on. When he walked up the path of No. 42 and rang the bell I expected him to run away, but his mother answered the bell and asked him how his first day had gone. I couldn't believe I had lived so close to the guy my whole life and never noticed him. We then made up for it by being virtually inseparable for the next twenty years, until he emigrated to America.

Mel Reilly came to Blackrock a year later than Gerry and me when he transferred from the college's junior school called Willow Park. He lived in a huge house on Cross Avenue and was the oldest of five boys. Mel is now a teacher in Dundrum and even today there is hardly a day goes by that I don't hook up with him.

Jerry and Mel weren't much into football yet that was what occupied most of our spare time in a jumpers-for-goalposts kind of way. Sometimes we would play on the hockey pitches at Belfield, over the road from us at University College Dublin, or in the car park of the Stella cinema, despite the fact that it was a steep slope.

Mostly, though, we would play three-and-in on Foster Avenue itself. The gateway of my friend Gary Byrne's house served as perfect goalposts. For a more elaborate and arguably somewhat grisly ball game called 'Sick, dying and dead' we used a wall on Owenstown Park at the entrance to UCD. Nowadays Foster Avenue is one long car park, but back then it saw hardly any traffic. After the game we would sit by Teevan's newsagent and eat Cowboy bars and drink Kool Pops or, if we had a little more money to spare, lavish 2d on a Trigger, a Flash bar or, the tastiest of them all, a Macaroon bar.

Dermot Morgan would sometimes join in our kick-abouts. He lived five doors down from Jerry on Wilson Road and in later life starred as Father Ted on TV. Dermot was a couple of years older than us and was in my brother Gerard's class. We used to call him Morgan the Mighty after the character in the comics.

Dermot wasn't the best footballer in the world and nor was his dad, Darragh, with his massive shock of white hair. Darragh would join us after he had finished work and was a bit of a character. He would charge around like mad kicking the ball for half an hour and then retire, absolutely bollocksed. I never hung around with Dermot, but by the time I went to UCD a few years later he was doing lunchtime sketch shows in the Arts building theatre to over a hundred people and trying to get on to TV. He was very funny; I never knew he had it in him.

In my pre-teen years, various friends came round to my house all the time and my parents always made them welcome. On Wednesday afternoons, when we were off school, we'd pull out both leaves of the dining-room table and play table football: the great Subbuteo.

We would take Subbuteo massively seriously. We had quite a primitive version and the players didn't have 3D facial features or even arms or legs, they were just lumps of plastic on a round base, but that didn't bother us. We were very strict on flicking the pieces only, no scooping. If we scored a goal, we'd run around the room: our celebrations were even more pathetic than the Premier League players today.

My dad sat in his chair, smoked his pipe and read the paper while we played. On the table next to him was a peculiar contraption: a crude, slightly rusty guillotine that he used to cut thin slices of plug tobacco. Barney would ground the slices with the thumb and forefinger of his right hand into the palm of his left, scoop them into the pipe and puff away happily. The whole process used to fascinate Jerry and Mel.

My father loved horse racing and would spend his Saturdays in front of the telly egging on every Irish horse, Irish-owned horse, Irish-trained horse or Irish jockey. I had no interest at all in this, although it didn't stop me jumping out of my skin when my dad suddenly started shouting as they headed into the home straight.

My dad was very much a homebody. He never really went out, except on Friday nights for a pint with his friend Jack Walsh in Byrne's of Galloping Green in Leopardstown. Other than that, he didn't really drink, and I remember when President Kennedy came to Ireland, a few months before he was assassinated in Dallas, my dad was invited to the big reception in Dublin Castle and took some persuading to go and take my mother. It was certainly the only time I ever saw him in a tuxedo.

Of my brothers and sister, I hung out the most with Gerard, who was the nearest to me in age. We shared a bedroom and plenty of adventures and we remain close to this day. I was close to Miriam as well but how many boys hang out with their four-year-older sister? She was also heavily into ballet: she'd come pirouetting into the room on tiptoes, and I'd raise my eyes to heaven and go back to whatever I was doing.

John and Peter had both left home by the time I hit my teens. They had moved to London, which seemed impossibly glamorous to me. In fact, whenever I read about Carnaby Street and swinging London, I felt like my brothers gave me a link to that exotic, tantalising world just across the water, even though I had never been there myself.

One major tradition in my family was the big annual summer holiday. In those days, ordinary families didn't vanish off to the Algarve or Tuscany, and we always went to exactly the same place: Bettystown in County Meath, about thirty miles from Dublin and five miles from my father's home town of Drogheda. We would go for about a month, to give him time to catch up with his family, and I loved it.

We'd rent a house right next to the sea with a grassy bank that led straight down to the beach. It would be a proper old-fashioned summerhouse, with wooden walls like a chalet, and we would play on the beach all day long, even if the weather was lousy which, of course, it often was. When the tide was out it was a long way to the sea, the water was bitterly cold, and the totter back up the beach to the house felt like torture.

Movies were always big news in our house. My father would take me to the Stella Cinema in Mount Merrion – which, sadly, is now a furniture shop – and the Ormonde in Stillorgan, which, I'm glad to say, is still open today. The Stella was a grand old-fashioned picture house, with two ornate kiosks to buy your tickets and your sweets, and beautiful sweeping staircases up to the balcony that we hardly ever sat in. I used to love seeing the usherettes walking through the cinema selling ice cream from their trays.

The movies were always screened either Mondays to Wednesdays or Thursdays to Saturdays, with a different bill on Sundays. Normally, there were double-feature screenings and my dad took me to a lot of Westerns. Saturdays would often be comedies, including some really, really bad ones interspersed with Pathé News.

As I got older, I would sometimes go to evening showings that began at 7.30, with friends from school. Sometimes we would be too young to see the films without a grown-up with us, so we would have to wait outside and ask an adult if we could go in with them. They would usually say yes because they knew us from around Mount Merrion, and they weren't X-rated movies – they just finished at 11 p.m., and unaccompanied kids had to be out of the cinema by then. There would be about ten of us, and once we got in we would make a beeline for the front row.

I have so many memories of wide-eyed nights in the Stella. I saw *Wait Until Dark*, the famous movie with Audrey Hepburn as a blind girl. Friends who had seen it already told me it had a really terrifying scene. At one stage Alan Arkin, playing a villain, killed one of his own guys by ramming a car into him.

I thought, 'Was that it? Big deal!' I relaxed – and a few minutes later, Audrey went to close a fridge and a man leapt out of it at her. Mother of Jesus! Thinking of that scene still gives me goose bumps to this day!

I was an avid moviegoer as a kid. Any trailer that I ever saw, I longed to see the film. I was an absolute sucker. I remember when I was slightly older, Jerry Coyle and I went to the Ormonde to see *The Prime of Miss Jean Brodie*, which had a real effect on me. Even at the tender age of 15, I thought Maggie Smith was brilliant.

Maybe I was always going to host a movie show, because as a kid I would write reviews of every film I saw in a little book that I made from pieces of brown paper stapled together. I would carefully write out the title, the director and names of the stars and then give it a critique and a mark out of ten. I am not sure my critical faculties were too honed back then; the only film I ever gave ten out of ten to was a totally obscure war film called *Tobruk*, starring Rock Hudson.

I read quite a lot as a kid – my mother made sure of that, and our house was full of books and literature. I was big into Enid Blyton with her Famous Five and Secret Seven and their mad adventures that always ended with farmers' wives giving them sandwiches and lashings of ginger beer. Her *Island of Adventure* and *Castle of Adventure* stories were the best. I was also fond of Richmal Crompton's *Just William* books – but when it came to reading, my major obsession was comics.

It started with the *Beano* and *Dandy*, with all the characters I can still picture now: the Bash Street Kids getting slippered by the teacher, Little Plum with his feather coming out of his head-band, Dennis the Menace knocking lumps out of Walter the Softie. In one story I particularly remember, Dennis came out of school with a book marked 'Sums'; Walter's was called 'Harder Sums'. My sister Miriam got the *Bunty* and *Judy,* and when she got too old for them, I started buying them instead. I didn't care that they were aimed at girls: the stories in them were just as good, especially the Four Marys, Lorna Doone with her magic dancing shoes, or the unfortunate heroine who would have her saddle loosened by horrid, wicked types who schemed to thwart her chances of winning the local gymkhana.

In my teenage years I took a bit of a step up with the comics, and – yes, I know this is sad – I can still remember the sequence that used to define my week. It was the *Hornet* on a Tuesday, the *Hotspur* on Thursday and the *Victor* on Friday. That was the big one: Friday afternoon, home from school, reading the *Victor* and eating fish and chips with the weekend ahead was definitely a major highlight of my week. I always sat at the same part of the kitchen table. I'd place the comic in the cutlery drawer, read bits as I digested the food and push the drawer back in when I went to the plate for a little more.

The Second World War stories didn't really do it for me. I could take or leave Matt Braddock VC or Captain Hurricane and his pint-sized batman Maggot Malone. Captain Hurricane had a 'ragin' fury' every week and would use guns, grenades and his filthy temper to wipe out 'krauts' and 'slant-eyed goons' – not terms you tend to hear in today's more enlightened, politically correct world. I much preferred Morgan the Mighty or Alf Tupper, the 'Tough of the Track', who always ate fish and chips before *and* after winning a race.

Dave Fanning

The *Hornet* always seemed to me to have the best stories and illustrations. Every week it had a serialised non-pictorial story over three or four pages in which Paul Terhune tried to solve some mystery or other, each instalment invariably ending on a cliff-hanger. As soon as a story finished, after about ten weeks, I would immediately go back and read the thirty or forty pages in one go. My favourite was a rather unlikely tale called 'Invisible Bullets from Nowhere' in which Terhune tried to work out why random citizens were being shot but nobody could find the shooter or the bullets. It transpired that a disgruntled employee at the local observatory high above the town had fitted the giant telescope with ice bullets and was taking pot shots at pedestrians he held a grudge against. Well, it made sense at the time.

Just reading the comics was never enough for me. They used to have competitions that I was soon compulsively entering. Quite often, I won. The first time I saw my name in print, I absolutely loved it. My mum used to read the *Irish Catholic*, and they had a competition asking readers to fill in the missing words in a limerick. I knew the answer because I had heard it before – in fact I can still remember it:

There was an old man quite weird,
Who shrieked, 'Tis just as I feared!
Four owls and a wren
Two larks and a hen
Have just built their nest in my beard.

I sent my answer in to the *Irish Catholic* and won £3, which was a small fortune to me. I wrote them a letter saying it had been fantastic to win, and they printed that too. The biggest buzz was just reading my name in the magazine: D FANNING, DUBLIN.

Fired by this triumph, I was soon entering all the competitions in my weekly comics. The *Valiant* asked readers to send in a cartoon, so I got hold of a copy of a religious magazine that we used to have in school called the *Word*. It had a cartoon of two guys on a pulley hanging off the Leaning Tower of Pisa, too far away to clean the windows, and I traced it and posted it to the *Valiant*. Let's face it, it was plagiarism, pure and simple, but the £1 postal order came in very handy.

I had no conscience about how I won the competitions. Once, I copied a joke from the *Beezer* and sent it to the *Topper*. I won. The question was 'What is the definition of a phone kiosk?' and I said 'A chatterbox'. They also asked for a definition of an alarm clock and I said 'Something that scares the living daylights out of you', which I thought was absolutely hilarious.

I entered and won so many competitions that the people at the DC Thomson offices in Scotland must have been saying, 'Jesus, not another one from that Irish guy!' The prize was normally a postal order, but on one occasion the *Beezer* sent me a walkie-talkie. It was two small hollow pieces of red plastic joined together by a foot of hollow black cord that looked like a piece of liquorice, and it was rubbish. But it was still as much of a thrill as ever to come home from school for dinner and find a parcel waiting for me next to my place at the table.

Like any normal, average young Dublin lad, I lived for music and football. There is much more to come in this book about music, believe me, but for a while in those early years football meant almost as much to me. The first games I ever went to were at Glenamlure Park in Milltown, the home of Shamrock Rovers. Dermot took me there every now and then. The ground was always packed. That was in the days when Mick Leech was the George Best of the Rovers team, and other star Irish players included Alfie Hale at Waterford and Freddie Strahan at Shelbourne. Glenmalure Park is now a housing estate, and many Shamrock fans have never forgiven the board for selling up.

I also saw a few international matches at Dalymount Park. It always struck me how much more physical the game was than it looked on television, how much more sweaty and grunty. You could easily be hit by flying spit. I remember seeing the great Noel Cantwell, who was always known as a true gentleman of football. As I gazed at him in awe, he glanced at the referee, then elbowed the guy next to him in the back of the head.

Yet most of my football watching was via television. I followed the English league closely, and in 1966, during one of our family holidays to Bettystown, I watched the legendary match when England beat West Germany 4–2 in the World Cup Final.

It was so exciting; so incredibly dramatic. We all watched it on a little black-and-white TV. At half-time I walked down to the beach, stared across the sea and told myself, 'I can see England, where the game is going on!' Then it was back in the house for the rest of the match. When Webber equalised for Germany and made it 2–2 in the last minute of normal time I thought, 'Uh-oh, this is going to go wrong!' Then Geoff Hurst scored that famous goal off the crossbar, which, let's be honest here, was never a goal. Unlike many Irish people, I had nothing against England winning the World Cup, but they certainly had all the luck.

Forty-four years later, in South Africa in the summer of 2010, again against Germany, Frank Lampard's goal would have made it 2–2 and kept England in the World Cup, but for the ref who decided that a perfectly good goal wasn't a goal. England never recovered.

At about 12, I decided that I was a Manchester United fan and followed the Red Devils avidly for the next two years. The Irish newspapers didn't have the in-depth coverage I wanted, so I subscribed to the *Manchester Evening News & Chronicle* – but only on the days after United had played. It would arrive in the post a few days after it had been published and I would cut the United articles out and glue them into my scrapbook.

I watched United – who at the time boasted the holy triumvirate of George Best, Bobby Charlton and Denis Law – beat Benfica 4–1 in the European Cup final in 1968. It was so emotional. It was ten years after the Munich air disaster, and Benfica were enormous in those days; they had just beaten Everton 5–0 and 2–0. Charlton scored two goals, Best got that famous one where he cheekily rounded the keeper, and Brian Kidd got the other, on his nineteenth birthday. I'll never forget it: right after Kidd scored, I went to the kitchen to make a cup of tea and my dad shouted out, 'Jesus, he's done it again! Exactly the same as the other one!' I ran back in, looked at the screen, and realised that my dad hadn't yet got his head around the concept of the instant action replay.

I once actually saw George Best play in the flesh. Manchester United were drawn against Waterford in an early qualifying game for the European Cup and they held the game in Daly-mount Park. United won 3–0, a Law hat-trick, and Best came on at half-time. One little kid got past security and ran up to him while the game was going on, and Best stopped and signed an autograph. He was just so cool.

Oddly enough, after two years I gave up supporting Man United and just followed football in general. The World Cup in Mexico in 1970 was hugely exciting. In those days the organisers didn't kowtow to European evening viewing times so the games were on live at two or three in the morning. It was school holidays, warm evenings and football in the middle of the night ... the muffled, atmospheric commentaries added to the sense of exoticism and novelty that marked that great summer.

One big family ritual was watching *The Big Match* on Sunday afternoons, hosted by Brian Moore. I will never forget how the programme used to start: Moore commentating and saying, 'Charlie George, who can hit 'em!' and George, with his long hair flying, hitting that amazing goal for Arsenal in the 1971 FA Cup final and then lying flat on his back.

Queens Park Rangers used to be on a lot, when Rodney Marsh and Stan Bowles were sexing up football. Marsh always seemed to score a hat-trick when the cameras were there. My oldest brother, John, was a mad QPR fan, and decades later, one of the proudest moments of his life came when he was about to retire from his advertising agency. John's favourite poet is Thomas Kinsella – he has even written a thesis about him – and his work colleagues had managed secretly to get hold of Rodney Marsh. At John's farewell party, they showed him a film of Rodney drinking a glass of wine and saying, 'Hello, John! I hear you're retiring!' Then he read him a Thomas Kinsella poem. Rodney's rendition from the autocue was somewhat idiosyncratic – I'm not too sure he entirely grasped the nuances and subtleties of what he was reading – but even so, what an amazing retirement present!

Football wasn't the only TV I watched. Absolutely my favourite programme as a kid was *The Avengers*. To my young mind, it was on a heightened, more surreal level than everything else on television. Patrick Macnee as Steed was so cool. Every week would start with him going to a big country house to see some retired brigadier-general or other who had a big moustache and would be re-enacting the battle of El Alamein on his kitchen table, moving toy soldiers around with a big stick. Steed would wander out into the garden, then go back in and the general would be lying dead, with an arrow in his head or some such.

I loved the fact that the Avengers had this ace, swinging London sort of flat. *The Saint* was the same. Roger Moore couldn't act, and actually still can't, but that didn't matter – he just had to look the part and drive his long, phallic-symbol white car. Pretty much every week would end with somebody saying, 'Thank you for saving my life – who are you?' And he would raise an eyebrow; that music would start; the halo would appear over his head; and he'd drive off.

As I got older, I was big into *Monty Python's Flying Circus* but – probably typically for me – I loved the albums more than the TV shows. There were five different albums, and I'm afraid I'm the sort of obsessive who can quote whole sketches left, right and centre. It's not something I am particularly proud of, but there you go.

Dave Fanning

One strange old tradition in Ireland is that a lot of secondary-school students used to go away for about a month to a college where they just spoke Irish. I had been quite proficient in our native language until I was about 12, but after that I lost a lot of it. In my second-last year at Blackrock, in 1969, I went off to an Irish College in Carraroe in County Galway. Jerry and Mel were there with me.

We asked – in Irish of course – if we could have a day off to mourn the death of Brian Jones, the Rolling Stones guitarist who died on 3 July. Our request was denied. While we were there, the three of us also watched on television as Neil Armstrong and Buzz Aldrin walked on the moon, and we were completely overcome by the sense that, for humankind, this was history in the making. We went out cycling through Carraroe later that night and I remember stopping my bike and just gazing up at the moon and saying to Jerry and Mel, 'Jesus Christ! There's two guys up there!'

So I guess I had a pretty normal, happy-go-lucky Dublin childhood, except for one major, glaring anomaly – by the time I was a teenager, I was absolutely obsessed with music, listened to it every waking hour, lived and breathed it and, in truth, cared for little else. It is the all-consuming passion that has dominated my whole life and shows no sign of dimming. Why, exactly, am I so fixated on music? That may be a little harder to explain ...

2

My parents used to have a piano in our house in Foster Avenue. My mother played it occasionally, but they got rid of it because my two oldest brothers, John and Peter, had not shown enough interest in it. If it had still been there when Gerard and I were old enough to give it a go, it might have been a different story.

Then again, maybe it wouldn't. I never had any great interest in making music. Unlike a lot of kids of my generation, learning the guitar never held any real appeal for me (well, maybe a little, but I was lazy) and even to this day I can't play a note on anything. I fell in love with music as an excited, passionate, hugely appreciative listener.

Being the youngest of six kids, there was always music about the house, right from my very earliest years. We had Elvis 78s from as early as I can remember and John had jazz records by people like Duke Ellington, as well as mysterious artists with exotic names such as Dudu Pakwana and Blossom Dearie.

Oddly enough, one of my first musical memories is the plane crash that killed Buddy Holly on 3 February 1959. I had just started infant school, and a teacher told a girl in my class called McCaffrey to sing 'I Guess It Doesn't Matter Any More'. She sang it beautifully: at four years old, I was in awe of her performance.

When I was about five, I became aware of the pop charts. It was when Lonnie Donegan was having hits with 'Tom Dooley', 'Battle of New Orleans' and, of course, 'My Old Man's a Dustman'. None of those were my first single, though – that was 'Calendar Girl', by Neil Sedaka. I had asked my mum and dad for it for my seventh birthday.

This was right at the start of the Sixties, at a time when Elvis had left the US Army and was doing crooner stuff such as 'Are You Lonesome Tonight?' On the other side of the Atlantic, we had Adam Faith and Billy Fury being pushed as stars, but the biggest figure for us was Cliff Richard.

I guess as a wide-eyed kid I liked Cliff. His debut, 'Move It', is still a classic. I believed in him and bought into what he was doing. I remember he had a hit called 'A Voice in the Wilderness' and I assumed that he really was lost and wanted help. He sounded broken-hearted and there was a small wee eedjit in Dublin feeling sorry for him.

It was hard to hear new music in those days, but a few things managed to get through. I'll never forget hearing the Beach Boys' 'I Get Around' during one Bettystown holiday and it just sounding absolutely fantastic. Also the Animals' 'The House of the Rising Sun' – that had a massive, massive impact on me, the first time I heard it.

It was the Top 40 charts that absolutely fascinated me, though. In 1959 my brother Peter subscribed to the *New Musical Express* (*NME*), ordering it from Teevan's newsagent at the top of Foster Avenue. (I took over his subscription when he left

Dublin in 1971 and finally cancelled it just after the Millennium, by which time that particular family subscription was into its sixth decade. That has to be some kind of record.)

It's impossible to explain how important the *NME* singles chart was to me in the early Sixties. I would devour it every week. Each entry had a bracketed number next to it, showing where the song had been in the previous week's chart. I would always know if a single was No. 12 up from No. 30, or No. 8 down from No. 3.

When there was a hyphen in the brackets, it meant it was a brand new chart entry. This was such a big deal: I remember in 1962 running in and excitedly interrupting my brother, who was studying for an exam, to tell him that 'Are You Sure' by the Allisons had gone straight in at No. 14. The *NME* would write about these artists in its 'New to the Chart' feature, and that was crucial reading.

Peter threw away all his *NME*s at the end of the 1970s but he cut out all of the charts and put them in a box. I still have that box at home and it's fantastic. The charts were on page 4, so on the backs of the cuttings are news stories. I love reading those headlines even today: HANK TO QUIT SHADOWS. CLIFF TO TOUR US. 'PICTURES OF LILY' NOT PORNOGRAPHIC, SAYS TOWNSHEND.

Yet rock 'n' roll was dying back then. Looking back now, it was all about crooning; Elvis doing sentimental ballads; people like Johnny Tillotson singing songs about young men dying in car crashes. In 1960, 'Telstar' by the Tornados became the first instrumental to be No. 1 in the US and the UK, and the UK's No. 1 for the following eight weeks was 'I Remember You' by Frank

Ifield, which featured yodelling. I guess it was all getting very safe, very nice.

At which point, two things happened that changed my world – the Beatles, and the arrival of television in Ireland.

Like every other kid alive, I had never heard anything like the Beatles. They electrified everything, and they electrified me. I was eight years old, and from the very first time I heard them, I was totally into them. It wasn't that I knew they were going to be big – I didn't know anything back then! I just loved them.

It started with 'Love Me Do' in 1962. I could not have been more excited than I was to see it in the *NME* chart at No. 17, with a hyphen in the bracket. (I still have that chart: Paul McCartney signed it for me when I met him decades later.) I remember sitting in the family car as my brother Peter was driving, near the shops on The Rise in Mount Merrion, when 'Love Me Do' came on the radio. I just looked out of the window thinking, this is wonderful.

Then along came 'Please Please Me', and the Beatles pretty much killed off all the good-looking boys with quiffs that were being pushed at us by impresarios back then. They saved rock 'n' roll. Being nearly ten years old when Beatlemania was exploding was a life-changing experience, and no mistake. John and Peter bought the very first Beatles albums, Dermot got *Rubber Soul* and *Help!*, and I was listening to them all avidly.

For my part, I bought every Beatles single and devoured the *NME* for every word about them. I joined the fanclub and got the posters and the Christmas flexidiscs every year through to the end of the decade. It got slightly easier to keep up when RTÉ launched television in Ireland in 1962. There wasn't much music on TV, but I loved what shows there were, such as *Thank Your Lucky Stars* and *Juke Box Jury*. Occasionally you'd get novel little filler items on the news: David Dimbleby saying 'She's only 16, but she's walking back to happiness in the pop chart!' and there would be a picture of Helen Shapiro walking through the school gates for the last time, much to the envy of all her class-mates. Or Dimbleby would say, 'He may be better known as a jazzman but Georgie Fame hits the top of the hit parade this week with a song called "Yeah Yeah",' and there'd be Georgie – a poster of a gig at Ronnie Scott's jazz club on his kitchen wall – making a cup of tea at home Even little things like that were exciting at the time.

Because we were so starved of access to music in the media, it is impossible to overstate the importance of *Top of the Pops* when it launched at the start of 1964. Suddenly, here they were – all the bands I was slavishly reading about in the *NME* every week, beaming out from our TV screen! It was almost too good to be true, and it was not to be missed.

Every Thursday night was a sacred routine. After tea it was *Top of the Pops* at 7.30, followed by *The Man from U.N.C.L.E.* and *Get Smart* – and *Top of the Pops* was by far the most impor-tant of the three. It may be a cliché, but it's true: *Top of the Pops* could change the way you walked through the world. In the school playground the next day, it was all that anybody talked about. At least, it seemed that way.

Top of the Pops could be totally overwhelming. I remember one instance when I was 13 and we rushed in from playing foot-ball for our weekly fix. Because the tennis was happening at

Wimbledon, the BBC had reduced the show from its normal thirty-five minutes to twenty, which I thought was an outrage, but even though it was a shorter show than usual it contained one piece of magic that blew me away. Procol Harum were on, playing 'A Whiter Shade of Pale', and to my teenage ears it was unique, a brand new sound that nobody had discovered before. When *Top of the Pops* finished and we ran back outside to carry on playing football, I played ten times better. I just felt like I was George Best – and all because of that powerful rush, that sudden fix of brilliance.

If *Top of the Pops* was the highlight of the week, the *Christmas Top of the Pops* was one of the most crucial programmes of the year – which always caused me major angst on Christmas Day. The problem was my father. Barney might have been one of the most easygoing men in the world but he had his routines and one of them was that a friend of his would always call round on Christmas Day and give him a present of a book about horse racing. I don't think he ever read one of them.

My father would have a glass of Christmas whiskey – which was the only time I'd ever see him drink in the house – then turn off the television and put on the one record that he owned. It was *Brendan O'Dowda Sings the Songs of Percy French* and it was packed with old Irish songs such as 'Delaney's Donkey' and 'Paddy McGinty's Goat'.

We'd have to listen to these gems, then it would come time for *Christmas Top of the Pops* and we'd plead with my dad for us to watch it. Like everyone else, we only had the one TV, and he thought it was better that it stayed off while his friend was there: he knew we loved the show, but I don't think he'd realised quite *how* much it meant to us. These occasions were the closest I ever came to a proper row with my dad. He seldom relented, so every Christmas Day, when we should have been reliving the year's biggest hits, we were enduring 'Up the Airy Mountain, Down the Rushy Glen'.

Like most households, we had one record player in the home and it was virtually never silent. Frequently we were queuing up to use it. When I got my turn, maybe when my mum and dad were watching some TV show like *Seven Days* in the other room, I would carefully line up nine songs to play in that forty-five minutes. My vinyl changeover time was super-quick – and each song had to be listened to with the lights out.

As a kid I was all about the pop charts and singles, but as I moved into my teens the idea hit me that I should be getting more concerned with albums. Luckily, my brothers were all seriously into music as well, so a lot of their taste trickled down to me, even if I didn't fully appreciate it at the time.

John had moved to England years ago by then and become my link to Carnaby Street and swinging London. It seemed a million miles away to most people, but the fact that John was there made me feel like it was on my back door. John was walking down Savile Row in 1970 when the Beatles played what turned out to be their last-ever show on the Apple HQ roof. He said you couldn't actually see anything from the road; everybody was just wondering what all the noise was.

Peter's tastes were more inclined towards folk music, and he had a Woody Guthrie box set when I was about eight. Bob Dylan was his big thing though. He was into Dylan from the moment his career started. In later years I got massively into him myself, and now he's right up there as undoubtedly one of my favourite artists ever, but as a kid I was annoyed when Peter was monopolising the record player with *The Freewheelin' Bob Dylan* or *The Times They Are A-Changin'* because it meant I couldn't play my chart singles.

Yet, over the years, I came to be grateful for Peter's liking for singer-songwriters. He was my portal to Joni Mitchell, one of my all-time favourites, and brought her *Song to a Seagull* and *Clouds* albums into the house. Leonard Cohen followed behind: Dermot and Gerard were the big supporters there, Gerard due to his love of poetry.

Gerard was a massive music fan, and although he was only two years older than me his tastes were very different from mine. I naturally got indoctrinated into a lot of things that he liked, even if I didn't realise it at the time. So many things that I love now I was indifferent to when I first heard them.

I wouldn't say Gerard was a hippy but that was the music he went for. He was hugely into the Incredible String Band and Van Morrison right from the off. As a chart tart, I only knew Them because 'Baby Please Don't Go' and 'Here Comes the Night' had been hits, but there was Gerard listening intently to *Astral Weeks* and *Moondance* and really getting them.

Through people like Randy Newman and John Prine, Gerard later went on to more folky things like Martin Carthy and Bert Jansch, not to mention Planxty and the Bothy Band. He took up playing the uilleann pipes and joined an Irish pipers club. They'd sit round in our kitchen playing their pipes all night. I'd love to say he was great at it, but he was pretty awful.

Yet the Beatles were still my big love, and the first album I ever bought – I'm not saying this just to try to be cool – was *Sgt. Pepper's Lonely Hearts Club Band*. For an impressionable 13-year-old music fan, this was not a bad place to start.

The purchase was quite a palaver. I knew *Sgt. Pepper* was due to come out in the summer of 1967, so that January I went to the local record shop, Golden Discs in Stillorgan, and put down a deposit on it. This was the mighty sum of ten shillings, which I had saved from my Christmas present money.

I bought all my singles at the time at Golden Discs so the guy behind the counter knew me a little by then and was just as excited as me by the whole thing. I already knew a few of the song titles from the album because I had read about them in the *NME*, and had spent many hours wondering what 'Being for the Benefit of Mr Kite', 'Lucy in the Sky With Diamonds' and 'Within You, Without You' would sound like.

The five-month wait for *Sgt. Pepper*'s release was intolerable, but eventually 1 June came round and I parted with the rest of the thirty shillings: a fortune for me, whose only income was an early-morning *Irish Times* paper round on St Thomas Road in Mount Merrion. Holding the album in my hands was over-whelming – it had lyrics written on the back, the songs all ran into each other and there were cardboard cut-outs of Sgt. Pepper's band. It was all too much for me – so much so that I didn't even rush home and play it straightaway. In fact, I think I even let Gerard play it first.

Even today, while it probably isn't the Beatles' best album, *Sgt. Pepper* sounds to me like a stone-cold classic, so you can only imagine the effect it had on me back then. Even my clueless teenage mind could tell they were opening up new possibilities in the studio, and the pre-Pepper 'Strawberry Fields Forever' single is the one song I'd take to a desert island with me. The Beatles were changing everything in those days; they were instigating a massive cultural shift and I was desperate to be part of it.

By my early teens, one whole wall of the living room had been taken over by albums. There was no couch or shelf in the room and the piano had long gone. Albums were encroaching like a tidal wave of vinyl; there must have been at least five hundred propped up in stacks against the wall and I would constantly flick through them.

The other main source for hearing new music in those days was Radio Luxembourg and its dodgy, crackly broadcasts. I'd listen in late at night to DJs like Alan Freeman or Jack Jackson and all the bizarre sponsors' messages. They used to play one advert to death: HORACE BATCHELOR, DEPARTMENT ONE, KEYNSHAM, SPELT K-E-Y-N-S-H-A-M, BRISTOL. To this day, I have no idea what Mr Bachelor was selling.

Kid Jensen was the main man on Radio Luxembourg late at night and one week he interviewed a Dublin band, Skid Row, on his programme. The name didn't mean a lot to me but it was still great to hear a local band talking on Luxembourg. I remember the Kid asked them all to introduce themselves, and when he asked Nollaig Bridgeman where he came from, instead of saying 'Dublin', Nollaig said 'Dorset Street' (with the emphasis on the 'set') in his thick Dublin accent. Don't ask me why, but I loved hearing that. Another night, the Kid returned from the Isle of Wight festival and said the band who blew everyone away was Taste. That again meant a lot: the festival had boasted a line-up of heavyweights, yet the Rory Gallagher-led Irish trio were the talk of the town.

In 1970, Kid Jensen made a big deal on Luxembourg about the fact he was premiering the next John Lennon album. I waited up to 1 a.m. to hear the first track, which was 'Imagine', and the Kid messed up – he said, 'John Lennon, "Imagine"', and nothing happened. Then he just said, 'Music', and the track started. I was taping it on a cheap battery-operated tape recorder and I played it twice down the phone to Jerry Coyle the next morning. I must have listened to that crackly tape a hundred times over the next six weeks until the song came out as a single, and even today, whenever I hear 'Imagine', I think of Kid Jensen's messed-up intro.

When I wasn't getting new music from *Top of the Pops*, Radio Luxembourg or my brothers' record collections, I was talking about it with my two best friends. Both Jerry and Mel were by now as hooked on music as I was, and we did little but try to get our hands on as much of it as we possibly could.

Our resources were not the same. Mel and Jerry often had a little more disposable income than me so, to be honest, I would try to coerce these guys into buying the records I craved but didn't have the money to get.

Every week I would scour the *NME* or *Melody Maker* and tell Jerry which albums I thought he should buy. Yet Jerry's big thing was buying records because he liked the cover. This led to a few dodgy purchases, particularly in the 1970s. He figured the first Black Sabbath album must be great simply because the sleeve had a picture of a mysterious veiled woman standing in a graveyard.

Jerry's tastes were eclectic and usually visually driven. He'd get seduced by the sleeves and buy albums by groups such as Gracious, Bakerloo or Piblokto. Mel bought the *Fat Mattress* album purely because the cover opened up into four big covers of the band sitting on a tree. Or maybe it was the fact that a former Jimi Hendrix Experience member was in the band. It was lucky the sleeve was striking, as the music wasn't up too much. Mel had more straightforward tastes as the Sixties ended – he was all about Cream, Jethro Tull and, obsessively, Led Zeppelin.

Mel and Jerry were also my company at the first gig I ever attended. Bands had started coming to Dublin in my early teens but I was just too young to go and see the Beatles or the Stones, both of whom played the Adelphi. Naturally, I memorised the reviews of the shows. Years later, I met Bob Geldof again and he told me he'd been to both of the gigs. Even decades later, I was still jealous.

The Adelphi was also the venue for my first gig, but the artists were of a different strain completely: the Bee Gees. It was just after they had a big hit with 'Massachusetts', which appealed to my chart-loving side, but they were also releasing albums with psychedelic covers. They were up there with the best pop music. Gerard had bought the debut album, *1st*, and they had released great singles – 'New York Mining Disaster', 'World', 'To Love Somebody'. The gig was full of screaming girls.

The support bands were also interesting: Dave Dee, Dozy, Beaky, Mick and Tich, who played their hit single 'The Legend of Xanadu' with Dave Dee jumping around stage with a sombrero and a whip. I'd remembered reading about Dave Dee. He used to be a policeman, and in 1960 had attended the scene of the car crash that injured Gene Vincent and killed Eddie Cochran. The other band was Grapefruit, one of the few bands that John Lennon ever signed to the Beatles' Apple label. We bought posters and sat upstairs and I absolutely loved the whole evening.

There weren't many gigs in Dublin at that time but we would go to anything we could get tickets for. The Stadium was where most shows of any size happened, and that was where Mel and I went in March 1971 to see his all-time favourite band, Led Zeppelin, touring the *Led Zeppelin IV*, or 'Four Symbols' album.

The band had played in Belfast the night before and played 'Stairway to Heaven' live for the first time, which was obviously a very big deal. While they also played it in Dublin, of course, I don't remember too much about it. The show was cool and I remember Jimmy Page playing his twin guitar with a bow and John Bonham banging his big gong. It was the songs from *Led Zeppelin III* that did it for me though, and it's still my favourite Zeppelin album.

Gigs were grand, yet for me albums came first. Every penny of my pocket money and my paper-round wage went on them. Each Christmas I would give my parents, brothers and aunties a list of the twenty records I'd most like, and hope for the best. One Christmas, through a mixture of presents and money saved, I hit the jackpot with big ones like *After the Goldrush* by Neil Young, *Atom Heart Mother* by Pink Floyd and *Layla* by Derek and the Dominoes. I also acquired craved-for obscurities like *Shooting at the Moon* by Kevin Ayers; *The Madcap Laughs* by Syd Barrett; *Loaded* by the Velvet Underground; *Twelve Dreams Of Dr. Sardonicus* by Spirit; *Fire and Water* by Free; Little Feat's self-titled debut album; *Lick My Decals Off, Baby* by Captain Beefheart & the Magic Band; *In the Wake of Poseidon* and *Lizard* by King Crimson; *12 Songs* by Randy Newman; Lennon's stark, masterful *Plastic Ono Band*; and, maybe, two of the very best in Soft Machine's *Third* and Dave Mason's *Alone Together*. There was also a great Island sampler called *Bumpers* in there. That really was a great Christmas.

If I had to pinpoint just one album which took me from the Sixties into the Seventies it would be *Blind Faith*, only album of the supergroup bearing the same name. Fifteen minutes were taken up by an awful Ginger Baker song but the other five numbers, including a Buddy Holly cover, combined to make this not just a great album, but an extremely important one for me. It single-handedly bridged the gap between the constant glory and magic of Sixties pop and the new world of progressive, album-orientated rock that was springing up all over the place.

It's hard to explain to kids in these days of constantly accessible websites and downloads, but just physically holding a vinyl album was half of the thrill for me. I would get a new purchase home, eagerly ease the record from its outer and inner sleeve, then spend hours mulling over the sleeve image and lyrics as it played.

Sometimes the inner sleeve had a Jolly Roger skull-and-crossbones and the sombre legend 'Home taping is killing music'. Personally, I thought nothing could kill music. I happily ignored the Jolly Roger's exhortations by recording hours and hours of music onto my own carefully selected 'Various Artists' cassette tapes. Mel, Jerry and I would play them, and always had a pencil or pen to hand, to carefully wind the tape back onto the spools as it inevitably collapsed in the tape deck. The 'Home taping is killing music' argument never convinced me. I just figured, how could I make these tapes without having bought the albums in the first place? I was killing nothing! I was never happier than when compiling yet another 'Various Artists' classic to take its place in the cassette-storage case I had got for Christmas.

To me, Various Artist compilations were an art form. There were no rules; you had to just feel your way to getting it right. A great cassette might have three classic reggae tracks, a very early curio by David Bowie and then a complete curveball such as 'Cottage In Negril' by Jamaican singer Tyrone Taylor. The tracks had to be obscure, brilliant and work together. I named my favourite instrumental self-compilation *Atmospheric* and was delighted when loads of my friends loved it. Sadly, I then betrayed my lack of imagination by naming its two eagerly awaited follow-ups *Atmospheric II* and *Atmospheric III*.

By the time I was at Blackrock College, my Irish teacher, Mr O'Shea, had taken to calling me *Fear Na Ceirnini* – the Man of the Records. I was always bringing albums into school, or he would see me out of school hours, walking up to Jerry's house with records under my arm. I was now a pretty fixated character. If I saw somebody in the street, even a complete stranger, with a record bag under their arm, I couldn't help going up to ask them what was in the bag. If it was Wishbone Ash, chances were they were pretty cool. If it was Brendan O'Dowda, well, maybe not.

Once an English guy came to live in Foster Avenue, in a house across the road from us. Somebody told me that he worked in the Irish office of Atlantic Records – I had never even known record labels had an Irish office. I used to watch him in awe as he drove off to what sounded to me the hippest job ever. I never dared to talk to him, but a neighbour did and got me Yes's *Time and a Word* at 25 per cent discount – nearly ten bob off!

Yes, the *Fear Na Ceirnini* was a very obsessed soul at this point, and his condition was about to get worse. I was already deeply in love with music – but I was poised to discover that it could sound even better and richer than I had ever imagined.

My father retired from his job at the Board of Works in 1972, after forty-seven years in the post. Unsurprisingly, his colleagues were keen to buy him a fittingly lavish retirement present, and my brothers and I, bored of our tinny mono record player, begged him to ask them for a stereo system.

Typically amiable and easygoing, Barney agreed. That shows the kind of father he was. He knew he would hardly ever use it, except maybe for the traditional spin for Brendan O'Dowda or Slim Dusty's 'The Pub With No Beer' on Christmas Day, but he also knew how much it would mean to Gerard and me. So our music room (that's what it was called by now!) in Foster Avenue received delivery of a state-of-the-art stereo record player – the only real litmus test for an album, as far as I was concerned.

By then I had listened to thousands of albums in that same room in the family home, but I'll never forget the day I set up the new system, with one speaker on a board balanced on the radiator and one on the dining-room table. I had waited for this moment for a very long time and in my head an excited little noise was nagging me: 'This is going to be my future for the next few years; it had better be good!'

The very first track I played in this brave new world was 'Carry On', the opening song on Crosby, Stills, Nash and Young's *Déjà Vu*. I COULD NOT BELIEVE THE DIFFERENCE. Obviously I had heard stereo systems before but never here, in my family home where I listened to and assessed all my music. It opened with a flurry of fast, acoustic guitar, then swept into an amazing vocal harmony that segued into a keyboard change – and it was like being blown away by a gust of wind on top of a mountain.

This was perfect! The dodgy old mono player, with the arm that creaked over, stopped in mid-air and clumsily plonked itself on to the crackly vinyl grooves, had been a loyal servant on a daily basis for close on a decade, but at that second it became no more than an outdated, occasionally cherished relic. Now I had a reason to revisit every album I owned and hear them exactly as the band and the producer had meant the music to be heard.

My parents and our warm-natured next-door neighbour, Mrs Maloney, scaled new heights of tolerance over the next few years as my listening routine developed. I would sit precisely between the speakers; the volume edging its way towards 11, with the curtains closed whatever time of day it was. I tried to unscrew the light-bulb, and when I failed, I accidentally-on-purpose broke it. I needed darkness, and top volume.

You may think this behaviour sounds extreme or even mildly disturbed, but to me it never felt that way. I was just indulging my life force, my all-consuming passion. I worked my way through all of my favourite Sixties albums again, with the Beatles and Dylan getting particularly forensic revisits, but Yes and Blind Faith also benefited from these intensive listening sessions.

I would sit between those two carefully balanced speakers for six or seven hours, my bum numb but my ears alive. I would have all the tracks on each album I wanted to listen to lined up in advance and never took more than ten seconds to jump up, take the needle off, put the album back in its sleeve, replace it and be back on my seat by the time the music began. I worked with pit-stop precision and it was always, always very loud.

My friends never even bothered to ring our doorbell any more. They simply knocked on the window. The telephone was in a cupboard at the bottom of the stairs but I never heard it ring, let alone answered it, although more often than not it was for me. It was a strange twilight existence, all alone, playing the music that I loved. You could almost say it was a future DJ doing some intensive career training.

3

In 1971, it came time to leave Blackrock College and I had a major decision to make. Except, of course, that it would be no decision at all. I would go to university because that was what my family did. Annie had only ever wanted two things for her children – for us to be happy, and to be educated. Every one of my siblings went to university except Dermot, and ironically he has worked as a porter at University College Dublin for over four decades. He wasn't alone – my sister Miriam worked in the UCD library for twenty years.

There was no doubt that I would be following John, Peter, Miriam and Gerard's footsteps to UCD. The university's Belfield campus was just across the road from our house in Foster Avenue. Sometimes in life the easy decision is the right one, and as there was nothing else I wanted to do at that time, I went along with it. I was to study English and Philosophy: I had the right qualifications for it, and it made as much sense as anything else.

But before I started at UCD, I took my first trip to England. My brother John was getting married to his girlfriend Kaye in London, and Dermot and I caught the boat over to Holyhead and then got a train down to London. We were there for about five days and I took advantage of the trip by going to see a few films such as *Straw Dogs* and *A Clockwork Orange* that were banned in Ireland back then. It's easy to forget what a strange, priest-riddled society we were – and in some ways still are.

When I started at UCD, I happily continued on my trajectory of being academically relentlessly average. This didn't mean I hated the course; far from it. Some of the texts made an impact. I loved and even memorised some of the classic phrases from Dickens, and for some reason Thomas Hardy's *The Mayor of Casterbridge* had a major effect on me – this strange tale of a poor eedjit who sold his wife to somebody and had his actions come back to haunt him when he became the mayor. I sat down by a roaring log fire to start reading that book at 10 o'clock one night and had finished it by seven the next morning.

I can't pretend, though, that I worked hard and came out of my English degree with a devout appreciation of the poems of Robert Frost or even a burning love for literature in general. When it came to the academic side of things, I did what I had to, and no more, which was reflected in my reliably ordinary exam results. For me, university was mostly about social life, girls, fun and freedom – and that was fantastic.

I had an absolute ball at UCD. Life was great, and exciting, and I felt like I was exactly where I should be. Having always been a fairly gregarious character, I found that I made loads of friends and there always seemed to be something to do, and somebody to do it with.

Obviously, with the arrogance of youth, I thought I was super-cool at college. Looking back, I clearly wasn't. I was always pathetically dishevelled, deliberately so, and a typical day would find me mooching about with my wispy beard and duffle coat, a copy of Solzhenitsyn or *The Hobbit* sticking meaningfully out of a pocket, quoting the *NME*'s The Lone Groover cartoon strip at every opportunity. Pretentious? Moi?

My hair was a source of great angst for me. The early Seventies was an era of being defined by your long hair and, sadly, my long hair was hopeless. Instead of growing straight down like Lennon it was curly and corkscrew and would stick out at ridiculous angles. My beard was even worse. My goal was to look as cool as *Let It Be*-era McCartney. I looked like Catweazle.

I lived at home all through my time at UCD. It never occurred to me to move out. This might have seemed strange to some of my college mates, whose sole ambition was to rent a flat that they could take women back to, but I was perfectly happy staying at home, where the atmosphere was looser, madder and freer than in any campus hall of residence.

I couldn't take girls back to spend the night but that was never really an issue. They weren't exactly queuing up – maybe it was the Catweazle beard that was the problem? Even so, our house in Foster Avenue soon became a major social centre for everyone to pile back to after we had spent the night putting the world to rights over a leisurely pint in the student bar.

My mother loved having my friends round at any time of the day or night. In no time, our house was more like a student flat in Ranelagh or Rathmines than a middle-class south Dublin home. Everybody would troop in, have a friendly word with Annie as she greeted them with homemade biscuits, then we'd all head into 'my' stereo-room to play records. My own late-night culinary skills were always appreciated – tins of salmon and beans on toast!

Even today, nearly forty years on, I meet people who claim to have been back to my house during their years at UCD. I once read in *Hot Press* the Irish justice minister, Dermot Ahern, saying that he went to Dave Fanning's house to listen to Pink Floyd. I am sure he did, but I have absolutely no memory of it whatsoever.

Friday and Saturday nights were always about going to a party, or trying to find one to gatecrash if you weren't invited to one. The routine was always the same – listen out in the student bar or the pub, try to get an address and a name, then just turn up as if you were expected and it was the most natural thing in the world. 'I know Dave! No, I mean Paul! Er ... Pete?' You would always be waving a six-pack of beer on the doorstep to show you were a good guest, but once you got inside you'd seldom put it in the fridge – it'd be gone in a second. Instead, you opened the first can and hid the rest in a secret place. Duffle-coat pockets were always good for that, even if it meant Solzhenitsyn or *The Hobbit*'s pages getting bent or wet.

My UCD years were not too dissolute but everybody smoked stuff they weren't supposed to and I was as enthusiastic as the next man. The first question at any gig you went to, to anyone you met, was always, 'Have you got any skins?' Sometimes it was relentless, and any paper or card in our path – beer mats, magazines, book covers – was in danger of being ripped up to use as roach papers.

Yet for all the enjoyable distractions, music remained my be-all and end-all, and university gave me more chances than ever to wallow in it. The Belfield student bar had cheap night-time gigs with free ones at lunchtime in the Theatre L in the Arts building, and in my three years at UCD, I hardly missed one.

Mainly, it would be local bands that were starting out, although I did see Paul Brady in his folk-inclined, pre-*Hard Station* era, and thought he was great. I also remember a band called Frruup from Belfast, who had just released a debut album called *Future Legends*, which I thought was brilliant. I saw one of them in a bar and had a bit of banter with him: 'I bought your album!' 'Oh, you're the one that bought it!' – that sort of stuff. That was interesting, because even then, I came away thinking, 'I can do that – I can talk to musicians ...'

Outside of college, I was still going to plenty of gigs. Horslips were the big local draw, and Rory Gallagher's gigs were rightly the stuff of legend. I saw Blodwyn Pig supported by Skid Row at the Stadium, and got very excited when Pink Floyd were due to come to Dublin, although in the end they never did, for some reason.

I went to a lot of gigs with Jerry and Mel and any number of others and, by now, Mel had got himself a Morris Minor car and had the four symbols from the cover of *Led Zeppelin IV* painted on the doors. His father owned a place in Clara Vale in Wicklow and Mel, Jerry and I would frequently spend weekends there, listening to my compilation cassettes on the way down and then playing albums on some cheap, tatty little record player that we took with us.

When it came to buying records, I had moved on from Golden Discs in Stillorgan to Pat Egan's Sound Cellar in Nassau Street, on the corner of Grafton Street and opposite Trinity College in the heart of Dublin. Sound Cellar was fantastic. You went through a tiny door that you would easily miss unless you were looking for it and then down two flights of stairs into a dingy, tiny little cellar. It had these great bargain bins and I would find some brilliant oddities and rarities in there.

Rummaging through those bins, I would come across Caravan, Gong, Weather Report, Todd Rundgren, J.J. Cale, Jackson Browne, Mahavishnu Orchestra and hundreds of others. There were some truly weird bands on the Harvest label and some excellent major-label samplers. CBS's *Fill Your Head with Rock* compilation was pretty cool as was Island's *Nice Enough to Eat*, which featured Quintessence, Free, King Crimson, Mott the Hoople, Nick Drake, Ireland's Dr Strangely Strange and Traffic, whom I still regard as one of the greatest English bands of all time.

Pat was eight or nine years older than me and seemed incredibly cool. He had been involved with weird underground bands on the Irish 'beat scene', which was slightly before my time, and as he and his mate and assistant Tommy got used to me being in the shop all the time, they'd call me up and tip me off about new releases.

It was a great system. Pat would phone me up and say, 'I've got such-and-such an album in', and I'd be excited because it wasn't due to be out for three weeks. He might only have one copy, so I'd ask him to keep it for me and then get in there as fast as I could. By then I was buying one album per week and I bet I got 80 per cent of them unheard – almost all on the strength of good reviews in the music comics, usually *NME* or *Melody Maker*.

The first Roxy Music album is probably my favourite debut album of all time. I was hooked from the first single, 'Virginia Plain'. It was all about sha-na-na, quiffs and Teddy Boys, which weren't really my thing, mixed with early 1970s glam rock, which *was*, the songs were magnificent and, crucially, it sounds as good today as it did then. Pat got copies of their next four or five albums a few weeks before their official releases and called me each time. I was usually in to buy it within the hour.

By the end of my first year at UCD, I was happily settled in to the student lifestyle and having the best time I could imagine – but I also had itchy feet. I fancied seeing a bit of the world and also earning enough money to keep me in albums for the next academic year.

One major perk of being a student was that you were eligible for a J1 visa, which allowed you to work abroad during university holidays – in America or nearer to home. A sizeable number of UCD undergraduates took off to Germany when term ended and in the summer of 1972 I decided to join them. As the term ended, I headed for Gross-Gerau, an industrial town twenty miles south of Frankfurt with my friend James O'Nolan. We had secured three months' work in a steel-pressing factory that made hinges and various other parts for BMW cars.

This was a hugely intimidating prospect for one very good reason – I had never done a day's work in my life. Sure, I'd had my early morning paper round for a year or two, but besides that and a week on a farm in Ballivor in County Meath, that was about it. Some kids might have had to clean their house from top to bottom before they were allowed to go and play but that had never been my parents' style and they'd never really made me do anything I hadn't wanted to. In truth, I'd had it pretty easy.

So on my first day I was pretty horrified as the factory foreman showed us around the thumping, clanking workplace full of vast noisy machinery. 'I don't know why you're bothering,' I was thinking. 'This is a big mistake and I'm out of here.' I'm pretty sure that James and a couple of others I was with felt the same – young, scared and a long way from home.

Given this trepidation, I felt very proud of myself that I stuck it out. It wasn't easy. We started work at 6 o'clock each morning, alongside a whole load of other immigrant workers who were mostly Turks or East Europeans. We were working on conveyor belts that turned flat pieces of metal into hinges, and given that each BMW had twenty-four hinges, there was no shortage of work. We'd make thousands of the things every day.

The factory was deafening, there were no earphones and the work was tedious and repetitive, so I survived the long days on the floor by pretending I was giving a concert. In my head, one minute I was Kevin Ayers and the next I was Roxy Music, on stage in Theatre L back in UCD. The foreman used to laugh when he came by and caught me singing my head off but I didn't care – it was my escape from the boredom.

I suppose it was a bit like Michael Caine as Harry Palmer in *The Ipcress File*. There is a scene where he is being tortured but he has a screw hidden in his hand. He grinds the screw so hard that it tears his flesh and blood seeps out but it helps him to survive the torture because it is his own pain; he's controlling it. OK, a bit dramatic, but that was how it felt to me, anyhow.

The four of us stayed in a little house next to the factory and we hardly mixed or learned any German at all. It was our childish way of rebelling against the banality of the whole experience. About the only language I picked up was *arbeiten* (work), *Fabrik* (factory) and *Förderband* (conveyor belt).

We were there to earn money and were so determined not to spend anything that we got into the bad habit of stealing stupid stuff from the local supermarket. I got particularly skilled at nicking coffee. I would walk around the supermarket, come out apparently empty-handed and the other lads would say, 'Ah, you couldn't do it today! No worries!' At which point I would open up my coat to reveal two huge jars of coffee nestling in the lining. I didn't even drink coffee at the time.

It was ridiculous. We even resented spending five Deutschmarks on potatoes, so we would go down to some huge local farm after dark and steal them from the field. We were doing that one night and a plane flew over us, unusually low. I somehow doubt the pilot could even see us or, if he could, was not too bothered about a handful of Irish eedjits nicking spuds but I remember yelling, in all seriousness, 'Hit the dirt!' and we did. There I was, face down with a mouth full of field and a German plane flying overhead, feeling like a wartime soldier from the *Valiant* or one of the other comics I used to read.

The best part about the German trip, by far, was that we got to a few major concerts. With Stephen Russell and Donal Foley and about thirty-five thousand others, I went to my first proper stadium gig near Frankfurt. Eighty per cent of the audience were American GI's, who were all smoking something: joints, pipes, bongs, whatever.

Dave Fanning

The Spencer Davis Group and Colosseum (with Gary Moore) opened up the show but the main draw were Sly and the Family Stone. They had never meant a lot to me but they were soul-funk legends and it was good to tick them off my list. Sly was pretty notorious for not turning up to shows, so when he appeared on stage the place went crazy. However, he did no more than twenty-five minutes before slouching off, leaving the crowd seriously unhappy. They wanted at least another hour.

Sly wasn't even the headliner. That was Rod Stewart, who at the time was enjoying worldwide hits with 'Maggie May' and 'Your Wear It Well' from the *Every Picture Tells a Story* album. This failed to win over the disgruntled GI's and I heard one of them grumble to his mate: 'We want funk rock, not faggot rock.' Rod and Sly share a surname and a chant soon started up: 'We want Sly Stewart, not Rod Stewart.' Rod seemed pretty oblivious to it all and the protest petered out after about twenty minutes.

A week later we were back in Frankfurt to see Frank Zappa, once again entertaining mainly American soldiers. The GIs seemed a pretty demanding bunch and Zappa wasn't exactly a 'play the hits', crowd-pleasing kind of performer, but he had enough authority and charisma to see off any audience revolt and lead them by the hand into fairly experimental areas.

The big-deal show of that summer, though, was the Rolling Stones playing an indoor gig at an ice-hockey arena. They were touring *Exile on Main Street* and Mick Taylor, Brian Jones's replacement, was in the band. You could see there was friction going on: at one point Mick Jagger went over to Taylor and ruffled his hair. Taylor looked at him like he wanted to kill him. After the gig we missed the bus, walked the ten miles home, got in at five in the morning and were back in the *Fabrik* on the *Förderband* by six.

My merry band lasted six weeks in Gross-Gerau and we couldn't wait to get back to Dublin and the pampered student life. We got the trains and boats back to UCD saying 'Never again!' so of course it goes without saying that I was back in the exact same factory the following year. This time I lasted more than three months – the others all quit and left before then, but things are never so bad second time around, and I wanted to earn as much money as possible. After all, those albums didn't buy themselves.

I was so fixated on saving money that I would sometimes hitchhike home across Germany and France to save the train fare. US GI's eager for company would often pick me up. On one journey, a young soldier asked where I was from. When I replied 'Ireland', he said: 'Wow! So have you seen the monster, huh?' It took me a few seconds to work out he meant the Loch Ness Monster. We then discussed this mythical beast for the next half-an-hour, during which I never had the heart to tell him it actually lived in Scotland.

Far more often, when I told people I was from Ireland, they asked about the unrest in Northern Ireland, or the Troubles, as they were called. I never knew what to say. It wasn't that I didn't care – I just felt so helpless and unable to do anything about a situation that looked insoluble. Whenever the latest bad news came on the television, I'd often just turn it off. It was a head-in-the-sand attitude, but I wasn't alone in adopting it.

In fact, I was much more interested in American politics. In my teenage years I had pored over *Rolling Stone* as much as I had the *NME*. They had a lot of political and social-issue coverage and American public figures just seemed so much more larger than life, vital and – let's face it – glamorous than the grey men of Dublin and Belfast. The assassination of JFK had been an incredible drama and I had been equally fascinated by Edward Kennedy's Chappaquiddick scandal, which began the day before the moon landing.

Many UCD students were consumed with anger after Bloody Sunday in 1972 and I remember an air of numbness around the campus that week. We had hated the mad tit-for-tat paramilitary response to everything and their intransigence in the face of just about any offer put to them. But this outrage was something else entirely. It took almost forty years, until the summer of 2010, for the British Government, in the person of Prime Minister David Cameron, to issue an admission of guilt and an apology.

If there was complacency of any sort, it was shaken in May 1974 when three car bombs went off in Dublin during the early evening rush hour. Nobody I knew was hurt (although within days we all felt we knew the victims) but there were tales of near misses and I guess for the first time it made us realise the huge shadow of fear that people in Belfast, just a hundred miles north of us, were living under.

As the summer of 1974 dawned my thoughts were very much over the Atlantic. I got to use my J1 visa again but this time I was giving Deutschland a miss – it was time for my first visit to America, with Mel as my equally pumped-up and excited travelling companion.

We flew into JFK but almost immediately our plans began to come apart at the seams. Mel and I had no fewer than three jobs, or potential jobs, lined up in or around the airport, but they all fell through when we arrived. So we bunkered down in Lefferts Boulevard, near the airport and right at the end of one of the subway lines, while we worked out what to do.

New York was amazing. I guess I always knew it would be, but the place was wonderful. It was almost too much to take in, and at first I was totally green and naive as I wandered around in the stifling summer heatwave. I strolled into a deli and asked for a 'baggle' rather than a bagel, which caused much hilarity at my expense.

In another café I ordered a Coke and asked the guy behind the counter, 'Can you put some ice in it?' He looked at me as if I had two heads, clearly thinking, 'Of course I'm going to!' But he didn't know that I was only too used to buying warm cans of Coke in places like the west of Ireland, where the can could have been in the window in sunshine for six weeks, with a few wasps buzzing around it.

I loved walking around the streets in New York. The sights are so familiar to us through years of watching TV – the yellow taxis, the hydrants, the steam coming up through the grates on the street corners – that it just felt like being in a movie. I loved even more the fact that all the clichés were true: on the rare occasion you clambered into a cab, for example, you really *did* have to shout your destination to a surly and uninterested driver with a very precarious grasp of English.

So New York was great but we were still stuck in that dodgy place at the end of the subway line with no income, and we were beginning to seriously stress out about our situation. It was time for Plan B. Two years earlier, my brother Gerard had come out to the East Coast and worked at a fairground, Shaheen's Fun-O-Rama Park, at Salisbury Beach near Boston. I had brought a brochure from home with the fairground's number on the slim chance that we needed to fall back on the place.

I phoned up the amusement park and because I was 'Gerry Fanning's brother' we were promised jobs on the spot. Our luck was turning. Mel and I went to Grand Central Station to buy tickets and an American guy called Bill Luce introduced himself by the ticket office and offered us a lift, saying he could use some company. He was a great guy and so we drove down in his big car, picking up a female hitchhiker on the way. It was grand: it all felt so cool, so American, so *right*. He even gave us his place to stay in overnight.

Salisbury Beach was in a place called Newburyport, seventy miles from Boston, and Shaheen's Fun-O-Rama was a typical old-fashioned amusement park such as you might find in Blackpool. We got our uniforms, which had red-and-white stripes like a Sunderland FC football kit, and we also got some important news: we would have to get haircuts.

This was the last straw for Mel. I couldn't have cared less, because my hair looked shite anyway, but Mel's hair was like Dave Gilmour's from Pink Floyd and was a statement of cool. He refused to cut it, worked one day at Shaheen's, told me, 'Fuck this place, I'm not doing this one day more!' and flew back to Dublin, where he worked all summer in Captain America's burger joint to claw back the money he'd spent.

So I was on my own in Salisbury Beach – but not for long. The park bosses billeted me in a house on the beach with five good-time, fun-loving party animals from Northern Ireland, including one called John Coll, whose cousin I knew in Dublin. All five of them were fiery, mostly redheaded heavy drinkers; I remember one of them lay on the beach for a whole day and got so sunburnt he had to go to hospital. I lived with this crew of likeable rogues for three memorable months.

The fairground work was no more intellectually demanding than had been the steel-processing plant in Gross-Gerau but it was a lot more fun. I would be working one of the rides, which involved taking the tickets off the customers as they walked up the steps, making sure they were safely strapped into the cars and pressing a button to set the whole thing moving.

There was a definite hierarchy to the amusement park. The big central ride was the rollercoaster, and all the cool American guys worked that, the jocks wearing accessorised red-and-white striped tops with blue slacks who would try to pull the girls as they helped them on to the ride.

I worked the smaller rides in the main part of the park and was just as interested in the music that was being blared out by Shaheen's on-site DJ. It was mostly the same few songs repeated all the time: 'Rock the Boat' by the Hues Corporation, 'Rock Your Baby' by George McCrae, '(You're) Having My Baby' by Paul Anka and 'Sugar Baby Love' by the Rubettes, which had been a big hit in Britain but had only just come out in America.

It was all a blast but, as ever, my focus was on making money to see me through the next term in Dublin and finance my trips to Pat Egan's Sound Cellar, so I worked like mad. The site didn't open until three in the afternoon but I would normally report for work at nine-thirty in the morning to clean the place up.

Then I'd be on duty on the rides until the fairground closed at 1 a.m., which made it an eighty- or even hundred-hour week.

The park was pretty quiet during the afternoons, as everybody stayed on the beach, but was buzzing every single evening as thousands of scantily clad sun-worshippers thronged the boardwalk. The weekends saw an incongruous, unlikely mix of parents with young kids and rowdy Spring Break types.

My sixteen-hour days might have been OK had I been able to relax and sleep at night but our place on the beach was party central. The Northern Ireland guys were all pissheads and loved to invite one-and-all back for parties of some description every night. Our Irish accents were a major plus point. It sounds daft, but we were almost celebrities.

Initially, I was a fish out of water after Mel had left, but living with this fun-loving group was a good experience for me, and they treated me really well. Because I was last in, all the bedrooms had gone when I arrived, but these lads, who were all a bit older than me, looked out for me and gave me a bed in the corner of the main downstairs room.

I had an eight-track machine beside my bed with two tapes – a Moody Blues album and the *American Graffiti* soundtrack, which is a collection of some of the greatest pop music ever assembled, bursting with short, sharp tunes of bobby-sox and pony-tail high-school stories. With bands like the Platters, Diamonds, Crests, Fleetwoods, Monotones, Silhouettes, Clovers, Cleftones, Spaniels, Heartbeats, Skyliners and a host of others from Flash Cadillac and Frankie Lymon to famous names like Buddy Holly and the Beach Boys, the mid-Fifties to early Sixties really was a glorious time for American pop music.

That bed in the corner of the room was where I was to lose my virginity. Frankly, it was not before time. I was 20 years old by then, and while I'd had flings with girls in the past, we'd never gone all the way or got even remotely serious. I had no interest at all in settling down with a steady girlfriend – plus, of course, I was still living with my parents, and I probably bored them all stupid talking about music!

The girl that finally popped my cherry was American. She used to hang around at the parties we held at our beach house of ill repute, and one night it just happened. I didn't have much confidence – in fact, as it became clear we were heading to what American frat boys called third base, I was thinking, 'Are you sure you want to do this with *me*, and not one of those blue-eyed, blond surfer dudes on the beach?' And the awful thing is that I can't even remember her name. Is that terrible – or is it just rock 'n' roll?

At the height of summer the fairground was heaving, I was getting a huge buzz every night, and 8 August 1974 was the most exciting evening of all (with apologies to the anonymous young lady above, obviously). President Richard Nixon had been increasingly at bay and besieged by controversy as the Watergate scandal erupted around him, and on the evening of 8 August, bowing to the inevitable, he became the first US president to resign while still in office.

This was massive news across the world, across America – and certainly on Salisbury Beach. Massachusetts was Democrat, Kennedy country, where Nixon had always been loathed. In the previous election, Nixon had won one of the biggest landslides in American election history. Forty-nine of the fifty states

voted for Nixon. The only one to vote for his Democrat oppo-
nent, George McGovern, was Massachusetts.

So Salisbury Beach celebrated in style. There were fireworks,
a lot of drinking, and a Wicker Man-style effigy of Richard
Nixon burning for hours on the beach. The air was thick with
heady talk of Tricky Dicky being tried for mass murder for his
1970 bombing campaign against Cambodia (obviously, this
came to nothing: instead, his vice-president, Gerald Ford,
assumed office and immediately granted Nixon a full pardon).
Yet for a US politics junkie like me, who had soaked in all this
stuff via the pages of *Rolling Stone*, this was amazing: I felt like
I was right at the heart of things.

The piss-ups continued unabated in the party house, but
unlike my party-animal housemates, I was also broadening my
cultural life. In my first week at Salisbury Beach, I had hatched
a cunning, if rather deceitful, plan, and it had worked like an
absolute dream.

In those days, music magazines as well as titles like *Reader's
Digest* and *Playboy* ran copious adverts for music clubs. The
deal was that you joined these clubs for a token two or three
dollars and were eligible for a fantastic introductory offer
whereby you could choose ten albums of your choice absolutely
gratis. The catch was that you were then obliged to purchase at
least one album per month at full price for at least a year – but I
knew that by then I would be back in Dublin and safely out of
reach.

I spent my first week at Shaheen's subscribing to these clubs,
cutting out forms and posting off my selections, and by July I
had parcels arriving at the beach house every single day. By the

start of August, I owned a hundred new albums and my record collection had doubled in size – and all for the princely sum of $25! I even joined a book club and got the complete works of Shakespeare for $2.50.

My only fear was that I would be travelling back to Ireland with my luggage a lot weightier than when I came out and could well get hit with a mammoth excess baggage charge. I had no need to worry. When I arrived at JFK in September, Orla O'Farrell, a friend of mine from UCD who was also working a J1 visa, was on duty at the Aer Lingus check-in desk. She waved my bags through with a nod and a wink and all was well.

Before I returned to Dublin though, I spent two weeks in New York, where I spent more money every day than I had in a week on Salisbury Beach. I stayed in a place in Bleecker Street and spent a couple of days trailing round Greenwich Village trying to find all the places Bob Dylan had played. It was my own little pathetic version of a Beatles tour of Liverpool.

While I was in New York that August, Frenchman Philippe Petit did his legendary tightrope walk between the Twin Towers, later immortalised in the *Man on Wire* movie. I would love to say I watched it, mouth agape, but I didn't even know it had happened until the next day. Nobody in Greenwich Village did. It's its own little world.

Mostly I spent that fortnight devouring New York and music. It was the dog-end of a scorching heatwave summer, the side-walks seemed to be melting, and the soundtrack to it all was Joni Mitchell's *Court and Spark* album and Eric Clapton's version of 'I Shot the Sheriff' – which, sacrilege as it might be, I have always preferred to Bob Marley's original.

Dave Fanning

Inevitably, I trawled record stores to add to the groaning haul of vinyl I had collected at Salisbury Beach via the unsuspecting music clubs. One mission was to find some music by Harry Partch, a weird old guy I had read a long article about in *Rolling Stone*. He had speakers under the floorboards in his house and only made music on found instruments. This guy made the Legendary Stardust Cowboy sound mainstream.

Poking around inside a musty old record shop, I asked the fella behind the counter about him. He unsurprisingly told me he had never heard of him and asked what kind of music he made. I could have said 'Avant-garde' or 'Experimental' but was honest and said 'Weird' – at which point, to my amazement, the guy pointed me to a 'Weird' section in a corner of the store.

Under the word 'Weird', about a thousand albums were stacked up. I took a deep breath, began flicking through ... and the second album from the front was *The World of Harry Partch*. I didn't even listen to it in the shop, just bought it straightaway, but a measure of exactly how weird it was is that when I got it home to Dublin, the first time I listened to it I played the entire first side at the wrong speed without even realising.

At the end of my NY mini-break, I joined eighty thousand other people at a huge outdoor concert at Roosevelt Raceway in Westbury that was being billed as the sound of California on the East Coast. At that time it was the biggest gig there had ever been in New York. Jesse Colin Young and the Beach Boys played first, then Joni Mitchell, and the headliners were Crosby, Stills, Nash and Young.

64

CSNY played for a long time and each member also played a solo set. Neil Young began his by telling us that, at the end, he would reveal the fate of Evel Knievel. The legendary daredevil had proclaimed that he would leap that day across the Grand Canyon on his motorbike. Young played a magnificent set and at the end, as he ambled off, said, 'It was a sham, it was a scam and he's still alive.' It was a fitting end to one of the best summers of my life.

Yet all dreams have to come to an end and, back in Dublin, I came down to a earth with a bump. I graduated in 1975 with a BA but no honours, which was pretty much what my minimal work-rate had deserved, and decided that I would take a one-year Higher Diploma in teaching.

I didn't make this decision with the best of motivations. All I wanted to do was to prolong academic life for one more year. I could take or leave teaching, it didn't have a great appeal for me, but I was also desperate not to leave university and slump into the nine-to-five grind.

Despite this, the H.Dip. course came as a bit of a shock to me. I had had it pretty easy on my degree course, where we only had to attend a handful of lectures every week, but this was a lot more onerous. I soon noticed that a few of the UCD heads who had spent most of the last three years stoned became pretty serious as they embarked upon their H.Dip. If I ever felt that I wanted to remain a student forever, the H.Dip. cured me of that folly. This was to be my shoehorn out of UCD.

Part of the course involved me teaching for a hundred hours during the academic year, which I did at St Peter & Paul's School in Walkinstown, about four miles south of Dublin. I spent a year heading there every day on the No. 17 bus, which followed the most circuitous and indirect route imaginable.

I was teaching English and a little bit of Geography as a supply or replacement teacher to 12-year-olds. It was an experience that I quite enjoyed without it ever feeling remotely like a vocation. The normal teachers would head off for a cup of tea, leaving me in charge of their class for an hour; then, in the afternoon, I would get the bus back to UCD, where I had lectures from four to six.

On Fridays at St Peter & Paul's the lessons were pretty relaxed, so I decided to school my English class in the works of Bob Dylan. Again, this was probably my attempt to prolong student life and kid myself that I wasn't now in the world of work. I also learned that Dylan's words definitely work better as song lyrics than they do as standalone poetry.

By now it was hard to believe that, as a kid, I had hated it when my older brothers played Dylan on the record player in Foster Avenue, thus robbing me of valuable time to play chart-pop. I absolutely worshipped Dylan and in that summer of 1976, I managed to see him live for the first time. The trip made no financial sense whatsoever. I had no money at all, but I still managed to scrimp and save enough together to get the boat to Holyhead in Wales and a train to London to see him play at Earl's Court.

This was Dylan's first UK show in years. He was touring the *Desire* album, which I thought was fantastic, and I was about fifty rows back. I loved being so close to him and yet the show itself was a tad underwhelming (my first, but by no means last, experience of being disappointed by Dylan live). Even so, I decided to stay on and bought a ticket from a tout for the next night's performance, ten rows from the front It was marginally better, but only marginally.

Back in Dublin, my teaching diploma year passed pretty quickly and I knew by then that I was living on borrowed time. My parents had never pushed me but they knew as well as I did that I had milked the studying thing as much as I could and it was time to face up to working life now that I was a qualified teacher.

For my part, I was naturally hugely in denial about this fact, and so immediately did the first thing I could think of to postpone reality. When September came around and there was no college for me to go back to, I vanished to Germany to work in a factory yet again, this time with Jerry Coyle in tow.

Jerry and I were working in a place called Krupunder on the outskirts of Hamburg, at the end of the U-Bahn line. It was freezing cold, winter was coming, and we were making wooden and cardboard boxes. It was pretty mindless work whichever way you looked at it.

This was my fourth working visit to Germany and I knew in my heart it was a trip too far. I felt like the student who graduates and then lives in the past, refusing to leave his university town, or the hapless loser who is still at a party at four in the morning when everybody else left hours ago. Jerry and I spent a few evenings in the local Bierkeller pretending we were having fun but I knew I was just avoiding the burning question of what I was actually going to do with my life.

After three months, Mel (who had joined us back down in Dusseldorf) and I set off on the nightmare journey back to

Dublin via a boat and train through France and then the ferry across the Channel. We arrived in London's Euston station at seven in the morning to find the tabloid newspapers raving about THE FILTH AND THE FURY. It seemed a whole new movement of bands had been brewing in London, dedicated to overthrowing the old musical order. They were calling it punk rock. I had been wasting my time making cardboard boxes in Krupunder and didn't know an awful lot about it.

It gave me a fillip, though, and I resolved to have one last determined go at finding work in music – even though I had no idea what kind of work it might be. My sole previous attempt had come four years earlier, when I had copied the address of a US recording studio off the sleeve of Elton John's *Tumbleweed Connection* album and written to them asking if they had any tea-making jobs going that summer. I never heard anything back.

So as I cast around for any way at all to make a living from my love of music, I settled into a fairly aimless period back in Dublin. In truth, I was stagnating and I knew it. I put in a few perfunctory applications for teaching jobs but knew in my heart that it was not what I wanted to do.

A few casual jobs kept the wolves from the door and maintained my album-buying habit. For a few weeks, I helped Neil Hickey, a friend from Foster Avenue, to man his market stall on the Dandelion Market. Neil was a maverick who had never even thought of going to college. His brother-in-law imported exotic sweets, so he started selling them on the market as a sideline.

Helping Neil out one day, I saw a skinny hand sneaking around the side of the stall to steal a chocolate. I rapped the offender hard on the wrist, only to be confronted by the indignant face of an adolescent whom I had taught a year earlier during my H.Dip. in Walkinstown. 'Jaysus, Mr Fanning!' he admonished me. 'It's only a Rolo!'

With a couple of great friends – James O'Nolan and his girl-friend, Martha McCarron – we bought some antiques and tried to sell them via a separate stall in the Dandelion Market but, as with my final labouring trip to Germany, all I was doing was killing time. My life was going nowhere, and fast.

I knew what I wanted, in an ideal world: gainful employment in the Irish music industry. This left me with one major hurdle to overcome: there was no such thing as the Irish music industry.

4

It was my mum who first saw the job advert. Annie was flicking through the *Irish Times*, as was her wont every day, and there at the back of the paper, in the Situations Vacant, were the words that jumped off the page the second she showed them to me:

EDITOR AND CONTRIBUTORS WANTED
FOR *SCENE* MAGAZINE

I knew all about *Scene*. In fact, I had read every issue. It was a monthly Irish rock magazine, the local manifestation of the DIY, semi-underground, punk-fuelled ethic that had inspired a host of cheap-and-cheerful independent music magazines and fanzines. It had been launched a few months earlier by Niall Stokes, a big music fan who was a couple of years older than me; I knew him slightly when we were both at UCD. A couple of friends, including Martha, also rang me about the ad.

At this stage, my music-journalism career amounted to no more than a lengthy essay on Joni Mitchell that I had penned for the UCD student newspaper, *The Campus Chronicle*, but this lack of experience didn't deter me from applying for the first job I had ever seen that would involve me making a living from music. I was hugely excited to be summoned for an interview at the *Scene* office near Portobello Bridge in Rathmines.

When I got there, I learned the situation in-house was far from ideal. Niall Stokes and the entire *Scene* staff had left to launch their own Irish music magazine, called *Hot Press* (which, of course, was to prove an enormous mould-breaking success, and which Niall is still editing today, more than thirty years on). The *Scene* publisher, Norman Barry, was thus casting around for a new team to keep his music title running.

Norman boasted a small and very idiosyncratic media empire. His handful of staff churned out four magazines per month: one was all about boats; one covered horses; one was packed with pictures of socialites in tuxedos and ball gowns at upmarket functions around Dublin; and the fourth was *Scene*. Norman freely admitted that he knew nothing about rock music and cared even less, and as only two people had answered the job advert, we became the new *Scene* team.

My colleague was to be a fella named Ken Ryan, a family man with three kids who had somehow managed to bluff his way into the publishing industry. Ken's main plus point was his infectious, game-for-a-laugh, try-anything enthusiasm. I knew everything about rock 'n' roll so Ken happily left that side of things to me and stayed in the office doing whatever it was that he did.

I threw myself into *Scene* with energy and optimism. The magazine was hardly a money-spinner and the pay was lousy, but I reasoned that at least a few people had heard of it, and it was the best, and indeed only, option I had. What did I have to lose?

Scene was a bit of a cowboy operation, and Ken Ryan and I were a pair of chancers making it up as we went along, but somehow we got a magazine out each month. A typical issue would contain interviews with local bands, live reviews, album reviews plus a fair chunk of advertising copy masquerading as editorial – and we always had the fall-back of photos of some local fashion party or other to fill the blank pages.

Scene was unlikely ever to be confused with *Rolling Stone*, then, but I was having a blast. Ken and I began a feature called 'Six Days on the Road', which involved me seeing a load of gigs every week and rambling on about them over two pages. Neil Hickey by now had a VW van to sell his exotic sweets from and this would be our transport to Dun Laoghaire to see a local band called Cool Breeze. I was also regularly writing about Stepaside at the Sportsman's in Mount Merrion, and any number of bands at the Baggot Inn and Toners in town.

With up to eighty pages per issue to fill, Ken and I were always desperate for feature material and nothing was too leftfield or obscure for us to cover. This constant hunger for copy led us to take an editorial decision in July 1977 that was to change my life.

We had been vaguely aware of a pirate radio station called Radio Dublin that had recently begun broadcasting a couple of pop shows every Saturday night. Looking for publicity, the station's owner called us one day, so we invited him in.

Eamonn Cooke was a decidedly bizarre character. A wizened, mature gentleman of indeterminate but possibly pensionable age, he drove an old white Rolls-Royce, styled himself Captain

Cooke and arrived at the *Scene* office carrying a shiny briefcase, which he promptly deposited on the interview table. I later found out that, *à la* James Bond, he had secreted a microphone in the case's lining and taped every word of our conversation.

Captain Cooke wasn't paranoid, as such, but conflicted – he was keen for some good publicity via what he regarded as a credible music magazine, but was also wary of what we might write. Yet as the interview progressed and he realised Ken and I had no hidden agenda, he relaxed and made us an extremely interesting offer.

The Captain explained that he was feeling ambitious and had resolved to expand Radio Dublin from its Saturday-evening-only broadcasts to also encompass a programme on Wednesday nights. He asked whether we would be interested in hosting a midweek show that would allow us regularly to plug *Scene* while also boosting his station's credibility. It was an idea to be seriously considered, given that his pirate was the only Irish radio station in existence outside of Radio Éireann.

Ken and I visited the Captain's tiny terraced house in Sarsfield Road in Inchicore in the southern suburbs of Dublin; a bizarre cave littered with wires, screwdrivers and customised bits of old radios. We met the lovely Sylvie, the station's sole existing DJ, and decided to give it a go. There was no debate over which of the two of us would be going on the air: Ken was married with three kids and had no intention of giving up his Wednesday nights to plug *Scene*. This one was down to me.

I was in two minds. Instinctively, I knew this opportunity was exactly what I was looking for, but I had to admit that I found the idea of talking on the radio a daunting prospect. Was

I really up for this? Yet Ken soon demolished my fears and put me at my ease with a typical Dubliner's logic: 'Sure, don't worry, it's not as if anybody will be listening to it!'

So August 1977 saw me host my first ever radio show, the first of thousands, via cheap twin decks and a dodgy microphone at the front window of a tiny terrace in Inchicore. It certainly didn't feel like the start of an era, but for what it's worth, the first record I ever played was 'Wishing Well' by Free.

Scene was still my main focus, of course, and Ken introduced me to a friend of his who wanted to contribute a few album reviews. Eddie Jordan is nowadays a multi-millionaire, and for some time was one of the biggest names in Formula One, but back then he was a clerk at the Bank of Ireland in Rathmines who owned a bashed-up old racing car that he parked outside his house.

Eddie didn't want his bosses at the bank to know that he was moonlighting reviewing records so he wrote under the pen name Jordache, which, come to think of it, wasn't the most impenetrable pseudonym ever invented. He was also a decent musician and his speciality was serious US guitar groups.

New local music was *Scene*'s lifeblood. One day in 1977, Fachtna O'Kelly came to our office to talk to me about the imminent, eponymous debut album by the Boomtown Rats. I had a lot of time for Fachtna. He was cool. Having been a music journalist on a national newspaper, he was trying his hand at management with the Rats, which was not proving an easy job.

A lot of Dublin scenesters and established musicians looked down on the Rats, feeling that they were all attitude and no talent and, worst of all in their eyes, hadn't paid their dues. I didn't share that opinion. I had seen them play Saturday night discos in Belfield and at Slattery's and thought they were great, with serious energy and thoughtful songs. They also came from my neck of the woods; my side of Dublin. I also slightly knew Bob Geldof, through his friendship with my brother Gerard.

So when the eponymous Boomtown Rats debut album came out a few weeks later, I loved it – in fact, it is still my favourite Rats record. I gave it the centre spread in *Scene* under the headline VINYL PROOF IS THE FINAL PROOF. It was, too. When it came to punk rock, the Clash and Pistols were kicking off in London, Blondie and Talking Heads were happening in New York, and we had the Rats and the Radiators.

I was intrigued and excited by punk – who wouldn't be? Yet I didn't share the scorched-earth attitude of its most extreme followers, who said that everything apart from punk was shit. For me, it wasn't about out with the old and in with the new: I loved the new wave but couldn't find it in me – or see the need – to turn my back on beloved old music.

Not that I didn't understand, and even admire, that strain of radical thinking. If you were 15 or 16 and consumed by punk, loving the new was all about hating the old, but just as I had been too young to be a hippy, I was too old to be a punk. In 1977 I was 23, and just wanted to soak up great music of every hue.

Nevertheless, it was still a major event on 21 October of that year when the Clash – the leaders of the punk revolution, and the darling of the London-based British music media – played their first Irish gig at Trinity College in Dublin. This was clearly going to be a legendary gig and I went along prepared to be utterly blown away. One problem: it was absolutely awful.

Was this Joe Strummer and Mick Jones's fault? I have no idea. I knew punk gigs were meant to be shambolic and in-your-face but this was just an excruciating blare of noise from start to finish. The fault probably lay with Trinity College, because a couple of years later I saw the Clash on the *London Calling* tour at the Top Hat in Dun Laoghaire and it remains one of my very favourite gigs of all time – if not *the* favourite.

At the other end of the musical spectrum, I developed an abiding love for Leonard Cohen, just the sort of literary, erudite artist who would be shunned by many contemptuous punks. Cohen played Dublin a dozen times in the 1970s, nearly always at the National Stadium, and I went to every one. Sometimes the ticket demand was so high that he would play a show at 5 p.m. and another gig later that evening, and there was no way I would miss either one.

Increasingly, when I wasn't at gigs in the evenings after I'd finished work at *Scene*, I was up at the tiny terrace house in Inchicore. Radio Dublin was by now broadcasting for ten or twelve hours most nights and I was on air three or four nights per week. Sometimes I would play my first record at 10 p.m. and go right through until 8 a.m., when a Trinity College graduate and friend of mine called Sarge – who would go on to co-found digital animation company Framestore – came in to do his breakfast show. After Sarge emigrated to London, John Clarke who many years later became the boss of 2FM, took over the programme.

Captain Cooke largely left me alone as he pottered around the house fiddling with wires and transformers but he didn't like my playlist of punk, new wave and new music in general, with the odd classic rock track thrown in. He was prone to suggesting I might like to add some Boney M to the musical mix; I am proud to say I always resisted that imprecation.

The Captain had more weighty matters on his mind at Christmas 1977. Radio Dublin's profile had been rising and we came to the attention of the local authorities, who promptly closed us down. We were only off the air for a few days and came back to find we had become a *cause célèbre*, with the *Evening Press* and *Evening Herald* both supporting this plucky little station in its David v Goliath struggle against The Man.

Yet despite our new folk hero status, Radio Dublin always felt like it was built on sand. The studio was a shambles, Captain Cooke didn't like my music and could have got rid of me at any minute, and he was an archetypal eccentric. I always thought he was a harmless one, mind you – which was why it was such a jolt, years later, to be phoned by a journalist wanting a reaction to the news that the Captain had been sent to jail for sex offences.

Given my misgivings about Radio Dublin, it didn't take me long to decide to jump ship at the start of 1978 when a rival network got in touch. James Dillon was part of a team of entrepreneurs who were trying to get the Big D off the ground, and clearly it was going to be a far more professional set-up than Radio Dublin.

The Big D was still a pirate, but rather than a chaotic cave in the suburbs it was to broadcast from a reasonably smart studio in Chapel Lane near Henry Street in the centre of Dublin. Dillon offered me a minimal weekly wage and offered me the midnight slot from Monday to Thursday every week. The plan was for the station to make its money playing chart pop during the day, leaving me free to do my alternative thing at night.

I jumped at the chance, even though the offer made very little financial sense. Every night I needed to transport forty or fifty vinyl albums from Foster Avenue to the studio; I would happily have cycled, but the sheer weight made the idea a non-starter. I had no choice but to get taxis to and from work every night, despite the fact they cost more than I got paid to do the shows.

Yet for the first time I felt that I was exactly where I wanted to be, doing what I was born to do. The Big D felt like a mission. I had always hated the fact that Irish bands had no outlet and so made an on-air appeal to be sent demo tapes. In no time at all, I was playing these cassettes as frequently as major-label vinyl releases.

It was lucky that the Big D had come along, as *Scene* was in trouble. Ken and I had lasted the best part of a year, put out twelve issues and even seen the publication turn A4 and glossy, but it was struggling commercially. It couldn't really compete with *Hot Press*'s greater heft and resources, and after about a year, Norman Barry pulled the plug.

Scene folded owing money to creditors, and humble reviewers were way down the list of priorities, meaning that Eddie Jordan, a.k.a. Jordache, never got paid his £10 for a Steely Dan album review he wrote for the final issue. (He has never been slow to remind me of this fact whenever our paths have crossed over the last thirty years; the debt was finally settled, or rather reversed, when I bumped into him in the Point a couple of years ago and gave him £20.)

It was sad to see the demise of *Scene*, although it h
run its course, but I quickly found another outlet for
ing. *In Dublin*, the equivalent to London's *Time Out*, ra
and movie reviews and was happy to use my scribbling
a useful outlet – and also introduced me to a man who
play a major role in shaping my career.

Ian Wilson was a bit of a name around Dublin. He had
the Ents Secretary at Trinity College, responsible for boo
all the gigs. He had also been involved in radical student p
tics and was now working on *In Dublin*. He was often in
magazine offices doing last-minute editing at weekends.
started off on nodding terms – but that would soon change.

It seemed like something new was happening every week in
that heady summer of 1978, when *Saturday Night Fever* dominated the airwaves during the day but new wave ruled on the
pirate stations at night. McGonagles, the hip and happening St
Anne Street club and gig venue, asked me to DJ on Friday, Saturday and Sunday nights. I eagerly accepted, and so was now in
the novel and distinctly non-lucrative position of working seven
nights per week at two different jobs, both of which started at
midnight in the centre of Dublin, and neither of which paid well
enough to cover my transport costs to get there.

Yet the Big D was taking off and I was having the time of my
life. It would have been hard for me to invent a better job (except
that some more money would have been nice). In the early hours
of the morning, I conducted erratic interviews with local bands
that turned up brandishing six-packs. Bassists fell asleep in the
corner and their snoring was broadcast all over Dublin. I did
every single show standing up – who needed chairs? We were

making it up as we went along but it felt real, significant and, most of all, fantastic fun.

Legendary local cult hero Smiley Bolger was the McGonagles DJ on the nights I wasn't there, i.e. Mondays to Thursdays, and also followed me on the air at the Big D when I clocked off at 3.30 a.m. Smiley would turn up with a beat box, change the light-bulbs to give the studio a clubbier ambience, then blast all sorts of music out until six or seven in the morning. It was all too much fun to go home, so I would often hang out with him.

We were still illegal, of course, and Big D's enhanced profile meant that a police raid was probably inevitable, but we just had to trust in the massive steel door at the bottom of the stage. I had probably grown blasé and assumed it would never happen by the time I went on a boozy boat-and-train journey to the Reading rock festival in August. The Garda struck while I was away: the DJ on duty was Denis Murray.

The Chapel Lane studio came to an end in somewhat mysterious circumstances. One evening Neil Hickey came in to hang out with me, and after I had finished my show we drove off in his orange VW van, inevitably filled with exotic sweets, to Big D owner James Dillon's house. I had left a tape of a pre-recorded show playing to fill the night hours and Neil and I tried to tune in to listen to it. Finding nothing, we assumed the transmission had gone on the blink.

You could say that again. The next morning we woke up to the news that the station had burned down and there was nothing left but a blackened shell. We absorbed this bad news, but within two days were up and running again with a new studio on St Stephen's Green. I couldn't help noticing that we were

using equipment that looked remarkably similar to what I had been using in Chapel Lane.

The St Stephen's Green studio was rather more salubrious and in a more gentrified part of town than Chapel Lane and, in truth, lacked its predecessor's edgy charm. Nevertheless, the Big D was growing in reputation and import, and soon not only local bands but also touring English artists were making their way up the four flights of stairs for interviews.

XTC were one of the best of the post-punk English new wave acts, but their Big D interview was cut short rather abruptly. As their record played, Andy Partridge complimented me on our smart studio and I idly replied that we were a pirate station and could get raided at any minute – at which point, one of the band jumped to his feet and bolted out of the door.

Probably my favourite punk album at that point was the second album by the Ramones, *Ramones Leave Home*. During my H.Dip. year it had been my personal soundtrack as I'd made that No. 17 bus journey to the school in Walkinstown, so it was a serious buzz for me when all four of the Ramones came into the studio one night. They were cool, laid-back and fairly philo-sophical about the many critics who wrote them off as cartoons or one-trick ponies.

I was in seventh heaven the next night when I went to their Dublin gig. Joey Ramone never said anything between songs apart from '1-2-3-4!', but as they fired into 'Babysitter' he drawled, 'This one goes out to Dave Fanning.' I heard it again decades later on a live bootleg, and it still gave me a thrill.

I thought the Ramones had a lot in common with the Under-tones and after I heard the Derry band's early singles that I had bought from Terry Hooley's Good Vibrations shop in Belfast, I raved about them on the radio. The late, great Bill Graham, chief *Hot Press* scribe, happened to be listening in the bath and jumped out, dried himself off and got a taxi down to the studio with a white label of their debut album.

Local bands such as the Blades and the Vipers sent me all their demos and came in for interviews, but I wasn't all about rebel rock and the shock of the new. I had formed an odd affection for Dire Straits when their debut single 'Sultans of Swing' came out in 1978, and played tracks off their first album when it came out, even though most punk and new wave fans hated them.

What followed was distinctly surreal. I had a phone call from an English guy who introduced himself as John Illsley, the bassist in Dire Straits. He thanked me for my support on the Big D and asked me if I wanted to go over to where he was staying, close to the Dublin Observatory, to interview him for the show.

This was most unorthodox, but the guy seemed pretty straight up and in those days crazy things were happening on a pretty serial basis, so I went along with it and headed out to his place. He was such a charming host and good company that, even though things didn't seem quite right, I invited him to come into the studio.

Before he arrived I talked to my producer and some of the other DJs and we all thought it might be a scam, but when 'Illsley' got in he was great value, cracking stories, dropping names such as David Bowie, and regaling us with anecdotes from Dire Straits' trip to New York a few weeks before. I was so puzzled that after the interview I went undercover to the hotel my guest had claimed he was staying in. Sure enough, they had a John Illsley booked into a suite. He had paid in cash.

Despite this, it was no real surprise a few months later when I interviewed Dire Straits to find that the real John Illsley bore no resemblance to the sharp operator who had fooled me so adroitly. Actually, that's not strictly true. Even on the night, we were just about certain he was an impostor, but the thing had taken on such a life of its own that it seemed a shame to spoil the fun and stop the rollercoaster. When I met the full band, I tried to explain to Mark Knopfler and the others what had happened. They clearly had no idea what I was talking about.

It was great meeting the touring English stars, and a large part of me was thrilled to be sitting chatting with artists I had read about for years in *NME* and *Melody Maker*, but my main drive on the Big D was still finding local talent and giving it its first break. At which point, enter the band who were to become the biggest Irish rock group of all time. So, what did I think of them? I was distinctly underwhelmed.

I had been vaguely aware of U2 for a little while. Or, rather, of the Hype, which was what they called themselves at that point. They played McGonagles one early 1978 midweek night, as the support act to Revolver, and I had wandered down but got there too late. For what it's worth, Revolver were pretty good.

By the end of 1978 the Hype had renamed themselves U2 and were playing McGonagles, as well as a few gigs in the Dandelion Market. They also started sending me demo tapes and initially I played them no more or less than other local bands. The band even came into the Big D for an interview, which was rare when they had not even got as far as putting a single out. But they were great to talk to, I loved the singer Bono's passion, wit and intensity – and they were certainly persistent.

One night in the Big D, I was interviewing Gavin Friday and his surrealist art punks the Virgin Prunes, who were also just starting out, when there came a knock on the door. I put a record on, ran down the four flights of stairs, and found Bono and the Edge standing there.

'I interviewed you two nights ago! What's up?'

'The Prunes – they're good friends of ours!'

I let them in.

U2 were not my favourite Irish band back then – I was more into the Undertones, the Rats and the Blades – but by late 1978 they were gathering pace, and on the strength of better demos I was soon championing them over any other of the new bands. They still had a certain gaucheness but the tapes they were sending me were getting stronger and I was getting to know, and like, them as people: Bono's motormouth enthusiasm, Edge's knowing calm, Adam's aloof irony and Larry's no-nonsense Dublin bluffness.

By this stage I was getting regular mentions in Hot Press and after one glowing nod where I got praised for championing Tom Waits, Niall Stokes asked me to write for the magazine. One of my commissions was to cover the Dark Space Festival, a twenty-four-hour 'happening' at the Project Arts Centre in Temple Bar.

The festival featured bands, art installations and a few films projected onto a white wall, and Niall sent two reviewers to cover it. I opted for my usual working hours: midnight to 6 a.m. U2 played at three in the morning, the worst time possible as by then the revellers were drunk, stoned, asleep, or all three. Most of the people still conscious were watching the movie. But Dave 'Scoop' Fanning of *Hot Press* was wide awake and filed the following report:

> Death Race 2000 *had passed its halfway mark when U2 took the stage to the hearty applause of the dedicated followers of fashion who had forgotten to bring sleeping bags. And the band's rock 'n' roll breakfast tasted just fine. With perfect posturing and dynamic delivery, Paul Hewson, straining every muscle and pulling the band forward, was always arresting. While they were always confident and competent, Dave Evans (gtr) and Adam Clayton (bass) belied the intermittent tendency to drag the music into the clutches of the age-old malaise of sludge metal, especially on the shadily atmospheric 'Shadows and Tall Trees'. The sound was crisp enough but Tayto it ain't. Yet on numbers like 'Cartoon World' and 'Another Time, Another Place' they showed enough bravado and intelligence to show anyone why this young band has hairs on their chest. 'Street Missions' was great. Their encore, 'Glad to See You Go', was energetic but it suffered slightly from its slower-than-the-Ramones pace. Not to worry. Their own numbers and enthusiasm will see them through.*

If I am honest, the review makes the show seem a whole lot more portentous than it was. I don't think there were actually more than ten people watching at any point in the gig. But my closing words were to prove prescient. U2 were about to get a very big break – and so was I.

5

As 1978 came to an end, my life was pretty good but not great. The positive aspect was that I was having the time of my life on pirate radio, meeting the bands I had always admired and living for new music – all I had ever wanted. The minus side was that I was perennially skint, living hand-to-mouth – and knew at any time the police could kick down the Big D's door and bring my playhouse crashing down.

It seemed impossible that I could carry on living this essentially idyllic lifestyle and yet do it legally, with confidence and security and for a decent regular salary. And then, suddenly, my dream came true.

RTÉ had for months been getting pretty hacked off with the scores of pirate radio stations that had sprung up all around Ireland in the wake of punk and stolen their younger listeners. Finally grasping the nettle, the state broadcaster announced that it was to do what it should have done years earlier – launch a national pop and rock music station.

A full twelve years after the BBC had launched Radio 1 in Britain, Radio 2 was to be our equivalent. The second I heard about it, I wanted in. I was not the only one. By now there must have been two to three hundred people working on illegal stations from Cork to Donegal. I imagine every single one of them applied for the twelve DJ jobs that RTÉ were advertising on Radio 2.

This was when I got very, very lucky. RTÉ were also looking for producers for their May 1979 launch and recruited Ian Wilson from *In Dublin*. They asked his advice on who should be presenting the shows, and, knowing Ian as I do, I've a shrewd idea of what he might have told them: 'Look, we need a rock guy at midnight and Dave Fanning is your man. He's doing the same show on the Big D, a lot of people like it, and what's more he's writing for all the music magazines, knows his stuff and is yer man about town. You'd be crazy not to use him.'

So that was it. Of course, I've no idea of what actually took place but there was never even anything remotely like an interview. I was to be RTÉ's late-night rock DJ from midnight to 2 a.m. on Radio 2, five days per week – my dream job, and it had fallen right into my lap. I jacked in the Big D and the DJ stints at McGonagles, and began preparing for the launch.

Even though Radio 2 sounded idyllic, initially I had reservations. Radio Dublin and the Big D had been raw, exciting and very amateurish, and I worried that RTÉ might prove too anodyne and sanitised by comparison. Would it all be just too corporate? Having been able to play and say exactly what I wanted to until now, I wasn't ready to give up my freedom to the suits.

I need not have worried. As we moved into RTÉ's swish studios on the Stillorgan Road, three-quarters of a mile from my home in Foster Avenue, it became clear it would be business as usual. Ian Wilson was to be my producer, and we would get together to plan the show, work out a rough playlist and a list of guests we wanted to invite on, and then hit the air.

Just before Radio 2 launched in May 1979, we had a charity football match in which the guest of honour was the Taoiseach, Charles Haughey. I thought Haughey was an odious little thug. He made me think of a TV mafioso who parrots the word 'Respect' while having no idea what it means. With his Aran sweater, his Kerry island and lord-of-the-manor attitude, he predated a character on *The Fast Show*, yet Charlie just wasn't funny.

As we lined up before the match, the Taoiseach made his way down the queue of players, shaking everybody's hand. I was holding a ball, and as Haughey reached me, I accidentally-on-purpose dropped it and ran off after it to avoid having any contact with him. It may have been pathetic, but it was my little act of rebellion.

The station launched with the in-your-face marketing slogan 'Cominatcha!' The management and producers had done a pretty decent job of assembling a strong broadcasting team from the off. Gerry Ryan moved over with me from the Big D, while other ex-pirates included Ronan Collins, Declan Meehan and Michael McNamara. Mark Cagney moved over from Cork local radio and a few DJs transferred from RTÉ's existing Radio 1 network: Vincent Hanley, Jimmy Grealy and Larry Gogan, who kicked things off by playing 'Like Clockwork' by the Boomtown Rats.

I felt pleased and flattered to be in such august company and was even more delighted to realise that, in Ian Wilson, I had a colossus in my corner. Wilson was just as committed as me to furthering the cause of new young bands and was hugely aware of the vast advantage of RTÉ over the pirates: we had proper studios, where groups could record sessions for the show.

Ian's attitude was that, night after night, I had been pushing new Irish music on the pirates for the previous few years. In many ways it had always been the centrepiece of my shows. I'd been playing Irish music, the officially released stuff from established or semi-established acts, but the big emphasis for me had always been the demo tapes, the new bands that never got a chance to be heard anywhere else. It was time to shift it up a gear.

RTÉ had always used its state-of-the-art facilities and top-of-the-range sound engineers to record major classical works, with the RTÉ Concert Orchestra pretty much annexing the lavish and spacious Studio 1 for rehearsals and performances. However, the smaller, rough-and-ready Studio 8 was frequently empty, and Ian donned his public-service hat to demand that we be allowed to use it for sessions by up-and-coming groups.

The RTÉ bosses were not at all keen on this at first. It was easy to see why. The sessions would cost money to record but not make any. Why should they give up valuable studio time for no financial return? But Ian was on a mission and argued that the hip quotient and profile for the network would be invaluable. A few weeks after Radio 2 launched, the Fanning Sessions were up and running.

Ian Wilson deserves the utmost credit for his prescience and persistence because it soon became clear that Fanning Sessions were as crucial to the show as they were to the bands. The routine was that a group would usually come in on a Monday and record four numbers, adding vocals and doing the mixing the next day. Suddenly, bands that nobody had heard of, who had never had even a sniff of a decent studio, could do their stuff and have four professionally recorded and mixed songs aired on national radio.

To my surprise and delight, in no time at all a session on my midnight Radio 2 rock show became the first rung on the ladder for wet-behind-the-ears Irish bands. It was their apprentice-ship. They would then send the tapes to record companies to try to get signed, and while successful submissions were still rare, it was even more rare to find a press release on the debut album of a newly signed band that didn't mention a Fanning Session.

People have praised me for this over the years and said some very kind things about my positive effect on the Irish music industry but I have always felt awkward accepting these plau-dits. Just because I'd already been doing this on my own for a few years, doesn't mean I would have had the tenacity or where-withal to take it to the level it needed to go to. Ian Wilson deserves the praise for that. I simply felt that really this was just the sort of thing RTÉ should have been doing years ago in exchange for its licence fee.

It was 1979. We were thankfully out of the 1950s and 60s de Valera era of social conservatism and repression. Young people were looking forward and outwards, the brash 1980s were about to begin, and it was only right that young Irish bands should have the opportunity for a major breakthrough.

Before the Sessions, they had no such outlet, and it's hardly a coincidence that so few Irish bands had made it past the starting line. There was Rory Gallagher, of course, and Thin Lizzy had a few hits in the UK, but even as late as 1977, it had been exciting to see a picture of Phil Lynott and Bob Geldof together in the *NME*, because that just didn't happen to people from Dublin.

So, almost immediately, demo tapes came in from all over the country. The Fanning Sessions probably took care of a large part of Radio 2's public service remit. They cost money, resources and manpower, sure, but as Ian had predicted, these negatives were far outweighed by the goodwill they generated towards RTÉ – and as many bands licensed Fanning Sessions for EPs and albums, they occasionally made a little money too.

Ian wasn't content for us to knock out just a handful of sessions. He said from the start we should aim to do at least forty per year. We listened to all the demos, and the bands we invited in usually stood out a mile and picked themselves. The process was hardly an exact science, although Ian's approach was a little more methodical than mine. Our only aim was to pick the best bands and help them do a good session. After that, it was out of our hands. If they split before Christmas, it wasn't our fault.

From the day we launched the Fanning Sessions, I began getting thousands of demo tapes, and they have never stopped. It was impossible to go anywhere without going home with a pocket crammed with cassettes. If I said on air I was going to a gig, I would arrive to be met by bands waving their demos. Once even, I was at the top of the Eiffel Tower with a friend and an Irish guy came shuffling over and gave me a tape.

So the Fanning Sessions began with quite a fanfare, and I could not have chosen a more appropriate band for the very first one: U2.

After my initial reservations – or at least less excited reaction than I'd had to a few other bands – U2's music had been growing on me, as had Bono's forthright and charismatic nature. They won a talent contest in Limerick where the prize was the chance to release a single via CBS Ireland, and between us we hatched a plot whereby my radio listeners would get to choose which would be the lead song.

U2 came in to the show for five consecutive nights and we interviewed them and played three songs: 'Out Of Control', 'Stories for Boys' and 'Boy/Girl'. (Looking back, that really was – and remains – such an unusual thing to do.) Listeners could write in to vote for which should be the A- and the B-side, with the song getting the least votes being jettisoned. We were pretty sure 'Out Of Control' would win, which it did, and in the end the band decided to put both of the other songs on the B-side.

I assumed those ancient interviews over five nights were long gone but they turned up recently, via the modern miracle of YouTube. It was so bizarre to hear, in crystalline sound, my voice asking questions of Bono three decades ago, and him in full flow assuring me that rock bands could matter – and that U2 would never play cover versions in their gigs around Ireland, even if the crowd *were* howling for 'Whiskey in the Jar' or Status Quo numbers.

On one of the five nights, U2 came in with two of the band dressed as Santa Claus. That was because they had just been part of a Christmas-themed mini-residency at McGonagles under the name Jingle Balls. Various acts had played on a stage that included a Christmas tree, and John Otway and Wild Willy Barrett had tried to climb it during their set – the night made even more fun by the fact that the 'Christmas' residency was in June.

Looking back, it's extraordinary that Ian and I majored so much on a brand new band, and it's all become part of U2 history and mythology, but we had no great master plan in doing it. It just seemed to make sense at the time. They were the local band I'd played more than any other over the previous few years and they hadn't broken up. We had no idea they were destined for future world domination: like them, we were making it up as we went along.

Later that year, U2 played four Tuesday nights at the Baggot Inn, supported by the Blades. I introduced the bands and DJ'd before and after the sets. U2 were on the up but the Blades by then had a bunch of singles behind them, all of which I still regard as classic Irish singles. Paul Cleary was a great singer and songwriter, and they had a strong working-class following, but their live thrill didn't translate to their first album. At the Baggot gigs, though, there were still people who came for the Blades and left when U2 came on.

Apart from the sessions, the recipe for my Radio 2 programme was not so different from the Big D – loads of punk and new wave and cutting-edge new music, with a few classic cuts thrown in. In some ways, I felt quite vulnerable, because it was a niche show that was never going to bring in huge audience ratings or vast amounts of advertising revenue to RTÉ. Yet if it was a niche, it was a big niche.

I was doing what I always wanted to do and I was doing it on national radio in the one slot where it could work. The show and the Fanning Sessions had a loyal core audience, and I think they could tell that I was having the time of my life and that the only reason I played a track on the show was that I loved it.

The rest of Radio 2 was strictly playlisted but I never came under any pressure from RTÉ management to alter my format or play a certain kind of music. To a large degree they left me to it, which was pretty laudable given that they must have realised that sometimes they could have played a repeat of the week's Top 40 rundown and attracted more listeners. I was also aware that Ian Wilson had covered my back and was absorbing and fighting off a lot of the political flak that would have otherwise come my way.

Ian may have been a fantastic producer and a huge driving force behind the show but he had his quirks and foibles. On one issue, he was hugely stubborn. He had a policy that all interviews had to be conducted live in the studio. We never travelled with a tape recorder, didn't pre-record conversations for later broadcast, and absolutely never coordinated with a record label to do a phone interview while we were live on the air with an artist in New York or Los Angeles. Interviews either happened after midnight in the studio or they didn't happen at all. Had Bruce Springsteen been in Dublin at the weekend and wanted to talk to us, we'd have told him no.

I went along with Ian's policy and it was never any major source of irritation to me, but I'm not sure it was the wisest move; it was better when we mixed it all up and took a different route in later years. Having said that, there *was* something about the 'Everything live' policy that added extra flavour after midnight.

Yet Ian and I were absolutely as one in terms of what kind of music we played. Not everybody got the point. There were still representatives of old-school Irish record labels, the kind that put out traditional show-bands playing cover versions, hanging around RTÉ. They would introduce themselves and hand over a single, with the hope that I might play it, and I would politely tell them, 'It really doesn't fit my programme.' Translation: 'Not in a million years!'

Ian's contributions towards my show weren't limited to the Sessions. He was keen to take the music around the country and so persuaded Radio 2 to instigate the Beat on the Street, which were major outdoor road shows that travelled the length and breadth of Ireland and always pulled in massive crowds of listeners.

Our vehicle for these on-the-road escapades was the Road-caster, which was billed as the first mobile radio studio in Ireland. Basically it was just a big old lorry with a studio built into it, and we could choose a location, publicise it in advance, park the Roadcaster and put the aerial up, and go on air from wherever we fancied. More often than not, we used the local RTÉ studios.

Ian's team for these trips was Radio 2's three late-night DJs: Gerry Ryan, Mark Cagney and me. The idea was that we would be like rock stars, entertaining the crowd with no more than a microphone and a pair of turntables, and people would come from miles around to see us making fools of ourselves. Yet the three of us had very different attitudes towards our duties.

I never dreaded the Beat on the Street shows but I was completely useless at them. The 'show' part wasn't really my thing. Playing new music was grand but I was way too self-conscious and awkward to do the big extrovert personality-DJ shtick and jump around for the crowds. When Ian realised this he would allow me to go on first, before it was dark and before people really knew what was going on, and then Mark Cagney would follow me.

Gerry Ryan was a different story entirely. He took to the road shows like a duck to water and was absolutely perfect for the last DJ slot, a worthy headliner. Gerry basically treated the Beat on the Street shows as if they were a rock festival and he was the singer in the main band, and he never disappointed.

Where I would be skulking at the centre of the stage muttering and playing records, Gerry would be climbing up and down the rigging and the speaker stacks like King Kong, launching himself into the audience and generally going totally insane. He would punch the air in time to the music's beat while trying to mouth the words, despite the fact that Gerry never knew the words to songs and couldn't be bothered to learn them.

The sole exception to this rule was the Waterboys' 'The Whole of the Moon', whose lyrics Gerry not only learned by heart but turned into a piece of inspired theatre. As the intro to the tune pounded out, Gerry would grab the mike and gee the crowd up for Mike Scott's words:

What do you see up there?!
I can't hear you; I said what do you see up there?!
Is it a quarter of the moon?
Is it a half of the moon?
No – it's the whole of the moon!

It looks ridiculous in print, but it worked. Although I didn't have it in me to do it myself, I used to love to stand by the side of the stage and listen to Gerry's blarney and watch his absurd antics and the crowd eating out of the palm of his hand. He always described his time on the Beat on the Street as his 'Led Zeppelin on the road' years, and anybody who ever saw him will know exactly what he meant.

Ian Wilson's other innovation was the Lark in the Park, and to be honest, these were far more to my liking. They were basically a free gig in Dublin's Blackrock Park or in Raheny, Cork or Galway, with four or five local bands playing sets on a makeshift stage. All that I had to do was to introduce the bands, play records in between, and then watch them play, which was a far less stressful routine.

Radio 2 had nothing to do with one of the more ridiculous sights I saw that year, which was at a big open-air Status Quo show at Dalymount Park. The comedy wasn't the Quo – you know what you get with them, and they never alter – but one of the support bands, new British metallers Judas Priest.

I was the stage announcer and was hanging around backstage before their set when I saw Judas Priest to the side of the stage. They were all standing next to motorbikes, in *Spinal Tap*-style fluorescent spandex trousers that were so tight you could tell their religion from fifty paces, talking amongst themselves and pointing nervously at the short, steep ramp that led up to the stage.

Singer Rob Halford sat revving his motorbike. The plan was apparently for them to all roar onto the stage and launch straight into something very loud and metallic, but there seemed to be some kind of problem. I didn't know what it was until their opening music came on and three roadies grabbed each of the band members by their backsides and shoved them and their bikes up the ramp and into view of the crowd. Clearly, with the steepness of the ramp and the tightness of their rock 'n' roll trousers, the Priest needed all the help they could get.

On my radio show, I loved the fact that I wasn't bound by any playlist and could rave about absolutely anything I wanted. I was never short of material. I must have championed a thousand bands who never equalled their debut album, another thousand who got better all the time but never piqued the interest of the record-buying public, and another thousand who I figured deserved to sell five million records but struggled to shift five hundred.

I unashamedly admit that some records became an obsession. Talking Heads were my favourite band for a few months and I played their classic 1979 third album, *Fear of Music*, to death. It was released the same week as another record I loved, *Self-Conscious Over You* by Northern Ireland punks the Outcasts, and for one entire show, I played nothing but those two albums.

I was less enamoured of a local punk band called the 4B2s, who in truth were fairly terrible, but they were very persistent when it came to sending in their demo tapes, which I would occasionally play. The band included a guy named Jimmy Lydon, and one night he came in for an interview with his brother John, who is better known to the world at large as former Sex Pistols singer Johnny Rotten.

Rotten's whole shtick had always been about being obnoxious in a fairly theatrical way, and his visit to my show veered from edgily entertaining to depressingly predictable. Sneering at me and my questions, he upped the levels of outrageousness by swearing on air, but the last straw came when he started spilling beer on the studio equipment. I asked him to stop, he refused, and Ian Wilson called security, who frogmarched him from the building. I put on a Ramones live album and played it straight through for twenty minutes while Ian and I mopped up and restored order.

Despite the fact that I played obscure music late at night, and had no interest in celebrity culture, there is no doubt that being on national radio gave me a certain minor fame. Whenever we left the studio to do a road show, the three of us would all be signing autographs non-stop, and not just on bits of paper: we signed tits, arses, the lot. Girls were definitely showing more interest in me, yet I had no real interest in finding a girlfriend.

It's hard to say why, exactly. I went on dates, but I didn't want to be tied down. After I had seen a girl for a month or two she'd want to go for romantic meals or have quiet nights in, and the sad truth was that I loved playing music, doing my own thing and hanging out with Jerry, Mel and others too much to think of giving it up. Maybe I was commitment-phobic ... or maybe I was just too young.

This situation changed towards the end of 1979 when I made my very first television appearance. RTÉ was to stage a somewhat strange event at Cork Opera House that featured a very eclectic array of talents, and John McColgan, who was producing the show, asked me to do one of the onstage announcements. The line-up included singer-songwriter Shay Healy, who was to go on to write Johnny Logan's Eurovision Song

Contest-winning song 'What's Another Year', as well as Twink from the Sixties all-girl trio Maxi, Dick and Twink. Twink was probably the nearest Ireland had ever got to a diva. Whenever she arrived at an airport, she wanted a red carpet and a school-girl to give her some flowers. At least, that was the image I had of her. It was an eccentric line-up but my job was straightfor-ward: to introduce the Celtic rock band Horslips.

The team that RTÉ had sent down to Cork included a girl called Moya Doherty, who worked in Radio 2 as a broadcasting assistant. I had very much noticed her around the office and quite fancied her, but had done nothing about it because I was too shy. In fact, I was 25 years old and had probably never prop-erly asked a girl out.

As I said, I was also not good in front of a live audience, so I was slightly nervous about introducing Horslips on TV, but then a very weird thing happened. I was in the wings waiting to go on and John McColgan was on stage. John said, 'Now, to introduce the next act, please welcome Radio 2's Dave Fanning ...' and then you couldn't hear a word he said, because the audience were all cheering and yelling so much. It was the last thing I expected and I was flabbergasted. It wasn't exactly the Beatles at Shea Stadium but it was proper pop star-style screaming, and while I realised the people round the country listened to my programme, it still totally surprised me. It gave me such a boost that when I bumped into Moya after introducing Horslips and striding off stage I was still sufficiently buzzing to ask her out on a date.

To my delight, she accepted, and in no time at all, Moya and I became an item. She was the first girl that I took home to meet my folks, who loved her. She also lived with her parents, which meant a lot of car journeys for me up to the north side of Dublin.

It was interesting, because Moya and I got on really well even though we didn't necessarily have all that much in common. She was not into my weird rock music and also not terribly interested in movies, which were my other main obsession. Theatre and dance were more her thing. I saw her act a few times (she was particularly good in one J. M. Synge play), and she was probably a lot more grounded and serious-minded than me, although bearing in mind what I was like in those days, that's not really saying a lot.

Moya was a great girl but, looking back, I'm not sure I was the best boyfriend. I was still living for music and generally enjoying a nocturnal student-like life. I was on the radio five nights per week at Radio 2 from midnight to 2 a.m., and when the show finished, Ian or somebody else would normally come back to Foster Avenue and smoke and talk until stupid o'clock.

It was often five or six in the morning before I got to bed and I wouldn't be up until two in the afternoon. My parents were fine with it and were happy because I was happy, although my dad found it hard to believe I actually got paid a decent wage for what I did. One weekend I went with him to see some of his family in Drogheda and he suddenly announced, 'Jaysus, he gets £175 a week for playing records!' He might as well have said, 'Holy fuck!' I knew what he meant: I woke up every day feeling like I had won the pools.

Christmas 1979 found me linking up yet again with U2, who had gone across to play their first few club and pub gigs in London. I went over to visit two friends, Tim and Maeve, and the sight that greeted us when we arrived showed that although the band had begun making waves in Dublin, they still had a long way to go in the UK.

Paul McGuinness seemed delighted to see me when I showed up at the gig. In all honesty, I think he would have been delighted to see anybody, and particularly a friendly face. At the time, there was a half-assed Mod revival scene supposedly going on in London, so Secret Affair were the headline band, with support from a similar group called Back to Zero.

U2 were first on and the number of people in the crowd was probably not even in double figures. It had the atmosphere of a non-league football match, an impression that was reinforced by the solitary dog skulking around by the mixing-desk. Despite this, they played like their lives depended on it, with the Edge in particular producing some amazing new noises from his guitar, and by the set's end, McGuinness was beaming with relief. There was no encore – the audience was a bunch of pretend Mods with no interest in U2 whatsoever – so we all piled back to somebody's nearby flat with a bunch of six-packs.

Back in Dublin, Moya was being pretty patient and indulgent of my music-obsessed and self-serving lifestyle. We were getting on really well together, so as the year ended we decided to hire a car and go on a romantic holiday together to Achill Island, the lovely beauty spot out in County Mayo.

It was Saturday 29 December, the last weekend of the decade, at six o'clock in the evening. I was driving near Ballinlough in County Longford. For some reason I distinctly remember we were listening to the Outside Track, Pat Kenny's show on Radio

2, and Brush Shiels – an original member of Thin Lizzy who had gone on to form Skid Row – was reviewing an album at the moment that we hit the black ice.

It was just how people always describe it: everything happened so quickly, and yet also as if it were in slow motion. We were going at about 40 mph and the car skidded sideways and hit a telegraph pole so hard that it broke the pole clean in two. It crashed down, luckily missing us as we turned right over and finished upside-down in a ditch.

Miraculously we were both still conscious and seemed fairly unhurt, but I could only think of the fact that I had filled the car up with petrol just ten miles back, so it could easily explode. Moya and I couldn't climb out of our windows because the car was wedged firmly into the ditch, but there was a glimmer of light around one of the back windows. She managed to roll into the back seat and then out and I followed her.

There was no way of getting to Achill Island without a car, so we ended up staying in a guest house above a pub in Ballinlough. Ironically, we had a great weekend, possibly because we were both hugely appreciative of being alive after our near-death experience.

As the new decade dawned I was making a bit of a name for myself on Radio 2. I always felt a bit odd when people stopped me in the street and said how much they loved what I did, or when bands told me I had helped to make their career, because I didn't feel I deserved such praise. I felt like the luckiest man going: I was being paid decent money just to play music I loved.

The first formal recognition that maybe what I was doing had a purpose came in 1980 when I was given a Jacob's Award

Dave Fanning

– Ireland's most prestigious broadcasting prize. It was the same year that John McColgan won for his Dory Previn special and Robert Kee won for his brilliant *Ireland – A Television History* series. I got the Best DJ prize, thus becoming the first person from Radio 2 to scoop a Jacob's.

Pat Kenny was presenting the awards live on TV, but after I had been given my gong I didn't hang around. This was partly because I still hadn't totally shaken off my too-cool-for-school student mentality and thought the event was a bit stuffy, but the main reason was that I'd just invested in a video recorder and was desperate to go home and watch it.

It sounds ridiculous in these days of 24/7 instant media access via iPlayers and the like, but in 1980 the idea of being able, should you so wish, to watch a movie at 2 a.m., even pausing it to make a cup of tea if the urge struck you, seemed exciting and truly groundbreaking. This was the future! The problem was it cost a small fortune to rent a movie back then, but I had splashed out on two – *Chinatown*, which I had already seen about four times, and *Butch Cassidy and the Sundance Kid*. I had quite a night coming up and there was no way the Jacob's Awards could compete with it.

I was still going to live gigs as many nights per week as I could, normally leaving before or right after the encore to race to the studio just in time for my show. It was also exciting to see that a festival scene was beginning to develop in Ireland. There had been smallish events in Lisdoonvarna from about 1978, but the ball really began rolling when thirty thousand people flocked to a major outdoor event in Leixlip, County Kildare on 27 July 1980.

My schedule at Leixlip was ridiculous. As well as doing the stage announcements, I had to find twenty minutes and a quiet spot to talk to Sting and Andy Summers from headline act the Police for my Radio 2 show, plus locate and interview some American new wave band called Skafish. On top of that, I was very keen to watch Squeeze and the one band I knew really well, the other support act, U2, who made a major impact on a crowd that maybe normally wouldn't follow local new groups very closely. I never did find Skafish.

Between Radio 2 and gigs, I didn't have time for much else in my life, so it was no surprise when Moya and I came to an end. In truth, we finished with a whimper, not a bang. There was no big argument or flashpoint: I just thought things were fizzling out and it was time to move on, and assumed she felt the same. I never really asked her, which is probably a good indication of just how insensitive I was back then.

After getting over the first few weeks of separation, Moya and I stayed on good terms and I'm delighted to say we still are. As soon as I was out of the way, things worked out brilliantly for her. She married John McColgan, the TV producer who had invited me to that fateful gig at Cork Opera House, and the two of them went on to invent *Riverdance*, which they produced and directed via their own production company. The rest, as they say, is history, and it's one Irish success story where I can genuinely say: 'It couldn't have happened to a nicer couple.'

Back on the radio show, Ian Wilson and I decided to introduce an annual listeners' chart of songs that we would call Fanning's Fab 50. The inspiration for this was John Peel, who had been running his Festive 50 on his BBC show for many years, but our poll differed from his in one respect: where Peel stipulated that all songs should have been released that year, we merely invited our listeners to choose their three favourite tracks of all time.

The winner in the first year, to our surprise, was 'Freebird' by Lynyrd Skynyrd, but thereafter U2 took a stranglehold on the top of the chart, winning for four consecutive years with '11 O'Clock Tick Tock'. In 1985 the Smiths usurped them with 'How Soon Is Now?' and for the rest of the decade it was U2 again, with the live version of 'Bad'. Radiohead and Smashing Pumpkins have also had a year each at No. 1, but ever since the early nineties it has been a rare year that U2 have not topped the Fab 50 with 'One'.

In life there are some events that affect you so deeply that you never forget where you were when they happened. They leave an indelible, visceral mark on you even years later. One of mine came on 8 December 1980 when I heard the news about the murder of John Lennon.

Lennon's death shocked me to the core. I was steeped in the world of new wave and new music on Radio 2 but I was also still the boy who had saved up his paper-round money to pre-order *Sgt. Pepper's Lonely Hearts Club Band* a full five months before it came out. The Beatles had meant the world to me and they always would.

I was fast asleep in bed at breakfast time, as usual, having probably only gone to sleep about two hours earlier, when my mum woke me. She said that John Lennon had been shot dead in New York and there was a Willie O'Reilly on the phone. Willie was the producer on Ronan Collins's Radio 2 morning show, and he asked me to go in to talk to Ronan about Lennon's murder.

Five minutes later I was in a car and in a state of shock. Jesus only knows what I said on the radio, because I wasn't thinking straight at all, and the rest of the day was given over to mourning Lennon. I got a tape recorder and taped stuff like Frank Bough hosting a tribute to John off the TV. A few days later there were vigils all around the world and I went to one in Dublin, where musician Jimmy Slevin played guitar and scores of people lit candles and sang 'Imagine' and other Lennon stuff.

It may sound sad or pathetic, but I genuinely felt deeper pain over Lennon's death than I would have if somebody I'd actually known, such as a distant uncle, had died. Like many people of my generation, I had lived an important part of my life through the prism of the Beatles. I felt a huge empathy for the guy: he'd been part of my thoughts, and of me, for more than twenty years.

It's a sign of how much the Beatles will always mean that, after a similar interval, George Harrison's death in 2001 also had a major impact on me. Behind all that stuff about the quiet one, he was an interesting, cool guy – he was the one who got the band into the Maharishi Mahesh Yogi and his first solo album was the most successful post-Beatles solo record. When Jerry Coyle and I were big Beatles fans as kids, George fascinated us. It was cigarettes that killed him. What a pity.

Though I never got to meet those legends, there are many iconic figures I *have* been lucky enough to meet, and they don't come any bigger than the man I had a surreal but characteristic encounter with on 6 July 1980. Once again I was on compère duties at a big outdoor event, this time a one-day festival at Dalymount Park. Dave Edmunds and Ronnie Lane had finished their sets and I needed to find out if headline act Bob Marley and the Wailers wanted me to announce their arrival on stage.

Making my way to the production area, I knocked on Marley's dressing room door. The great man himself opened it and, cliché though it might be, I could hardly see him for the clouds of ganja smoke that were billowing out around him. We had a polite three-minute conversation in which he explained that he didn't need introducing because they would follow their usual pattern: backing vocalists the I-Threes would go on first, the Wailers would follow them, and Marley would slip into the middle once he had caught the groove. True to his word, that was exactly what they did.

If meeting Marley was special, I was even more excited around the same time to encounter Tom Waits. I had been hooked on Waits ever since I had caught him on *The Old Grey Whistle Test* in 1976, growling out 'Waltzing Matilda' for an avuncular Bob Harris. I had played him to death on Radio Dublin and the Big D, so when he played a series of shows at the Olympia in 1981, I was always going to be there.

Waits did four or five memorable, idiosyncratic shows, and I was there for every one, even getting to shake his hand and have a quick chat backstage one night. The last night was a close call: I was on my way to it with Dublin scenester B. P. Fallon when smoke began billowing from under the bonnet of my relatively new Renault 5. Totally in denial, Beep and I ignored it and bumped on until the car ground to a complete halt, at which point we abandoned it and grabbed a cab to the Olympia.

A major decision that I made during the summer of 1981 – and, looking back, it is ridiculous how important these things seem when you are young – was to shave off my perennially hopeless straggly beard. By now well into my mid twenties, and making more frequent television appearances, it no longer seemed to make quite so much sense to be rocking the over-grown-student look. I will never forget shaving it off on holiday in Crete, over a copy of *Sounds* open at a two-page feature about a new British heavy metal band called Def Leppard. Little did I know how much their singer would later mean to me.

Newly shorn, I was ready to help play nursemaid later that year to the birth of a major Irish music institution. There had not been huge festivals in the country for years, but the success of the Police-headlined event at Leixlip the previous year led a brave promoter to chance his arm at staging a huge event in the natural amphitheatre at Slane Castle.

This was the first time Slane had been used for a huge-scale gig such as this, and as ten or fifteen thousand people buzzed around out front, the atmosphere backstage next to the River Boyne was very much of people hoping for the best and making it up as they went along. Smiley Bolger was sharing stage announcement duties with me and the bands he introduced received a much better reception than his attempt to perform his own, novelty single, 'Half Mad Irishman'.

The line-up featured County Fermanagh hard rock band Mama's Boys, Belfast metal band Sweet Savage, Australian rock band Rose Tattoo and British new wave group the Bureau. Hazel O'Connor did her art-rock thing and inevitably U2 were on the bill as they tenaciously pursued a breakthrough that by now seemed tantalisingly close. It was certainly encouraging to hear the crowd react enthusiastically as I introduced them.

Everything ran roughly to schedule, possibly more by luck than judgement, but the evening really came alive when the whirr of rotor blades cut through the night sky and a local old-school rock god descended amongst us. When Phil Lynott swaggered out of the helicopter, it was the first time I had seen a star step from a chopper straight onto stage, and Thin Lizzy played a thrilling set that reminded us exactly why they were one of the few veteran bands that the punk generation accepted rather than rejected.

As much as I was using my privileged position on Radio 2 to champion local talent, I was also managing to tick off my list a number of rock legends I had always loved from afar while never even remotely imagining I would get the chance to meet them. Bob Marley and Tom Waits had been pretty special, but for me, the bar was raised even higher in 1982 with Joni Mitchell.

From album to album, well before my long hot summer in America in 1974 when *Court and Spark* was the soundtrack of Greenwich Village, I had followed Joni's career closely. I had devoured the exquisite follow-up, *The Hissing of Summer Lawns*, and the magnificent road album *Hejira*, so when Joni came to play a single show in Dublin, I knew I had to try to make contact with her.

She was notoriously publicity-averse and had done no more than a handful of interviews in the previous seven or eight years, but Ian Wilson and I figured, as we so often did, that we had nothing to lose. We took the most direct route imaginable: before my show began, I phoned the city centre hotel where I knew she was staying, asked for her room and told her we would send a car if she would come down and talk to us. To my utter amazement and excitement, she said yes.

When I went on the air that evening, I proudly said, 'Well, we're expecting Joni Mitchell shortly!' Mark Cagney, who had just finished his show in the studio next door, is almost as big a Joni fan as me and barged in to tear me off a strip as I played a record. 'Don't be ridiculous!' he began. 'Just because Joni Mitchell is in town tonight, she is hardly the sort of star who drops everything to do an unscheduled live interview ...' He didn't get a chance to get any further, because at that point the door swung open and in walked Joni and her husband, Larry Klein.

Mark was gobsmacked and silenced and, to be honest, so was I. We introduced ourselves, Joni sat down to begin the interview and for probably the only time in my life I was tongue-tied and star-struck. I even had to employ that infamous last resort of the scoundrel DJ – gratuitously playing a record while I tried to work out what to say.

Yet after that unpromising start, I think I only played one more song until we finished chatting ninety minutes later. She was a sharp and superb interviewee, as you would expect from a woman who has written some of the most erudite and intelligent rock songs in existence, and I really felt we had given any fans who were listening a genuine insight into her creative muse. The interview has been used in Joni biographies and on various websites, and even today it remains one of the career highlights of which I am most proud.

Mike Oldfield was a rather less productive encounter. The punk generation had no time for the man whose *Tubular Bells* album had broken all sales records a decade earlier and launched Richard Branson and Virgin Records into the strato-sphere, but I had a soft spot for him. Apart from *Tubular Bells*, he'd played with Kevin Ayers – a guy whose music I'd loved ever since I stumbled across it in the bargain bins in Pat Egan's Sound Cellar – and his Whole World band on fantastically eccentric albums such as *Whatevershebringswesing* and *Shooting at the Moon*.

I was therefore pleased to learn I was to spend a whole Sunday with Oldfield for a feature for *Hot Press* but Mike didn't seem to share my enthusiasm. When I picked him up with his partner Sally from their city centre hotel, he was courteous but distant and exuded the definite air of a man who would rather be some-where, anywhere, else rather than here.

Sensing his ennui, I suggested a drive out of Dublin and we finished up on Killiney Hill, where Oldfield momentarily perked up, fascinated by a group of hang-gliders fearlessly leaping off a nearby cliff. Yet his moroseness returned when we sat down to talk and he struck me as an unhappy man with a lot of emotional baggage who hated the interview process. Perhaps he sensed that his Eighties would not be as stellar as his Seven-ties had been. Or maybe my questions simply weren't as excit-ing as watching hang-gliding.

A camera on the Radio 2 studio wall would have caught some memorable footage when Willy DeVille came in to Radio 2. Willy, the singer with New York punk band Mink DeVille, who had been the house band at CBGBs, came in straight from the airport from a transatlantic flight. He told us that he might be a bit jetlagged. I was more inclined to think he was totally off his face.

Willy looked wild-eyed and extremely exotic and began our chat by producing two cigars and offering me one of them. When I declined, he ignored me and crammed it into my mouth anyway. As I played his signature song, 'Spanish Stroll', Willy crawled around the studio on all fours, shouting up at us that he was looking for a light and a guitar.

Ian Wilson was losing patience and was in favour of turfing Willy out, but then Aonghus McNally, a Radio 1 DJ who had been on air a few doors up the corridor, got wind of the commotion and wandered in. He was a Mink DeVille fan, and as Willy continued to demand a guitar, confided that he had one in his car and went out to fetch it.

Willy was extremely grateful but could not get over what he felt to be Aonghus's unusual name: 'Wow! Are you named after a Scottish cow?' He tuned up and eventually, with a cheroot dangling from his lips and looking like an extra from *The Good, The Bad and The Ugly*, sang a song about a drunk falling off a bar stool, which both seemed very apposite and also showed what a major, natural talent he was. When he died recently, only in his fifties, of pancreatic cancer, it was a huge shame.

Later that year, I was back at Slane Castle for the follow-up festival to the previous year's Thin Lizzy extravaganza. The organisers had certainly pulled a rabbit out of the hat this time. The support acts were no more than lukewarm – the J. Geils Band and the Chieftains – but the headliners more than made up for any down-the-bill deficiencies: the Rolling Stones.

There is no doubt the Stones were past their peak by then. Thirty years on, they are still trundling round the globe, so I hate to think exactly how past-their-sell-by-date they are now.

Even so, it was still an amazing thrill to be so close to one of the greatest rock 'n' roll bands to have ever existed.

Pat Kenny was manning our outdoor studio at Slane, doing his Saturday evening show, *The Outside Track,* and I had to go in and chat to him about the Stones just as they came on. Then I just soaked up the show. By that time, the Stones were not without their showbiz element and they certainly knew how to entertain a massive audience; nobody can strut down a ramp into the crowd quite like Messrs Jagger and Richards.

By the end of 1982, I had broadened my writing activities from *Hot Press* to also include reviewing gigs for the *Irish Times.* This dovetailed neatly with my stints on Radio 2, giving me time to take in a band, race down to the *Times* office on D'Olier Street to file my copy, and then head off to the studio with – on a good night – half an hour to spare.

The great thing about writing for the *Irish Times* was that my mum loved it. Books and literature had always been her life and the *Times* was her newspaper: indeed, that was where she had spotted the job advert at *Scene* that had been my lucky break.

Over the years I've occasionally been lucky enough to get behind a band I like right from the start, and that was certainly true of Michael Stipe and R.E.M. By early 1983 there was a mini-revival of what were being called 'paisley' groups in the US and I was getting probably twenty or twenty-five debut albums by American groups every month, but R.E.M. stood out as soon as I heard them.

For a while, I played them to death. An RTÉ kids' TV show called *Youngline* decided to do a ten-minute item called 'A Day in the Life of Radio 2's Dave Fanning', and filmed me from a bridge driving along the Stillorgan dual carriageway. When the producers asked me which music I would like played during the sequence, I said 'Radio Free Europe', the opening track on the R.E.M. debut album, *Murmur*. Nobody had heard of them, least of all the school kids watching the show, but I just wanted to push the band at every opportunity.

In contrast to R.E.M, New Order were big news in 1983, even if they seemed not to want to be. After the suicide of Ian Curtis in 1980, the remaining members of Joy Division understand-ably had gone to ground before deciding to continue under the name New Order, and they'd produced no publicity at all around their patchy, hesitant debut album *Movement*.

They decided to do a handful of interviews around the release of their second album *Power, Corruption and Lies* and came into the Radio 2 studio. The interview was a disaster. They had nothing to say and no interest in saying it, and I couldn't work out if Bernard Sumner and Peter Hook's offhand truculence was a studied pose or down to genuine awkwardness and nervousness.

It was a complete non-starter and I was glad to see the back of them, although to give them credit, they came over to me at an event in London years later and apologised for being so uncooperative, admitting they were just being bolshie. I was impressed with that, but less impressed when I later read them quoted in a book saying that the first ever New Order interview had been with 'pixillated' Irish DJ Dave Fanning. Were they trying to imply I was drunk? I have no idea, but it didn't sound great, especially as I have never done an interview pissed. I had been to their gig that evening but not even had one drink.

As 1983 began to wind down, Radio 2 made some changes to its schedule. This was absolutely fine by me. I had enjoyed a wonderful five years on the midnight slot but would not have wanted to go on working those anti-social hours indefinitely, so a switch to an earlier, evening time-slot, with no alteration in the music I played, made a lot of sense to me.

I certainly went out with a bang. For my last midnight show, we managed to fix it for Robert Plant to come in for an exclusive, extremely rare interview. This was quite a coup: it was only five years earlier – although the shift in attitudes occasioned by punk made it seem longer – that Led Zeppelin had been the biggest rock band in the world, blazing a trail of dissolute mayhem across the globe.

Yes, a Robert Plant interview was a seriously big deal, and as a result, I wasn't alone in the studio. Mel, the man who had worshipped Zeppelin so much he'd had their famous Four Symbols painted on the doors of his little green Morris Minor, was there, of course, sitting quietly in the corner soaking up the aura of a legend. B. P. Fallon, who had worked with Zeppelin in the Seventies and was now presenting a weekend show on Radio 2, was also there. And completing our number was Bono. He'd rung me before the show and asked if he could pop in. U2 were by then coming on in leaps and bounds: their third album, *War*, had topped the UK charts and they were making real inroads into America. Yet they were nowhere near the level of Zeppelin's all-consuming success and Bono was typically keen to get to know a true rock legend.

If he was eager to meet Plant, he certainly hadn't dressed to impress. Mel still talks occasionally of how Bono showed up to the studio in a pair of old brown cord trousers with a big, black ink stain under one of the bum pockets. He looked like he'd just finished doing his homework.

The interview was candid and wide-ranging. Plant was happy to discuss Zeppelin's sex and drugs and 1970s rock 'n' roll and yet I got the impression from the singer that he never wanted to lead that lifestyle again. He wasn't making any apologies for Zep's hedonism and debauchery, but tacitly implied that if he were to do it all again, he would do so more sensitively, less frantically and with rather more concern for other people.

Robert stayed for the entire programme. When it was over, he and Bono launched into a remarkably intense but seemingly satisfying tête-à-tête and then we all retired to the Pink Elephant in Mr Plant's limo for further refreshment and negotiations. It was certainly a major high to end a memorable and truly special era of my life.

Some people may possibly find it odd that while I was leading this occasionally highly glamorous lifestyle of broadcasting on national radio and meeting ever more stellar rock stars, I was also still living at Foster Avenue with my mum and dad. All I can say is that it never seemed remotely odd to me. I had been happy there since the day I was born, Barney and Annie were the most patient and understanding parents you can imagine and we still got on like a house on fire. I had simply never seen the need, or had the slightest desire, to move.

Yet as the great George Harrison said, all things must pass, and in 1983 at the age of 29, I temporarily moved out of my family home. Neil Hickey had invited me to take a spare room in his house up in Dun Laoghaire, in a pretty little square just around the corner from where Bob Geldof had famously been a latch-key kid.

Neil and I had always got on well and the move worked like a dream. He was still in the speciality sweet game and would be off first thing in the morning with his van loaded up with exotic confectionery to flog at the various markets around the country. If I had a day off, I occasionally went with him to help out, just for old times' sake.

Even though I had technically moved out, I still spent a lot of time at Foster Avenue and, in truth, was probably spending as many nights sleeping there as I was down in Dun Laoghaire. And I was home on the morning of 25 November 1983; the day that my father died.

He died of a heart attack on a 46A bus on the way to visit my brother Gerard, who was now living in Artane. Ironically, it was on St Stephen's Green, where he had worked at the Board of Works for forty-seven years. He had never been sick, never been in hospital, but I guess it can't have helped that he had smoked cigarettes right up until fifteen years before he died. Even when he had given them up on health grounds, he had done that daft thing people often do of going on to smoking cigars and a pipe instead, kidding themselves that in some way it is not so lethal.

The ambulance people had found a piece of paper in Barney's pocket with his address on it, and so the Gardai came to Foster Avenue to break the news. I was the only person at home. My mother had gone into town on the bus, as she did every Tuesday and Thursday morning, and as usual I was fast asleep in the middle of the morning when two policemen rapped on the door.

As they told me what had happened, I could see my mum over their shoulders, walking up the road on the way home. She saw the police but wasn't at all alarmed. I'd got a couple of parking tickets in my time, so she assumed something similar had happened again. As Anne reached us, I took a deep breath and told her straightaway.

The rest of the day passed in a horrible daze. I phoned Dermot and Miriam, who both worked over the road at UCD, and they came immediately. We tried to talk but we were just mouthing words; not making sense. It was impossible for me to believe I would never see Barney again, sitting in his arm chair rolling tobacco with his contraption, watching horse racing as if his life depended on the result or pottering around watching the football at Belfield.

It slowly sank in as the next few weeks dragged by that it wasn't some ridiculous, unfunny joke, and Dad really had gone for good. The whole grieving process was a delayed reaction, like when you bang your elbow and it doesn't hurt for a few seconds and then is suddenly absolute agony. The pain really hit us at Christmas.

Dad had died exactly one month before Christmas Day, and as we all gathered at Foster Avenue on 25 December 1983, there was a gaping hole at the heart of the family where Barney should have been. As a long afternoon slowly passed, I thought the words I had never imagined would cross my mind: I would give anything right now to hear *Brendan O'Dowda Sings the Songs of Percy French*.

6

You don't easily get over the death of a parent. It's not the sort of thing where you sigh, take a deep breath and carry on as if nothing has happened. We all knew we had to move on from the loss of Barney, but I began 1984 carrying a dull ache and a sense of profound emptiness everywhere I went. It only went away when I didn't think about Dad, and most days that seemed to be impossible.

My mother coped much better than I had feared she would. She was heart-broken at the time; she had always adored my dad, and I hardly remember a cross word between them. But Anne had that true Dubliner's get-on-with-it mentality and her religion saw her through. I abhor organised religion, a point I'll come to in a lot more detail later, but I could see Mum's faith was a great crutch to her when she needed it.

We all have different ways to deal with tragedy, and I did it the only way I knew how: I threw myself with even greater gusto into my work. It was probably lucky that I had these extra levels of energy because suddenly, my weekly schedule was getting ridiculously demanding.

My Radio 2 show moving from the midnight slot to 8–10 p.m. should in theory have made my life a lot more straightforward but it actually complicated things severely. The main problem was that I was still reviewing gigs for the *Irish Times*, the vast majority of which were obviously happening when I was due to be on the air.

One capability that has always marked my career is the ability to juggle, and as I took over the evening show in 1984, I realised that the only way I could keep all the balls in the air was by cheating. I quickly developed a system that apparently allowed me to be broadcasting live on national radio at the same time that I was reviewing a band across town.

Arriving at the RTÉ HQ about 7 p.m., I would pre-record the last hour or so of my show. If there were two or even three studios free, I would be hopping between them, recording links, intros and comments and lining up records as Ian Wilson trailed along behind me doing his producer thing.

I would go live at 8 p.m. and then at about quarter to nine or so we would stick on the pre-recorded tape and I would hotfoot it down to the Point, the Stadium, the Baggot, the Tivoli, Whelan's or wherever else that night's gig happened to be. Usually arriving just as the band came on, I would catch as much of the set as possible – I still wince at the memory of having to write a review of the Smiths based on only three songs – and then race across to the *Irish Times*, where I would have thirty or, on a good night, forty-five minutes to file my copy in time for the City edition.

By the time my 11 o'clock deadline came round I would feel I had had a pretty full and manic evening. I would be buzzing and far too wired to sleep, so then it was time to socialise. I never cared for the scene in Leeson Street with its sleazy basement pick-up bars fleecing all-comers with their over-priced bottles of wine, so most nights I would end up in the Pink Elephant, where I would always know somebody – normally a disgruntled musician happy to while away a few hours moaning about his record deal. I could stay as late as I wanted: after all, there was no need to get up early the next day.

Anybody hearing this routine might suspect that I had a cavalier disregard for my radio show, but nothing could be further from the truth. It was just the way I worked. In truth, it still is. I have always liked being loose and spontaneous on the radio: the world of playlists and rigorous pre-planning is anathema to me. I always figure the ideal show should sound as if you've popped around to see me in my flat, and I'm saying to you, 'Oh, by the way, listen to this new single, it's great!'

The most important elements for my programme are that I should know my stuff and be enthusiastic, and hopefully I have always scored pretty highly on both counts. And if you love a record, you listen to it way more than once. I have never seen anything wrong with playing a track at the start of the show and, if it was great, whacking it on again at a quarter to ten. It may not be how most people do it but it makes total sense to me and, thankfully, I've always got away with it.

My attitude has always been that my radio show is the be-all and end-all, the core of what I do, and anything else that comes along – magazine writing, introducing bands at festivals, and so forth – is a bonus. When RTÉ offered me a new project during

1984, I was initially extremely wary, but on a personal level it was to prove a life-changing experience.

The TV show was called *Jobsuss* and it was about work and the world of employment around Ireland. The idea was that we would travel about the country going to factories, start-ups and small businesses and seeing what made them tick.

I couldn't see any link in this to what I did and told RTÉ and producer Claire O'Loughlin that I was probably the wrong man for the job. They changed my mind by telling me we could have a band on the show each week, which I would be able to choose. My co-host on the show was a girl called Susan Byrne, who did the proper, serious journalism side of things (actually, she didn't: she was as clueless as I was) and in no time at all, I fell for her hook, line and sinker.

To my delight, this feeling turned out to be mutual. Susan and I started dating and things were fantastic. She was the first real girlfriend I'd had since Moya, and right from the start we hit it off and became close to inseparable. They say you should never work with your partner, but we seemed to do just fine.

Susan and I had a great time doing all the usual things together: gigs, movies, meals, holidays. She wasn't particularly steeped in rock music the way I was, but I was hugely impressed when she told me that, not only had she taken the cover shot for the Horslips' *Live in Belfast* album sleeve, she had taken the cover photo of U2's second single, 'Another Day', back in 1980. She hadn't even known the band: she had just taken a photo of Blackrock train station in Dublin and given it to them, and they liked it and used it.

Life gives with one hand and takes away with the other. As I was getting used to being in a grown-up, genuine relationship with Susan, and loving it, Jerry Coyle told me that he was emigrating to America.

Jerry had always been a restless soul. I had stayed close to him since the day we met, as I had with Mel Reilly – even with my mad lifestyle of TV shows, radio and gigs, it was a rare day that I didn't see at least one of them, and normally both. However, Jerry's life had taken a very different route from mine.

After we left Blackrock, Jerry didn't go off to college. It had never appealed to him. Instead he had worked in the family business – his father's abattoir and meat-processing plant in the middle of Dublin. Unsurprisingly, he didn't greatly care for that, but since then he'd just done bits and pieces of jobs, as well as going off travelling for about six months.

When Jerry got back, his feet were too itchy to stay in Dublin and he fancied another adventure. His younger brother Des had gone to study in America on a scholarship to Pepperdine University in Los Angeles and was now running a tree-surgery business. Being pretty handy at physical work and at this time working in the same business in Dublin, Jerry went over to join him.

One of the last things we did before Jerry left was to recreate the main thrust of Werner Herzog's *Fitzcarraldo*. The movie was the truly daft story of an Irish rubber baron. He dreamed of building an opera house in Iquitos, and the film showed him trying to organise a team of men to pull a vast steamship over a hill in the Peruvian rain forest. We didn't go *that* far, but we went to a market where we bought an old-fashioned gramo-phone player like the one on the HMV logo (minus the dog, of course). Jerry's dad had some Vera Lynn and opera music on heavy old 78rpm vinyl waxings and we brought along a few needles for the player's arm. They were like nails compared to the tiny, thin stereo needles we were used to.

You could rent out tiny motorboats at Bulloch Harbour in Dalkey and cruise out to Dalkey Island, where the only inhabit-ants were goats. So on a beautiful sunny Sunday, Jerry and I navigated through the glitterati sipping gin and tonics on their expensive boats, blasting out scratched opera records as we went. They sounded great.

It was clear that Jerry would not be coming back for a very long time, and while I tried not to be self-indulgent, it was quite hard on me to lose one of my two best friends in the world so soon after my dad's passing away. Still, I knew the routine by now: throw myself into work even more obsessively.

This was not hard to do. For a start-off, my love for Talking Heads was rekindled by the release of Jonathan Demme's fantastic live concert movie, *Stop Making Sense*. It had been filmed on the previous year's Heads' tour, when David Byrne had brilliantly taken his subversion of rock 'n' roll clichés to another level by wearing his absurdist over-size white suit at all the shows. One of the greatest concert movies ever made, *Stop Making Sense* won a host of cinematic awards, and deservedly so.

It's a sign of its popularity and influence that the Ambassador cinema at the top of O'Connell Street showed *Stop Making Sense* on Friday nights for nearly three months. I went to almost every showing, on each occasion dragging along yet another person to convert with evangelical glee.

The film's allure for me was so strong that I started to get the itch every Friday evening, longing to get the pub session over with so I could see the movie again. This was new territory for me. A cinema in Rathmines had shown *The Rocky Horror Picture Show* every Friday night for a decade and I had gone once, but the whole thing with the audience in costumes, throwing rice at the screen and shouting out the catchphrases, had left me cold. It just wasn't my thing. *Stop Making Sense* was different: for a few weeks, I felt like John Travolta in *Saturday Night Fever*, fiending for my weekend fix.

Every showing seemed better than the last, until one weekend, on about my seventh or eighth visit, something seemed wrong with the experience. I couldn't put my finger on it at first, but then, about twenty minutes into the screening, I realised it wasn't loud enough.

Leaving my seat, I made my way to the back of the cinema and found myself confronted by some crusty old steps that looked as if they had been laid some time in the last century. Reaching the top, I pushed open a door and found myself in a dingy, smoky little room with rolls of film whirring noisily on huge spools. The old guy sitting smoking his pipe and reading the *Irish Independent* under a flickering lamp didn't seem at all perturbed that I had just sauntered into his den.

I asked this laid-back projectionist if there was any chance he could turn the sound up just a little and he nodded at a dial on the speaker and said, 'Sure, go right ahead.' It was on five so I wrenched it round to ten, at which point a roar erupted from the auditorium below us. By the time I got back to my seat, most of the audience were dancing in the aisles.

It got even better. At the end of *Stop Making Sense*, David Byrne sprints around the stage as the concert reaches its climax with 'Naïve Melody', and that particular night the Ambassador's audience, most of whom had clearly enjoyed a long night in the pub pre-cinema, decided it was only polite to join in. The sight of two hundred people running the length, width and breadth of the grand old cinema as David Byrne yodelled away was truly something to behold.

This was around the time that I first interviewed Byrne, and I was totally thrown by his idiosyncratic mannerisms and awkward conversational hesitations. He definitely seemed as herky-jerky and self-conscious as I expected, and after I lobbed him my first question, he didn't speak for a few seconds. On the radio, silence is dead air, so I panicked and straightaway blurted out my next question, which received the same (non) response.

This was worse than New Order! I gabbled out another question, and then another, and it wasn't until I paused for breath that Byrne gave a cogent and considered answer to the first one I had asked. At which point, I realised that he would answer them all, if I just shut up for a few seconds and gave him a chance.

I probably asked him twenty questions in ten minutes and Byrne answered three of them, but he wasn't trying to be awkward. He just let my queries sink in and collected his thoughts before speaking rather than answering on autopilot as most artists did. The next time I interviewed him I knew the drill and tried not to interrupt even when he tugged his hair, scratched at his ankle and gave a nervous giggle before reply-ing, because once these funny little rituals were over, his answers were well worth waiting for.

Few interviewees are as intelligent and enigmatic as David Byrne, but one who certainly is is Leonard Cohen. I had loved Cohen ever since Dermot and Gerard had introduced me to his music as a boy, and my feelings had changed to idolatry after going to every one of his consequent live shows in Dublin.

I interviewed him in a hotel in London, first in the bar and then in his room, and he did not disappoint. He was a study in effortless cool, sitting in his long coat and working his way through a pack of Gauloises while answering questions with a slow, deliberate precision. His forensic intelligence was bracing and he remains one of my favourite, most impressive interviewees.

It was a major thrill to meet Joe Strummer, even if the Clash had jettisoned Mick Jones and were fast disintegrating as they released the disappointing *Cut the Crap* album. Strummer was just as impassioned and authentic as I had hoped but was also a model of decency and consideration. He could certainly have taught his fellow punk Mr Lydon a few lessons about manners.

Away from my music work, things with Susan just kept getting better and better. We were still filming *Jobsuss* together as well as just hanging out and enjoying each other's company. It all felt very right, especially when we enjoyed truly wonderful summer holidays together in Cyprus and the west of Ireland. I also got on brilliantly with her parents. It wasn't that I had much in common with her dad – he was the president of a Dublin golf club – but he was great fun, as was her mum, a lovely woman who sometimes drove us down to Wicklow to go horse-riding. That was Susan's passion and I pretended I liked it. I was terrified.

I was living between Susan's place in Dublin, Neil's gaff in Dun Loaghaire and crashing at my mum's house in Foster Avenue. The appeal of living out of an overnight bag was a new one for me and, to be honest, I found I liked it. Susan was renting a flat in Monkstown, which as it happened was right across the road from where the Edge was living with his then wife, Aishlinn.

Christmas 1984 was inevitably a bittersweet occasion. My work could not have been going better and it felt great to be hanging out with Susan, but it was impossible to have Christmas lunch at Foster Avenue and not recall the previous year's sorrow as we reeled from Dad's death. Nevertheless, I was going into 1985 on top of the world – and my career was about to take a decided right-turn from the margins into the mainstream.

RTÉ had decided to launch a pop quiz TV show and asked Gerry Ryan and me to be the team captains. This was a highly interesting new development. In some ways, it was the obverse of my career to date: I had been tucked away on late-night radio playing obscure new music, and this was RTÉ 1, prime-time, after the news at 7 p.m. every Wednesday night. This was still the time of four or five TV stations, compared to the four or five hundred you can see now.

There was probably a small, snobby, punky voice in the back of my head that wondered if I was selling out, but it was drowned out by me thinking it sounded a fantastic idea. I knew Gerry so well that the chemistry would be good, and if the programme didn't work out, so what? I could always leave! If I lost a bit of cool factor ... well, what was cooler than having fun?

I could not have made a better decision, because *No. 1* was fantastic right from the off. We'd record the whole series in about three weeks, shooting multiple episodes each day. Gerry and I would finish an episode and go off and change our clothes while the next guests were wheeled on, to give the impression that it was another day. So we could easily be sitting in Santa costumes in the middle of July. Over the next few decades, Gerry often talked about the possibility of resurrecting the show; he felt it was the most hassle-free, enjoyable experience he'd ever had.

The format was that we started off at No. 20 in the chart and moved up one place every time we got a question right, with the winner being the first to No. 1. The teams were each made up of the captain, a member of the public and a star from a band, who with the greatest respect, didn't tend to be terribly A-list.

The point of the show was to entertain and have fun rather than to win, which, to be honest, was just as well from Gerry's point of view. If nothing else, I know my music inside-out and am not without my anorak tendencies, while Gerry was more of an all-round entertainer whose grasp on music was, frankly, sketchy.

Gerry was not a musical idiot. If he was into something, as he was with Frank Zappa, say, he could be very well informed, but his general music knowledge was shallow rather than deep. The producers of *No. 1* would prime him and give him a few answers beforehand, to try to even up the contest. If anything, it made things worse.

The producers would tell Gerry: 'We will ask you "Who made 'Gimme Shelter'?" and the answer is the Rolling Stones. Then we will ask you, "Who made *Sgt. Pepper's Lonely Hearts Club Band*?" and the answer is the Beatles.' Gerry would be only half listening, so the show would start, quizmaster Dave Heffernan would ask him, 'Who made "Gimme Shelter"?' and he would say 'the Beatles'.

Nobody minded. It all added to the mood of anarchy and general hilarity and *No. 1* was a riot to film. With Gerry, it was never about knowing the answers; it was all about having a laugh. As he was genuinely the funniest guy I've ever met, it was his humour that allowed us to keep it loose all the time.

Our guests had a blast as well. I remember one week the guest star was Steve Coogan's brother Martin, who was singer in a band called the Mock Turtles, and he loved it so much he begged to be allowed to do another show. He was trying to change his flight home, extend his hotel stay, everything.

No. 1 was great fun but 2FM was still my main passion, and on the evening show the guests kept coming. Morrissey was the hottest property in the UK music press and on late-night radio when the Smiths recorded their third album, *Meat Is Murder*, and I was looking forward to talking to this genuine cult idol. The interview was as spiky as I'd hoped, with Morrissey keen to stress that he absolutely condoned physical violence against the 'murderers' who ran slaughterhouses and butchers' shops.

Live Aid was also a major busy day for me. I was in the studio as usual broadcasting but also linking to Wembley and keeping the listeners updated with what was going on at Bob Geldof's enormous gig, staged as a reaction to the poverty in Ethiopia. It was a sign of how seriously both the concert and Radio 2 were taken that I got to interview the Irish prime minister, Garret Fitzgerald.

For many people, U2 stole the day at Live Aid, and were about to do the same a lot nearer to home. Radio 2 were still running the Beat on the Streets and the Lark in the Park all through the summer, meaning I was travelling all around Ireland, and the most memorable Lark in the Park of them all came on 24 August 1985 at Lee Fields in Cork.

Ian Wilson and I had known for weeks that we had something very, very special lined up. It was hard to keep the secret but we told nobody. Remarkably, everybody on the Lark in the Park production team who was in the know also kept quiet, which meant that when the big day came around, it caused an absolute sensation.

It was a decent late-summer day in Lee Fields and the crowd had been basking in the sunshine and the free live music by local artists such as Cypress Mine and Freddie White. When I made an announcement that we had one more surprise guest to come if people didn't mind hanging around for half an hour, it triggered mild interest but no great excitement. One of the roadies had on a Moving Hearts T-shirt, and an immediate rumour swept the crowd that these veteran folk-rockers would be appearing.

It's hard to imagine the pandemonium, then, when I went back on the stage and handed over to Freddie to announce U2. By then the band were far too big to even think of doing something like this. The previous year, their album *The*

Unforgettable Fire had topped the charts and they had played to packed stadiums across the globe – including, crucially, in America. These were bona fide world superstars striding on to a makeshift stage on the back of a dodgy old truck in a public park in Cork.

I could hardly believe the hysteria as Bono greeted the crowd and U2 took their marks. It was lucky the St John's Ambulance staff were more prepared. As the opening chords of 'I Will Follow' rang out into the evening sky, hundreds of people who had already left and were heading down Grand Parade turned around and came charging back to Lee Fields. By the end of the first song, the ambulance crew were dealing with more casualties than they had seen all day. There were no injuries, as such, but a handful of people fainted through sheer disbelief.

The backstage area was absolute chaos – well, it would have been if we'd had a backstage area. All we had was the tiny area we called 'backtruck' at the Lark in the Parks; a small space for our production equipment, surrounded by a few cheap crash barriers. Out of the corner of my eye, I caught a glimpse of Ali Hewson trying to gain entrance by convincing a security guard that, yes, she really WAS the singer's wife.

The gig was electric on that crazy, beautiful night in Cork. The crowd alternated between pinching themselves and going mental as U2 ran through 'Sunday Bloody Sunday', 'Gloria', 'Pride (In the Name of Love)', '40' and Dylan's 'Knocking on Heaven's Door'. The next day's local paper write-up was pretty close to definitive: *'For years to come, a generation of Cork music fans will be remembered thus – those who were at the Lee Fields, and those who weren't.'*

As I watched what remains one of the most memorable U2 gigs I have ever seen, my mind went back to an earlier, even more odd event. A few years earlier, U2 had played on a dark night on the roof of a block of inner-city Dublin flats in Sheriff Street. I introduced the band on Bono's microphone but there were only a handful of curious people down below.

As they played, windows opened around us, with some people unhappy at the noise. On a lower roof just out to the right a slightly overweight, inebriated woman was dancing and by the second song she crashed the ground. She seemed pretty concussed, so Adam Clayton and I took her to the nearest hospital, where she quickly sobered up. It was an odd one: nobody who saw U2 that night knew who they were, there were no cameras and there was nothing in the papers the next day.

As U2 were making their way into the rock firmament, another major rock star was sadly exiting stage left. Thin Lizzy star Phil Lynott had been dogged by drug and alcohol problems for years and collapsed at his home in London on Christmas Day 1985. His body had just given up, and after two weeks in hospital, he died four days into 1986. He was just 36.

This was terrible news not just because Thin Lizzy were a great old-school rock 'n' roll band but also because Phil was both a genuine star and a gentleman. He had appeared on my Radio 2 programme a number of times, including one occasion when he was decidedly the worse for wear on God knows what. He had to lean against the desk to keep himself upright, and Ian Wilson eventually swapped Phil's microphone for one with a heavier base so it wouldn't collapse when he kept slumping against it.

I had great memories of Philo. Once he turned up at Radio 2 with Terry Woods of the Woods Band and later the Pogues to record a great session. Another time I was driving home with Joe Breen, a friend from the *Irish Times*, from a trip to Galway and we heard on the radio that Lizzy were playing that night in Cork. Abandoning our night's plans in Dublin on the spot, we swung right at Athenry, down through Loughrea and Nenagh, and saw a superb show, with Lynott on top form.

Phil was not one for a quiet night in and he never tried to hide his proclivity for wild living, pills and powders, but there was one time when I thought he might be slowing down and mellowing. With his wife, Caroline, he showed me around his house in Sutton in the mid-1980s and talked excitedly of solo albums, and a small book of poetry and lyrics he was poised to release. He signed a copy for me and we sat on the beach behind his magnificent house just shooting the breeze for an hour. Phil genuinely seemed to think his rock 'n' roll excesses were behind him. Sadly, they caught up with him in the end.

Meanwhile, RTÉ seemed to be pleased with my performance on *No. 1*, even though I was largely filling my traditional role as Gerry Ryan's straight man. Together with producer Billy McGrath, I was asked to take on another TV show. *Visual Eyes*, notwithstanding its dodgy title, was a fairly serious programme that focused on different areas of media and technology each week. It ran for two series.

Even as somebody who had never had any great ambitions apart from playing music and seeing where the fates took him, I could sense my career was taking off. Despite this, *Jobsuss* did not get recommissioned after its second series. Susan was eager to find a decent follow-up programme quickly, but as the weeks went by, nothing appeared.

She and I were still getting on grand, but it's disheartening for anyone to feel unemployed and/or under-used, especially if your partner is thriving. Susan became convinced she wanted to try her luck in the media in London, and long, anguished conversations followed as we worried into the night, trying to find the best way forward for us.

Susan left for London towards the end of 1985. I was deeply upset to see her go but she was adamant it was something she had to do and we convinced ourselves we could still make things work. We would both be back and forth; I would go over to London every other weekend, maybe even pick up some work over there – we could survive this temporary setback, right?

Wrong. Anybody who has ever tried to conduct a long-distance relationship knows just how hard it is – the pain of separation; the resentments; the difficult phone conversations, the pressure on you to have a good time when you finally meet up. I was willing to give it a go, Susan said she was too, but I have to say, when she got to London, I think the world looked a lot different.

Susan was making a brand new start, she was in an exciting, vibrant new city, and I guess Dublin suddenly seemed a very long way away. What's that line in the Carly Simon song: '*You gave away the things you loved, and one of them was me*'? In any case, I had made no more than three of my planned fort-nightly weekend trips to London when she finished with me.

I had not seen this coming and I really, really did not want it to happen. If your lover wants to end a relationship, you can't talk them out of it, but at that moment I realised what it is that great songwriters mean when they talk about being heartbroken.

A number of drunken, self-pitying nights with Mel or Neil followed as I tried to put myself back together and come to terms with what had happened. But, really, how do you survive these things? You do what everybody does who has been in the same horrible situation over the years: you pick yourself up, dust yourself down and carry on.

Work has always been my salvation in times of crisis and so it proved. RTÉ were delighted with Radio 2, where the listening figures were healthy and the reviews were excellent. People seemed to like the evening line-up of me from 8–10 p.m., Gerry Ryan at 10 o'clock and Mark Cagney from midnight, and it seemed a major vote of confidence when *Hot Press* put a photo of the three of us on their cover under the headline 'The Right Stuff'.

I scored another notch on the bedpost of meeting my heroes in 1986 when Neil Young came in to my evening show. He was right up there with Leonard Cohen and Joni Mitchell, the two other Canadian singer-songwriters that I venerated. Again, my brothers had got me into him at an impressionable age, and then I had followed him avidly through stone-cold classic albums such as *After the Goldrush* and *Tonight's the Night*.

Never one for record-label mollycoddling, Neil made his own way into the studio by taxi and arrived alone except for a certain Otto. Otto was a hand-held camcorder, which is a very common thing to see nowadays but back then seemed as futuristic as any unlikely contraption debuted on *Tomorrow's World*.

Neil Young is quite the gadget freak and wondered aloud at the miracle of a device that was, as he put it, 'no bigger than a box of popcorn' and yet could record everyday life at the flick of a switch. As he held forth, I realised that I had misunderstood his accent. He hadn't quixotically named the gadget Otto: he was showing me the Auto, as in auto-focus.

Neil Young has made some wondrous albums but he's also churned out a few stinkers over the years and I had to admit that his latest offering, *Landing on Water*, was not my favourite. I tried to convey this politely but he interrupted me, amused and not at all offended, to ask, 'Are you trying to say this is a piece of crap?' When I indicated that this was, indeed, my opinion, Neil carefully explained why it might be worth my while to give it a second chance, and was also happy to talk through his vast musical history, from Buffalo Springfield onwards, in no little detail. They say you should never meet your heroes, but Neil Young certainly didn't let me down.

I was fortunate, for Young could be notoriously prickly, as could Ray Davies of the Kinks, who also dropped into Radio 2 for a chat. The nervous tension was upped considerably by the fact that accompanying Ray was his fellow Kink and brother Dave Davies, with whom he enjoys a famously volatile relationship.

I was expecting fireworks but in the event got cool conversation and great anecdotage. Ray had great stories of touring with the Beatles, even though he did betray a certain, probably justifiable, resentment that the Kinks' more avant-garde, experimental work never got the critical recognition it deserved.

Ray and Dave seemed to be getting on fine, but an interesting insight into their relationship came when Dave dropped a conversational howler. 'This first time I heard *Sgt. Pepper's Lonely Hearts Club Band,'* he told me, 'I was with that singer Val ... Val Doon ... the one from Belfast ...' 'Van Morrison?' I suggested. 'Aye, that's the one, Van Morrison!' Ray pounced on the error with relish, pointing out to his brother with amused scorn that he really ought to know the difference between Van the Man and Sixties MOR crooner Val Doonican. Yet that night at least, there didn't seem anything more malicious to their banter than good old-fashioned sibling rivalry.

One thing I loved about the Radio 2 show was that it gave me the chance to interview not just established superstars such as Messrs Young and Davies but also total newcomers. This was very much the case when Fachtna O'Kelly, who had first contacted me when I was at *Scene* about the Boomtown Rats, got in touch to tell me about a new artist he was managing: Sinéad O'Connor.

Sinéad had previously been in a couple of local bands, In Tua Nua and Ton Ton Macoute, but was now recording solo material. She had just recorded a single with the Edge, 'Heroine', for the soundtrack of a movie called *Captive* and was working on her debut album. Fachtna warned me that she was 'a bit different' and could be unpredictable, but the interview went fine and I didn't understand what he was talking about. Our paths were to cross many times in future years, when all would become clear.

After Live Aid, there was a spell in the mid-Eighties when open-air benefit concerts were *de rigueur*, and I was called upon to do my usual stage-announcing duties for Ireland's most significant contribution to the genre. Held on 17 May 1986, Self

Aid was intended to focus minds on Ireland's large-scale unemployment problem, with more than a quarter of a million people out of work at the time of the show. As well as 'honorary Irishmen' Elvis Costello and Chris Rea, the cream of the Irish music world turned out, from Rory Gallagher to Van Morrison, Paul Brady, Christy Moore, Clannad and the Pogues in a fourteen-hour extravaganza.

It was a big day for Bob Geldof. Self Aid represented the Boomtown Rats' last ever show, and, four months after Phil Lynott's death, he was also to sing with the surviving members of Thin Lizzy in a moving tribute to Philo. Before they went on, I was running around backstage trying to get hold of a cassette player and a Thin Lizzy album on tape so that Geldof could reacquaint (or was it just acquaint?) himself with the band's tunes and lyrics.

The tribute, and the day, passed off fine, and as I took to the stage for the final time to introduce the concert's inevitable headliners, U2, I felt a sense of relief, as well as privileged to be up there amongst the cream of the Irish music industry. I didn't know at that moment that by far the most important person of all was not up on stage with me but watching from deep in the crowd.

7

In 1986, my friend Neil Hickey was now living in a swish apartment in Sorrento Heights in Dalkey. His flatmate was Ursula Courtney. She worked in the *Irish Times* while Neil, for his part, had by then left the world of exotic sweets and begun working as a rigger, building stages for big gigs.

Ursula's parents were both from Galway but were living in America. Her father was a well-respected jeweller who in the past had not only been a top engraver for Tiffany's and Cartier but also engraved commissioned pieces for John and Jackie Kennedy and the Rockefellers. He was now running his own jewellery shop and business in Jacksonville in Florida.

When the Courtneys relocated to Florida, Ursula realised it wasn't for her – there was too much emphasis on pick-up trucks, guns and Jesus, not to mention too much Journey and Styx on the radio! Having struggled through a few weeks, she decided that she and Florida had to part ways, and she returned to Ireland.

Neil knew Ursula slightly through her sister, Deirdre, who had a spectacularly cool job. Deidre was the personal nutritionist to Brian Wilson, which meant she lived in a house on the beach in Malibu, California, with the reclusive genius who had penned the Beach Boys' slivers of Sixties pop genius.

Ursula had come back to Ireland, Neil had just sold his family home and both were looking for a place to live. She'd got herself a full-on job in the advertisement department of the *Irish Times*, persuading major companies to part with large sums for back-page ads and the like. I may well have seen her in the office, but really I don't think I ever did. I was never there in normal working hours, just making occasional pre-midnight visits to type up gig reviews, though – after four years of reviewing – that had now changed, for I'd just switched to having my own weekly half-page column, largely dedicated to the week's new album reviews.

The chances are I had met Ursula before, however, as in those days I regularly went to a handful of bars just off Grafton Street at weekends; places like Keoghs, the Bailey and Tobins. There was a little scene going on there – Neil was part of it, as was Deirdre before she went to LA, and Ursula occasionally went down with Deirdre. She is convinced that we met there in those days and although I don't remember, I am sure she is right.

I may not have noticed Ursula then, but when she came back from America I became very aware of her indeed. I found a lot more excuses to call round and see Neil. It turned out she had been in the crowd at Self Aid, watching me introduce U2, and she had also travelled down to Cork with Neil for one of the Lark in the Parks. It seemed like our paths were increasingly crossing, and the more I saw of her, the more I liked her.

People sometimes ask what the initial attraction was when I met Ursula, and despite the fact that I make my living by the

At Dublin Zoo with my dad, Barney, on my First Holy Communion Day when I was 7. Dad was bald and always wore a hat or a cap. He'd leave it on top of the telly to keep it warm.

In the garden of Mr Barry's house in Dublin's Phoenix Park.

Dad and pipe.

My mum, Annie (the greatest Irish mammy, ever).

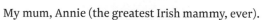

Standing up, left to right: Gerry Coyle, me and Mel Reilly in Carraroe, Galway, a few days before the first moonwalk in July 1969.

Sartorially challenged: an on-air shot in Big D Radio in Chapel Lane in the centre of Dublin in 1978. Inset: broadcasting on Radio Dublin in Sarsfield Road, Inchicore, Dublin in 1977.

Left to right: Larry, Edge, me, Adam, Bono at RTÉ Radio 2 at the start of the Eighties.

Early Nineties 2FM with Edge and Ian Wilson.

With Bono in the mid Eighties.

With Jim Kerr of Simple Minds and Bono a few years earlier.

One of my favourite photos with U2, taken onstage at Lakeland in Florida. A minute later, they started their first ever Zoo TV gig.

Clockwise from left: Blondie; Robbie Williams; Depeche Mode.
Left to right: Jackson Browne; Bob Geldof; Bryan Adams.
Left to right: Pamela Anderson; Björk.

Left to right: Sir George Martin; Morrissey.

Clockwise from left: Rod Stewart; Ringo Starr; Michael Hutchence of INXS; The Corrs; Sir Cliff Richard.

Left to right: John Paul Jones of Led Zeppelin; Lyle Lovett; Colin Farrell with my son, Robert.

With David Byrne of
Talking Heads.

In Paris with Bono and Robert.

With Bono in Italy on the Joshua
Tree tour, May 1987.

The annual U2 live radio interview in the year of *The Joshua Tree*. 'Let's change things,' says Bono.
'Let's take our clothes off. That should make for a different interview.' It did. That's Bono's felt-penned
autograph on my lily-white back.

Joni Mitchell in 1983. One of my heroes and the best female artist of the Seventies.

The first of many meetings with REM. With Bill Berry and Michael Stipe, following the release of their second album, *Reckoning*.

With the Governator, Arnold Schwarzenegger.

an ordinary photograhh of two extraodinary people, love, Bono + Ali

On holiday in Crete in 1988 with Gerry Ryan.

Top right: 'An ordinary photograph of two extraordinary people, love, Bono and Ali' – Bono tries his hand at photography with this shot of Ursula and me.

With Ursula (left) and Dolores O'Riordan of the Cranberries at Dolores's wedding in Tipperary.

The Rolling Stones. Left to right: Charlie Watts, Ursula, Keith Richards and Mick Jagger.
Inset: The same picture, just to prove I got my head in. Keith was more interested in Ursula.

David Bowie, the best male artist of the Seventies. When he rang me at home, I was in the loo. Met him six or seven times and always gives good quote.

A thousand bands passed through the 2FM studio. Pre-megafame, Oasis dropped in at the time of the release of *Definitely Maybe*, their debut album.

Shane MacGowan. In London. In a pub.

Clockwise from left: Noel Gallagher with my son, Jack; Nick Cave; Lenny Kravitz.
Left to right: Bryan Ferry of Roxy Music; Ray Davies of the Kinks; Iggy Pop.
Clockwise from left: Lou Reed; Damon Albarn of Blur; the Housemartins, with Fatboy Slim (left).

Left to right: Cindy Crawford (and Concorde's steps); Paul McCartney in his London office.
Left to right: Willie Nelson; Beyoncé; M People.
Left to right: Phil Lynott, a Thin Lizzy fan and bearded Dave; Ursula and Beach Boy genius Brian Wilson in Malibu; with two giants of Irish music, Rory Gallagher and Christy Moore.
Left to right: Mick Jagger; Sinéad O'Connor's first ever interview.

Left to right: Gerry, Ursula, Me, Morah, Mel and Christine on our wedding day in Wicklow, August 1990.

A very young Jack Fanning!

With Elvis Costello at my wedding.

The Fanning family in Disneyland, LA.

Mum with the kids.

Ursula and Hayley.

In Kildare in summer 2010.

Erudite genius: the lyrical
Leonard Cohen.

My third Canadian singer-
songwriter hero, Neil Young.

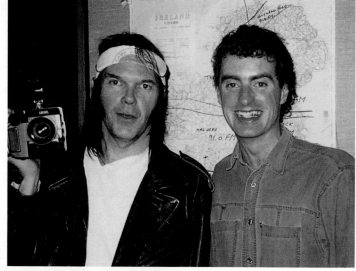

The Ramones, one of my
favourite punk bands.

spoken and written word, I am hopeless at answering questions like that. I go tongue-tied and struggle to express myself. The best way to explain it is this: I thought she was charming, funny, sexy and utterly fabulous on every level. In fact, I still do.

I resolved to do the thing I have always been completely useless at and ask her out on a date. It's probably indicative of my awkwardness that, rather than invite her face-to-face, I took the mildly cowardly option and did it on the phone. If she said no, I felt it would be slightly less embarrassing for both of us that way.

So I called the *Irish Times* one afternoon and asked for her. I must have been pretty nervous, because when another girl answered and said, 'Yes, I'll get her, who wants her?' I made a lame and totally pointless joke and said 'Neil'. This could have easily backfired, because Ursula came to the phone clearly very work-stressed, and barked, 'Jesus, Neil, what do you want? I am really busy here, you know!'

Feeling kind of stupid, I told her, 'Look, it's not Neil; it's Dave,' and she went very quiet. Plucking up my courage, I invited her to go with me to an event the next night in a space that was sometimes used for parties in Dublin Cathedral.

The cathedral event was some kind of MTV launch. MTV had made various inroads into Ireland through the 1980s and everyone knew our own MTUSA show hosted by a guy called Vincent Hanley, or Fab Vinny, who had been a launch DJ on Radio 2. The launch was a fairly nothing event but we had a great first date and decided we would like to have a lot more.

I would have fallen in love with Ursula even if she loathed all music, but the fact she was a big music fan was a huge bonus.

Her tastes were similar enough to mine, although she tended more to the Todd Rundgren/Van Morrison/Graham Parker school of rock. She had attended a lot of gigs with a previous boyfriend, she loved music enough to have gone to London for Live Aid with Deirdre the previous year, and it turned out there were plenty of artists that we both admired – especially Nick Cave.

When you meet the person that, for want of a better phrase, you might call your soulmate, everything falls into place. Ursula was gregarious, funny and was as happy going out in a gang and having a great laugh as she was cooking on a quiet night in. In addition, I soon realised that where I have always been chronically disorganised and all over the shop, Ursula was level headed, pragmatic and together.

Neil landed a rigger's job on U2's mammoth *The Joshua Tree* tour and was out of the country for months at a time. *The Joshua Tree* was the album that truly marked U2's arrival as the biggest band of the 1980s and went on to top the chart in more than twenty countries around the globe, including America. The band asked me to conduct an extensive and far-reaching interview with a view to providing an EPK (electronic press kit) for use on US radio programmes. I interview the band about the new album, the full interview gets sent to radio stations all over the US, and each one has the choice to leave in my questions or take them out and just leave the answers from the band. (I did this again a number of times for subsequent U2 albums.)

Anyhow, I went to Ardmore Studios in Bray in Co. Wicklow, where the band was shooting the video for 'With or Without

You'. This later became the first single from the album and the first of three to hit the No. 1 spot on the US singles chart. Myself and Ian set up a small 5-mic studio. After filming for a few hours with director Meiert Avis, the band came over feeling they'd done enough to have bagged a few decent takes. Bono asked me if I'd heard the album; I'd only heard it once or twice at that stage. He thought, correctly, that we'd have a better interview if I'd lived with it for a while, so we scrapped the recording and reconvened a fortnight later at the Factory in Dublin.

I had an advance copy for a couple of months before it came out, and it was our personal soundtrack when Ursula and I had our first long weekend away together in Kerry. It was clear to my ears that the band had made a quantum leap and that there was every chance world domination could follow. All they had to do was release a great album. They did.

In March 1987, when I accompanied U2 to Modena in Italy, Pavarotti's hometown, to make an RTÉ documentary about *The Joshua Tree* tour with producer Billy McGrath, I got some idea of the madness and adulation that follows the band around. It was hard to believe just how manic their Italian fans were. It was also interesting to note how differently the band members react to obsessive fans: Larry and Adam can get pretty cheesed off with it, Edge lets it wash over him, and Bono simply laps it up. The highlight of the trip was U2 being awarded the freedom of Modena, though the stuffy officials, daft medals and ridiculous ceremony for this was the stuff of a *Carry On* film. I could almost hear Sid James's cackle.

Shortly after *The Joshua Tree* was released, U2 came into Radio 2 for their traditional launch interview. We had naturally set the whole two-hour show aside for this major event. Adam and Larry were there promptly for the 8 p.m. start, the Edge showed up as the news bulletin finished, and Bono tumbled in late just as the first song from the album came to an end.

After all the tiny gigs and support slots, all the hard work and slogging around the globe, all the interviews we had done on two-bit pirate radio stations, U2's time had clearly come and the band were in celebratory mode. Bono in particular was in great spirits and, as is his occasional wont, set the conversational ball rolling by telling a couple of jokes. I thought they were pretty funny.

'This sandwich walked into a bar,' he chuckled. 'The landlord told him, "We don't serve sandwiches."' Now, this routine is not likely to give Eddie Izzard any sleepless nights, but there was such a buzz of joy around U2 on that night that we all found it inexplicably hilarious and fell about.

Pleased with his success, Bono tried his luck again: 'Mary and Josephine go to England for a few days. Mary buys a skunk and wants to bring it back to Dublin but Josephine warns her they will never let it through Customs. As they get to the airport, Josephine asks Mary what she is going to do with the skunk, and Mary says, "Put it down my knickers." "What about the smell?" asks Josephine, and Mary says, "If it dies, it dies ..."'

Things got even more bizarre. In ebullient spirits and keen to be as silly as possible, Bono declared that the interview would be far better if we conducted it naked. We didn't all initially take too kindly to this suggestion – for very good reasons, I am never keen to expose my torso unless absolutely artistically necessary – but Bono was typically insistent and eventually we all went along with it. The band even sang impromptu a cappella versions of 'Puppy Love' and 'Lost Highway'.

So it was that when RTÉ's head of radio, Michael Carroll, came wandering in with his son to see how the big celebrity interview with U2 was going, he glanced through the studio glass to find five naked men drinking beer and killing themselves laughing live on the air. It certainly was not what he was expecting and I have no idea what he was thinking, but at least he was smiling. It was certainly a long way from de Velera's Radio Éireann.

A few days later, U2 played two triumphant homecoming gigs in Croke Park. It was the ultimate local-boys-made-good show and the newspapers were full of THE BOYS ARE BACK IN TOWN-type headlines. The local TV news programmes went to town, tracking down everybody from the band's old Mount Temple music teachers to roadies to stagehands. Their finest moment was undoubtedly an in-depth interview with the owner of a local hearing-aid shop called Bono Vox.

Around this time Bono had bought a new house in Killiney in Dublin and one day he showed me around as Ursula chatted with Ali in the kitchen. From a balcony, he pointed down to a small building at the end of the garden that led down to the beach. 'See that gazebo? I'm painting down there at the moment,' he said. 'Oh yeah? What colour?' I asked. 'No, Dave – I'm *painting*.' Ah. Right.

If I felt I had maybe contributed a tiny amount to U2's success, via my support on the radio, in print, and so forth, I was at least always able to do so from the sidelines, on my own terms. When another music superstar came to Dublin in 1987, I got trapped in the glare centre-stage and I absolutely hated it.

Elvis Costello had long been one of my favourite post-punk new wave artists and I loved his trenchant, caustic lyrics and way of twisting a classicist melody. When he played a few nights at the Olympia Theatre on his Spinning Songbook tour, on which he revolved a giant wheel bearing his song titles and played the song that the needle indicated when it came to rest, I was naturally eager to go and see him.

Actually, that's not quite correct. Elvis didn't spin the wheel. It was members of the audience that did that, and when the wheel came to rest, they were then obliged to go across to a giant cage on the other side of the stage and dance for the crowd's entertainment for the duration of the song.

There are clearly plenty of extroverts in Dublin, because every time they asked for another audience member to spin the wheel, there would be a forest of hands in the Olympia as everybody strained to be picked, like primary school kids who knew the answer to teacher's question. It looked to be a hideous experience to me, but I was enjoying the show at the back of the hall with fellow music writer Ritchie Taylor.

B. P. Fallon was the evening's compère, so I should probably have seen what was coming next, but I really didn't. Halfway through the show, Beep was back on the mike doing this 'OK, who's next?' banter. 'I know someone who'd love to get up here to take part in some spin 'n' boogie,' he announced. 'Dave Fanning!'

Beep had planned the whole thing and I never stood a chance. The second that he said my name the lighting guy trained a spotlight on my face at the back of the hall. Ritchie was no fool – he turned and legged it out of the hall the second the light hit us. I was on my own for this one.

People may think I have a fair degree of natural confidence from being on the radio and TV and conducting thousands of interviews over the years but this was something else entirely. I swear I was shaking as I walked down the centre of the venue, climbed on stage, shook hands with Elvis, who had a nicely evil glint in his eye, and turned the Spinning Songbook wheel.

I was in such a state of shock that I didn't even notice which song the wheel stopped at and to this day I could not tell you which song I danced to. Suffice it to say that I simply cannot dance, or even lurch, not even after a barrel of Guinness. This was infinitely worse than acting the fool on the Beat on the Streets, and as I twitched and juddered in the torture cage for the longest five minutes of my life, my pain wasn't eased by seeing Bono and Larry sitting in a side-box a few feet above my head, laughing themselves stupid.

It's strange how I found being in the public eye in that way excruciating and yet was perfectly happy being on TV or the radio all the time. I was still having the time of my life filming the RTÉ 1 pop quiz show, *No. 1*, and in 1987 there was a change of personnel on the programme that unexpectedly brought a new, very close friend into my life.

After a couple of years, Gerry Ryan had had enough of being my rival team captain (well, all those defeats must get to you) and the producers cast around for a replacement. I expected them to choose another Radio 2 DJ or a local scenester, but instead I suggested Joe Elliott, lead singer of British heavy metal band Def Leppard.

Joe was not somebody I would necessarily have expected to bond with. His band's music and metal in general I like, but it's never been top of my list. Joe had come to live in Dublin a couple of years previously for tax reasons, after *Pyromania* had sold crazy numbers in America and made him a fortune. He had grown to love Dublin and in no time at all, to my surprise and delight, I came to really like the guy.

Joe was perfect for *No. 1* because despite Def Leppard's stellar unit-shifting status – their *Hysteria* album actually knocked Michael Jackson's *Thriller* off the top of the US charts – he had remained utterly down-to-earth and unpretentious. The band members had gone from working factory production lines in their native Sheffield to being music megastars, but they had never forgotten where they had come from.

Gerry Ryan's was a big chair to fill but Joe Elliott did it. For one thing, he is a major pop trivia buff and he loves music, especially early Seventies glam such as T. Rex, David Bowie and Mott the Hoople. He took to *No. 1* like a duck to water, launching himself at the show and its foibles with an almost childlike enthusiasm.

Since we became friends, over the years I have interviewed Joe many times, on radio and TV, and he has never been less than accommodating and scurrilously entertaining. The first time we chatted was for a TV show, and we conducted the whole interview while playing pool in our underwear at his house in Stepaside. I don't remember whose idea that one was.

During the interview, I talked to Joe about life on the road and he freely admitted that when Def Leppard broke big and were suddenly finding drink, drugs and groupies wherever they went, they availed themselves of everything going. 'Of course we did!' he said. 'We were young kids in our early twenties and every night was party night. We thought all of our birthdays had come at once!'

Joe is also happily aware of the *Spinal Tap* aspect of his band and, rather than piously denying it, he revels in it. The group's drummer Rick Allen famously only has one arm, after losing the other in a road accident, and during one interview, Joe loved telling me the tale of US cops trying to arrest Rick for grievous bodily harm after a carry-on in LA airport. 'They couldn't work out what to do with the handcuffs,' he laughed.

Def Leppard's music is not my bag, apart from occasional songs such as 'Animal', and Joe knows that but couldn't care less. He was unfailingly punctual and diligent when it came to filming *No. 1*, and on the sole occasion when he had apparently adopted rock star timekeeping and turned up an hour late, there was a typically *Spinal Tap*-style reason for his tardiness. His part of Dublin had suffered a power cut, so Joe had been stuck sitting in his car in his driveway, unable to open his electric gates. Eventually, fretting that he was late and couldn't contact us (this was a long time, remember, before mobile phones), Joe had climbed over the gates and hailed a taxi.

Around the same time, I got a call from the modest, unassuming, Roddy Doyle. He had written a book and he wanted me to launch it. I told him I wasn't really the book-launching type but asked him to send it to me anyway. It was called *The Commitments* and was the story of a Dublin soul band. A couple of hundred A4 stapled-together pages arrived that week in a thin red sleeve: its black type had been knocked out on one of those pre-electric manual typewriters. I still have the manuscript: I was hooked by page 20.

It was great to get a couple of mentions within the story but that had nothing to do with the fact that this was the funniest book I'd ever read. Roddy's description of the band's chaotic first school gig and particularly the small crowd's reaction to it was both hilarious and, from many of my own experiences, spot on. Five years later, the Alan Parker movie of the book was launched in Dublin in a wave of good-time publicity; launches, great gigs at the Waterfront, interviews, soul music on the radio – everyone had smiles on their faces. More than twenty years on, the film regularly hits the No. 1 spot in the list of Greatest Irish Movies and Roddy has deservedly gone on to a stellar career as a writer and novelist.

At home, when Neil Hickey returned from his year-plus of U2 adventures on *The Joshua Tree* tour and got ready to head off again on another long tour, Ursula and I were still blissfully happy. We decided to move in together, rented a very swanky and much bigger apartment up on Sorrento Heights, and kept a room for Neil, even though, as it turned out, he was seldom in the country.

The apartment looked out over Dalkey and had a stunning view of the bay. It was a pretty cool and sexy place, and it cost us crazy money, but in truth I never liked it all that much. Maybe I had been spoiled by all those years in Foster Avenue, just around the corner from RTÉ and town. Now the commute in to work was too long and I felt a bit too far from the action.

Still, this was a minor gripe. Life was pretty good, the TV work was coming in, and my radio show, which as ever was my main focus, was ticking over nicely. When I got deputed to interview Peter Buck from R.E.M. in Los Angeles during 1987, I seized the opportunity to tag a few days on to the end of the trip and catch up with Jerry Coyle.

Jerry had had mixed fortunes since he had emigrated. Having started off working in his brother's tree surgery business, he had then bumped into a Dublin guy called Pat Hanley who worked with a lot of Hollywood directors and producers such as Joel Silver and Steven Spielberg. Pat became a good friend and Jerry started to work as personal assistant to Whoopi Goldberg

I spent a day with Jerry in Whoopi's house in Amalfi in the Pacific Palisades area of Los Angeles. The house was just up the road from Tom Hanks's and opposite Bill Cosby's place. I was morbidly fascinated by it, having read about it in a couple of books many years earlier. A couple of decades before the well-publicised shenanigans of the Frank Sinatra, Dean Martin, Jerry Lewis etc. playboys, Hollywood's Errol Flynn-led 'rat-pack' hung out here. Way over to the left of the front door – where now a framed 'Dear Whoopi' letter from Bill and Hillary Clinton hangs thanking Whoopi for staying in the White House – lies a door where, on the other side, stone steps lead down to a wine-cellar. In 1946, as David Niven and friends played a game of hide-and-seek after a dinner party, his wife, 28-year-old Primula Niven, opened the door thinking it was a cupboard. She died from the fall down the stairs.

Jerry loved working for Whoopi, was always very protective of her and loved the buzz of the movie stars who called and the madness of Oscar week in the years that the show was presented by her.

Back in Ireland, Gerry Ryan, Mark Cagney and I were still travelling around the country during the summer doing the Beat in the Streets and the Lark in the Parks. Ursula took a few days off work and came with us at one point and really got into the madness of the whole caper, plus she had a bit of a buzz at seeing how the three of us were inexplicably treated as celebrities.

We had a wild trip to Sligo and also spent an entire week in Cork during which I swear we hardly slept. Our hotel had at least four different discos rocking at any given time, and when I was off-stage it seemed like I did nothing but sign autographs. If that sounds ridiculous, well, it was. If you're not careful, it can go to your head and you start living in your own little bubble, but thankfully Irish people are never too slow to bring you back down to earth.

I had a memorable comeuppance in Cork. As we were checking out of the hotel at the end of a riotous few days, the receptionist smilingly passed me a piece of paper and began the following conversational exchange:

'Will you sign, please?'

'Of course! You know, it's terrible, I've been here nearly a week and I still don't know your name!'

'It's Mary.'

'OK, shall I make it out to Mary?'

'There's no need. It's the bill.'

That minor humiliation was far from a one-off. On a separate occasion, I was on the balcony in the Ambassador at the top of O'Connell Street, watching a gig with Ursula and a few friends, and went downstairs to buy three pints. Heading back to the stairs balancing three glasses, I was confronted by a bouncer telling me I could not go up that way.

I politely explained that I had just come down that way but the bouncer shook his head and pointed me towards another door, about fifty feet and four hundred people away. He didn't say this with total conviction, so I started to ask him, 'Do you know for sure I can get in that door?' I had got as far as 'Do you know ...' and he abruptly interrupted: 'Yeah, I DO know who you are, and you still can't come in this way!' One–nil to the bouncer. I headed off across the dance floor.

You really are best advised not to get too bigheaded in Ireland. Once, Ursula and I were walking around Dromoland Castle with her sister, Deirdre, when a guy approached us in a state of some excitement. 'Jesuschristohmygod!' he spluttered. 'Can I get an autograph?' Whipping out my pen, I had got as far as 'Dave F...' when the suddenly crestfallen fella said, 'Oh, you're that DJ guy. I thought you were Eddie Irvine ... Ah, sure, finish it! You might as well!' The two girls were in knots, but I didn't personally feel that being mistaken for Eddie Irvine was the worst disaster in the world.

Gerry Ryan and I always got very different types of attention. Because of his public image and the nature of his show, some people were quite confrontational with Gerry. Thankfully, I just get people asking 'How are ya, Dave?' and sharing their views on music or movies.

During 1987 I was still presenting the technology/media/arts show *Visual Eyes* on TV, which gave me the chance to meet one of rock 'n' roll's all-time great heroes and iconoclasts: David Bowie. Bowie was on his spectacular, technology-heavy Glass Spider tour and the lavish production was at Wembley on its way to Slane Castle. I flew over to film a special on the making of the tour. I got my hotels mixed up, the interview was slightly blighted by pushy PR girls, and the Glass Spider tour itself, all acrobats and giant arachnids, was getting poor reviews, but Bowie was charming and courteous. Although I didn't know it then, our paths were to cross again over the years.

Radio 2 was nearing the end of its first decade by 1988 and marked the occasion with a major facelift. RTÉ rebranded the station as 2FM and introduced some fairly radical changes to its schedule. I was relatively unaffected by this and my show remained in the same slot, but the major shift saw Gerry Ryan move from his midnight music programme to host a morning talk show.

By then, Gerry's ten-to-midnight show had a cult following among students and music fans. A naturally subversive and irreverent soul, Gerry sent up all the listeners who called in to his *Lights Out* show and took the piss out of just about everyone. Most of them were in on the joke: when they didn't know what was going on, it just made it even funnier.

When 2FM boss Bill O'Donovan told me that he was thinking of moving Gerry to host a morning current affairs magazine programme, I couldn't decide whether the decision was brilliant or crazy. Late at night, his outspoken comments and surrealist Monty Python-style humour were fantastic, but I was by no means sure that his anarchic style would transfer to the mainstream.

The move was an undoubted success. Within six months Gerry had the country eating out of his hand. He quickly became 2FM's *enfant terrible,* sure, and the number of complaints to the station rose by 200 per cent, but the more important statistic was that the listening figures rose by 400 per cent. Bill O'Donovan had his work cut out defending him against some of the more conservative listeners but he knew that it was worth it.

Gerry always polarised listeners, and people as a whole, but he was a funny and talented broadcaster and I think he deserves a huge amount of credit for helping to pull Irish radio and general societal attitudes into the twenty-first century. He helped to put the de Valera and Cardinal Newman years behind us so much more quickly, and I think we should all be grateful for that. What was it that Joni Mitchell said in that song? *'Don't it always seem to go/You don't know what you got till it's gone ...'*

By the summer of 1988, I had been going out with Ursula for nearly two years. No relationship of mine had ever gone further than that point and yet I could not imagine this one ending. I don't want to get too Mills & Boon here, but everything between us still felt as fresh and exciting as it had done in the beginning, and I had never for one second doubted that she was the woman for me.

Despite this, when Ursula first mentioned the idea of us getting married, my stomach did a little leap of panic. It was just not something I had ever imagined doing. We had just come back from a two-week sun, sea and sand holiday in Greece with Gerry Ryan and his wife Morah, and had bumped into Pat Kenny and his wife-to-be Cathy while we were there. We had laughed, drunk and played and had an idyllic time, but still I felt hesitant about going the extra step and making everything legal.

I didn't want ever to be without Ursula again; that much I knew. I also didn't want to marry her. It's hard to explain exactly why that was without sounding, well, stupid. It wasn't that I was too young, because I was well into my mid-thirties by then. Nor was it that I had more wild oats to sow, because I hadn't exactly been giving Casanova any reason for concern before Ursula came into my life.

Thinking back, I guess I was being a typical Irish male trying to cling on to his single status as long as possible and not get 'tied down'. In the depths of my subconscious, marriage represented conventionality, a door closing on youth and independence, and probably I felt that it was just not something that fitted in to what I was doing.

I am no psychologist but my attitude to marriage definitely had echoes of my behaviour at the end of my H.Dip., when I took off yet again to Germany to work in a factory for the nth time rather than knuckle down, look for a teaching job and face adulthood responsibly. There was an attitude, a lifestyle that I just did not want to give up, and in my head I was waging a pathetic and yet determined battle to hang on to it.

Ursula and I didn't exactly argue about my reluctance to marry but we did reach an impasse and it was hard to see a resolution. I was happy rubbing along exactly as were, and she was not. At which point, as 1988 began to head for the home straight, she dropped a bombshell: she was going to give up her *Irish Times* job and go to California to house-sit a place in Malibu with a friend of hers, Anne.

This wasn't presented as an ultimatum. Ursula was not suggesting she was leaving me because of my chronic immaturity and failure to commit. We were still very much a couple; she was going for a great adventure, and the future remained open-ended and unwritten. Nevertheless, as a coded message telling me to get my act together, it was nothing less than brilliant.

Ursula headed out to California with Anne, moved into the condo in Harvester Road, Malibu, and also hung out with Deirdre, who was still at Brian Wilson's place nearby. If ever I had doubted just how happy I was with her, and how much I would miss her if she were gone, now I knew. The Dalkey flat felt like a morgue, I pined for her like mad, and in a matter of days I had booked some time off 2FM and was heading off on holiday to stay with her.

We had a fantastic time in California. One night we went to a launch party at the Whiskey A-Go-Go on Sunset Strip for a Keith Richards solo album. The guests weren't given the usual laminates but instead were obliged to wear T-shirts that bore the legend: 'Who the fuck are the Rolling Stones anyway?' Keef spent the evening wandering around the room accompanied by a beefy minder whose sole purpose appeared to be to keep him vertical.

And our paths crossed with U2's yet again. The band were in Los Angeles putting the finishing touches to the *Rattle and Hum* album and accompanying movie, and had rented a big house up in Beverly Hills, just a few doors from where the Menendez brothers were to murder their parents less than a year later. We hung out with the group at this HQ, where they showed us the artwork they had chosen for the album: a shot of Bono, Edge and a spotlight that had been taken during a live performance of 'Bullet the Blue Sky'. It was noticeable that Larry was making a lot of creative and merchandise decisions.

The cliché says that the only way to see New York is to walk and the only way to get around LA is to drive. Like most clichés, it is absolutely true. Bono had heard of a Vietnamese restaurant he wanted to try out. There was talk of us walking down there, but eventually we all piled into a convoy of cars. It was just as well: the restaurant turned out to be fifty miles away.

I cadged a lift with Adam, who was driving some cool old two-seater relic of a car and was characteristically blithe about the fact that he wasn't entirely sure where we were heading. He had the *Rattle and Hum* double-album on two cassettes and used the journey as his first opportunity to hear the freshly mixed album as a whole, so I also got a sneak preview as we blasted it out loud as we drove through the Hollywood Hills. Ursula and Anne followed behind, which was probably a bit silly as they knew the roads far better than Adam.

The next night U2 took Ursula and me to an INXS party. The Australian band's music had never done anything for me but I figured a rock 'n' roll party in West Hollywood's infamous Chateau Marmont was too good to miss. Ursula and I travelled with Larry and Bono's wife Ali in a minibus-taxi, but when we got there, the bouncer wouldn't let us in, saying he had no idea who we were. Ironically, he was wearing a U2 T-shirt and I couldn't resist pointing at it and then at Larry, saying, 'See yer man here on the left of the picture? That's him, right there!' At which point we got in pretty quickly.

INXS had billed the party as their end-of-tour bash, which was bizarre as they were only halfway through their dates. The event was fairly rock 'n' roll, with loads of women wandering round wearing only a thong, nipple tassles and a big smile, and we enjoyed soaking up the absurdities as we gazed out over the city.

My decision to follow Ursula to LA proved intensely valuable for us both. If she had gone there partly for an adventure and partly to make me show my hand and indicate my intentions, it worked. The fact that I had immediately gone haring out after her spoke volumes for how much I cared. I didn't go down on one knee and propose marriage on Sunset Boulevard, nothing like that, but by the time we said goodbye and I flew back to Dublin, with Ursula to follow on a few weeks later, we knew that everything was fine with us and we were going to be OK.

U2's publicity machine began to roll and as *Rattle and Hum* saw the light of day in October 1988, the band were invited back to LA by Westwood One, America's largest radio network, for a major interview to be syndicated across the States. The corporation's executives were surprised and possibly slightly miffed when Bono said U2 didn't want to go back to California but would do the interview in Dublin with a DJ called Dave Fanning.

Westwood One clearly weren't used to hearing the word 'No' but they needed U2 so we reached a compromise solution. They would bring over their own production staff and I would jointly interview the band in RTÉ with their man, Timothy White, the cerebral, bow-tie-sporting former *Rolling Stone* writer who was by now editing *Billboard*.

It was all quite a palaver. Our usual 2FM studio was too pokey to accommodate all of Westwood One's team so we adjourned to the far larger Studio 10. Around the table were Timothy White; myself; the four U2 members; and Phil Joanou, the director of the *Rattle and Hum* movie. Two US radio producers jostled with Ian Wilson at the studio's helm.

The interview was live but could not have been more stop-start and staccato. Timothy White had clearly eaten a dictionary for breakfast, with a thesaurus for dessert. Even Adam, who fancies himself as a bit of an intellectual on the quiet, was soon staring at him with his mouth hanging open. The conversation never got out of first gear because every time something interesting was said, we had to break for yet another ad break or message from a sponsor.

After ninety minutes the Americans said thank you and packed up, and U2 and I stayed on the air until well past midnight, falling gratefully into our natural 2FM interview mode of laid-back chatting, joking and putting in ad breaks at points that didn't break up the conversation. It was way more relaxed and, dare I say it, ten times better than the uptight earlier segment.

Also in 1988, I hooked up with a large bunch of journalists and radio-types from all over Europe to accompany the Scottish band Big Country on their groundbreaking tour behind the Iron Curtain. Early signs weren't good. As the plane came in to land at the airport in Moscow – and just a couple of hundred feet off the ground – the pilot suddenly decided to climb back up again to at least 2,000 feet, landing back on the runway fifteen minutes later with no explanation from anyone as to what caused his initial change of heart. The DVD *Peace in Our Time* documents the band's live tour, the first time a Western band had played live in the Soviet Union promoted by a private individual (not the state) and before the general paying public (not an invited audience). Unique maybe, but there was nothing particularly memorable about it besides a couple of receptions in large, austere rooms off Red Square.

To my huge relief and delight, Ursula returned from Malibu and we resolved to find somewhere else to live. I had never totally warmed to the chic flat in Dalkey and was bored stupid of the daily commute to Dublin, so we settled on a place called the Elms off Mount Merrion Avenue in Blackrock, not far from RTÉ.

Hopefully, the landlord knew we were OK for the rent: his name was Joe Elliott. Shortly after we moved in, Gerry Ryan and I were hosting an awards ceremony in which Def Leppard won something or other. Gerry announced the winner thus: 'And here to collect the award ... Dave Fanning's landlord!'

So as 1989 dawned, we were happily ensconced back in town. While she was out in California, Ursula had done some work with a legal company, and back in Dublin she joined a small but highly motivated team that was working on an exciting new start-up venture. Based out of an office in Windmill Lane, TV3 was to be a national commercial TV rival to RTÉ, and Ursula threw herself into the project with enthusiasm.

For my part, as 2FM celebrated its tenth birthday, I was still enjoying life on the station as much as the day I had left the Big

D to join the launch team. As another, less welcome anniversary loomed – my 35th birthday in February – I was fairly keen to keep it quiet, but some people had other ideas.

Ursula had claimed she had arranged a quiet meal out with Gerry Ryan and Morah for my birthday night, which suited me down to the ground. We all headed out, but Morah asked if we would mind if we briefly called in at a club called Mother Redcaps, where there was an art exhibition she was keen to see.

We swung by the club and wandered in to an upstairs room, at which point everything went bananas. All around us there was cheering, whooping, and five or six cameras all went off at once. Gerry and Morah quickly scarpered to one side, leaving Ursula and me in the middle of a hundred-strong crowd that I suddenly noticed included Bono, the Edge and Paul McGuinness.

It was a secret birthday party, and as Alf Tupper, 'the Tough of the Track', might say in *The Victor*, I had been done up like a kipper. After the initial shock and embarrassment had faded, though, I had a great evening. Gerry Ryan was the evening's MC in his own inimitable style and Paul McGuinness made a speech and presented me with a gift of a huge radio adorned by a gold plaque that rather preposterously proclaimed me to be the World's Best DJ.

Every good party has its scandal and controversy and this was no exception. A few weeks earlier I had been asked, or rather told, by 2FM to take part in a local anti-smoking government campaign. Back then I was the kind of half-hearted puffer who occasionally lights up after his third pint, so I told the campaign organisers it would be fine to put posters of me around Dublin with the slogan 'Don't Smoke'. When the posters appeared, this phrase had rather mysteriously changed to 'I Don't Smoke'.

It was ironic, then, that when pictures of my party appeared on the local papers' gossip pages, they all chose to go with one of me and Ursula arriving at the party, in which my mouth was hanging open in shock and a cigarette was clearly visible in my right hand. A couple of them even ringed the offending hand in question, just to make sure that their readers got the point.

U2 were then probably about as big as R.E.M., a band whose career I had avidly followed ever since their debut album, *Murmur*. Michael Stipe and Bill Berry had been in to Radio 2 for interviews over the years, I'd encountered Peter Buck a few times, and when the band released the sumptuous *Green* album in 1989 and came to Dublin to play the RDS, there was no way I was going to miss it.

R.E.M. were great, as ever, but I never liked the acoustics and feel of the RDS, which I always thought was the worst venue in Dublin, so I was amazed a few weeks later to read *Rolling Stone* and learn that R.E.M. considered it to have been the best gig of their whole tour. However, I did really enjoy the support band, the Go-Betweens, and Ian Wilson ended up organising a free Lark in the Parks show by them on the cricket pitch of his alma mater, Trinity College.

RTÉ also sponsored a few free outdoor summertime shows such as Cork Rocks, one of which starred a new band from Limerick who had sent us a demo tape. The Cranberry Saw Us were so shy that lead singer Dolores O'Riordan played the whole show with her back to the audience. She has rather more confidence now they are called the Cranberries and have sold 15 million albums worldwide. Years later, I stumbled across the original demo the Cranberry Saw Us had sent. It included five tracks, and Ian Wilson had marked four of them as worth playing – none of which later surfaced on any albums. The only song we rejected was 'Linger': their breakthrough single and most popular tune!

When Ursula and I decided to get married, the obvious next move was to hand in our keys to Joe Elliott, give up on renting and buy our own home. The house-hunting process went on for a few weeks and we must have looked at forty places at least before we found one that we instinctively both liked – a little house directly opposite Carysfort National School on Convent Road in Blackrock.

An architect cousin of Ursula, John Smyth, turned the garage into a very sexy room, complete with spiral staircase and cool glass roof, for me to play music and keep my records in. RTÉ liked that room so much that when I later started filming *The Movie Show,* they recorded many broadcasts in there.

Somehow, at the end of the Eighties, so much of what I did seemed to be bound up with U2. New Year's Eve 1989 found me on stage at the Point as the band played the second of two gigs to see out the end of what had been for them a decade of spectacular progress and achievement. They were due on stage at midnight, and it was my job to count down the clock to the Nineties and then introduce them.

The countdown began at thirty, and I led the packed Point in the chant of 'Thirty! ... Twenty-nine! ... Twenty-eight! ... Twenty-seven! ...' Except that as we reached around eighteen, I looked at the huge clock at the back of the venue and realised that something had gone badly wrong and there were only actually ten seconds to go.

Panicking, I skipped eight or nine numbers and started bellowing 'Ten! ... nine! ... eight! ...' which meant that we hit the start of the new decade spot on but with the entire arena hopelessly confused. Maybe I should have ignored the clock and just carried on the original countdown – we had been doing perfectly well, and after all, what is ten seconds in a decade?

I began the Nineties standing with Ursula at the side of a stage watching U2. At the end of the set, Bono told the adulatory Point that U2 were going to go away for a while and 'dream it all up again'. The comment was received with widespread cheers and unthinking, celebratory bonhomie. I don't think any of us there, least of all me, began to realise just how much he meant it.

8

Throughout the Eighties, my career had been pretty exclusively based around Ireland. There had been occasional jaunts and junkets around the globe for a big-name interview, a trip with U2 or a feature for the *Irish Times*, but mostly I had been all about my show on 2FM and RTÉ. This all changed as the Nineties dawned and London began to play a far bigger part in my life.

The catalysts for this change were Anita Notaro and Avril McRory. Avril had spent many years at RTÉ but had since moved across to Channel 4 in London where she was in charge of a few departments, including music. She asked me and my agent of the time, Eamonn Maguire, if I would be interested in presenting a new live TV music show that was to be called *Rocksteady*.

Rocksteady was to be broadcast out of Channel 4's studios in Charlotte Street in the heart of London. There would also be live music broadcasts from a number of venues all over England and at the Cork Opera House and Barrowlands in Glasgow. Avril stipulated that I needed some live TV broadcasting experience. I had very little, if any, of this, but I glossed over the point – I mean, how hard could it be?

I was severely rethinking this extremely blasé assumption a few days later as I stared into the abyss of my first *Rocksteady* assignment. Eric Clapton was playing one of his legendary lengthy residencies at the Royal Albert Hall, and I was sent to film a pre-recorded interview with him at the venue before introducing a song live on air during the TV show.

The interview was absolutely fine. I was no stranger to doing them on TV, and Clapton and I sat on an Albert Hall balcony overlooking the stage for a detailed and sober discussion of his art. He clearly took himself fairly seriously and was concerned that original blues artists have not been treated with enough respect by the hundreds of rock bands who have plundered their music then whitened it up in order to make millions.

The live link was something else entirely. The *Rocksteady* producers impressed on me that it was paramount that my timing was perfect. They would finish an item and cut to me. Clapton would be finishing a song and, as he did so, I had to walk, talk, follow a camera and introduce the next song pithily and bang on cue, ensuring all the time that Clapton was firmly in shot behind me. Nikki Horne, my *Rocksteady* co-host in the studio, would be talking into my ear all the way through, and depending on how far into a song Slowhand was when they joined me, my bit could take anything between ten seconds and three minutes. After it was over, I had to quickly sprint to another part of the venue to back-announce the performance.

A producer handed me a twenty-five-page running order – four times longer than anything I had worked with before. There was page after page of time sequences, camera shots, videotape inserts, location positions and presenter cues, plus a list of seventy or eighty people involved with production, logistical and technical duties. At the top were the names of producers Andrew Holmes and Andy Hudson, and above even them, three accusing words: PRESENTER: DAVE FANNING.

As I stood on the stage of the beautiful but, on that particular day, uniquely intimidating Albert Hall during rehearsals, among the mess of cables, cameras, laminates and coffee stations, I wondered exactly how wise I had been to bluff my previous live TV presenting experience so convincingly. I genuinely seriously pondered telling the producers I was not up for it.

The trick with high-pressure, seat-of-the-pants live TV such as this is to ooze nonchalant confidence and not give a damn, but that day I did the exact opposite and was a nervous wreck. One ally was the show's researcher, Richard Fell, who acted as a PA on broadcast nights and had the precious knack of being hugely efficient yet able to stay relaxed and chuckling as the pressure mounted and the on-air moment neared. As I watched Richard, I realised that that was exactly how I was on my 2FM show, where I felt totally at home and in control, and I vowed to reproduce that attitude for Channel 4.

Rocksteady sent me off to see an ear specialist in Harley Street, who fitted me with tiny bespoke microphone devices so that producers, directors, engineers and, for all that I knew, the tea lady could bark instructions at me while I was on the air. I still have those sleek, customised gadgets unused in their boxes. I would much rather rely on a floor manager. If he or she is any good at their job, they can filter this information as they get it, tell you what's needed and let you know all time cues via hand signals. Why complicate matters?

So began an absurdly busy time of my life when I was flying off to London every week for *Rocksteady*. Some weeks I had other trips to do for the show: I went to Cork with Hothouse Flowers and Glasgow with Daniel Lanois. I was still writing my *Irish Times* column, so I had to deliver more than a thousand words each week to the Arts section editor. There was hardly a week when it was not submitted at the very last minute, and I often boarded a flight in a blind state of panic with a blank sheet of paper and got off at the other end with my column completed.

It never rains but it pours (what was that we were saying about all clichés being true?) and the day I got back to Dublin from my semi-terrifying debut on *Rocksteady* with Clapton, Anita Notaro, an RTÉ producer and great friend, called me into RTÉ for a meeting. She wanted to talk to me about hosting a new series of thirty-minute interviews with rock stars that was to be titled, with mind-bending originality, *Fanning Profiles*.

This naturally appealed to me, and while part of me wondered quite how I would cram it into my schedule alongside the daily 2FM show, *Rocksteady*, the *Irish Times* and whatever other bits of random work were always coming up, I quickly agreed. I'm delighted that I did, because I have now been making that style of TV programme under various titles for twenty years.

Yet *Rocksteady* and London were now taking up a large amount of my time. Some weeks I would have to fly over twice, and so Eamonn Maguire and I negotiated a deal with British Midland whereby I guaranteed I would fly with them around a hundred times a year in exchange for a special rate. My schedules were so tight and demanding that I probably missed a quarter of my pre-booked flights.

Dave Fanning

I became so well known to the British Midland check-in staff in Dublin and Heathrow that we had quite a routine going. I would jump out of my taxi late or park my car with minutes to go, and go running up to the departure desk hopefully. They would shake their heads and point at the sky. No words were needed. The message was clear: 'You've missed it. Again.' Luckily, flights were so frequent in those days that it was no more significant than missing a bus.

Occasionally I had to pre-record a 2FM show with Ian Wilson's help, although I avoided doing this unless it was unavoidable as, despite my host of new commitments, I still regarded 2FM as my primary and most important job. Sometimes I would fly to London the day before *Rocksteady* and present my show live from the BBC's Broadcasting House, which had the advantage of gaining us access to quite a few artists who were not due to be in Ireland.

Broadcasting from the BBC also gave me the chance to hang out occasionally with John Peel, the legendary veteran alternative DJ with whom I was lucky enough to occasionally be compared. Peel was every bit as urbane and witty as you would expect. I gave him a bunch of demo tapes of Irish bands. He could quite easily have ignored them – he received literally hundreds of demos each week as it was – but he not only listened to them, but even played some of them on his show over the next few weeks.

I also picked up some more work in London when I connected with a legendary music industry Irish ex-pat. Vince Power was originally from Waterford but had moved to London in the 1960s while still in his teens and worked as a labourer before opening a small string of second-hand furniture stores. The money he made from these enabled him to pursue his first love: music, and specifically country & western.

Vince had opened his Mean Fiddler club in unfashionable Harlesden in northwest London in the early 1980s and brought over some of the very biggest US superstars to play, such as Roy Orbison and Johnny Cash. A lot of Irish guys came in and Vince invited me to DJ there every Sunday night. I used to mosey down, play the same bunch of records every week, such as 'Sally MacLennane' by the Pogues and the Specials' 'Free Nelson Mandela', and then fly back home on Monday mornings.

When Vince launched the Fleadh, an annual festival of Irish and Irish-inclined music in Finsbury Park, north London, I guess he figured I was a fairly obvious choice to handle the stage announcements. The event was fun, even though it seemed to attract bad weather and turn into a mud bath more years than not, and I basically introduced a string of bands, a lot of whom I knew already, in front of London's Irish diaspora.

Over the years I had a few encounters with the Pogues and they were natural headliners for the Fleadh. Shane MacGowan and I have had both good interviews and some excruciatingly horrible ones, and the latter have always been because Shane has been off his face. His manager, Frank Murray, was always assuring me that Shane was clean, but with all respect, I was never too sure and figured I would believe it when I saw it.

One year I ended up going with the Pogues to some particularly shitty London pub after the Fleadh and can hardly remember a more depressing evening. Shane was trashed, the night had a real vibe of bad, heavy drugs, and I couldn't wait to get out of there and back to my hotel. People say Shane MacGowan is a genius and he has certainly written some amazing songs, but it is equally valid to see him as a major creative talent who has largely pissed it all up against the wall.

Back in Dublin, promoter Dermot Flynn launched a series of Rollercoaster tours and asked me to host them. Bands such as Kerbdog, the Frames and the Pale toured student unions and local venues, and I spent my evenings drinking, talking music, collecting demo tapes and generally having a laugh. By the end of each tour, I felt I had done enough drinking to last a year.

Throughout the Eighties I was the 2FM night-time guy. In terms of popular music, as in, say, the staple diet of daytime radio, the Eighties, with the passage of time, hasn't enjoyed great press. That's probably because, say, compared to the Sixties, it *was* pretty awful. What did we get in amongst the MTV and synth pop on any sort of regular basis? Huey Lewis, Wham!, Whitney Houston, Donna Summer, J. Geils Band, Journey, Madonna, Frankie, Bon Jovi, George Michael, Queen, Van Halen, Eurythmics, Michael Jackson, Police, Tina Turner, Phil Collins, Cher, Human League, Lionel Ritchie, Sheena Easton – that's about one-tenth of what you might hear on the radio at any one given time and just about all of it disposable and dull.

I don't suppose the Eighties was the best decade for alternative stuff either but, nonetheless, great music was all around. As usual, all you had to do was scrape beneath the surface. If the Nineties gave us grunge, Britpop, indie, and nu metal, and the Seventies spread out often with influences from soul, funk and Latin music to soft, glam, hard, progressive and punk rock (not forgetting metal), the Eighties gave us new wave, hardcore

punk, rap, hip-hop and alternative rock and a few other catego-
ries which, in themselves, make about as much sense as the
categories I've mentioned. And that's not even the half of it. So
I remember playing albums by the Pixies, Replacements,
R.E.M., Talking Heads, Eno, Tom Waits, Marshall Crenshaw,
Jam, Smiths, Jesus and Mary Chain, Japan, Wire, Aztec Camera,
Cure, Prefab Sprout, X, Faith No More, Psychedelic Furs,
Hüsker Dü, Dinosaur Jr, XTC, Cocteau Twins, Laurie Anderson,
Minutemen, Jane's Addiction, Ramones, Depeche Mode, DB's,
Feelies, Blue Nile, Smithereens, Dead Kennedys, Violent
Femmes, Echo and the Bunnymen, Beastie Boys, Cramps, Sonic
Youth, Throwing Muses, Go-Betweens, Church, Wedding
Present, Fall, Mekons, Triffids, Camper Van Beethoven, Shriek-
back, Scritti Politti, Soul Asylum, Sugarcubes, Robert Wyatt,
Soft Boys, Orange Juice, Pere Ubu, Killing Joke, Felt, Primal
Scream, Wonder Stuff, Yo La Tengo, Long Ryders, Screaming
Trees, Gun Club, Au Pairs, Chrome, Yello, Swell Maps, Gang of
Four, Del Fuegos, Fugazi, Dead Milkmen, Lemonheads, Beat
Farmers, Pavement, Pulp, Slits, Loop, Crazyhead, House of
Love, Jonathan Richman and many many more. I even remem-
ber great stuff from Screaming Blue Messiahs and Stitched-
Back Foot Airman. Simon Vincent was the main guy in that
band, which hailed from Southampton. This is stuff I shouldn't
know.

Interspersed with all of these was a huge bunch of Irish bands
on vinyl, across a thousand demos and hundreds of sessions.
Besides the obvious names from Philo and Rory for the first
part of that decade to Van and Bono for the full ten years, I'll
pick one name, if only because, when I think of the Eighties, I

usually find myself mentioning Stephen Ryan. He played with Stars of Heaven in that decade and the Revenants in the Nineties.

He wrote great songs and his voice was plaintive, authoritative, lived-in, resigned, world-weary and beautiful. I liked the way he held his guitar. Stars of Heaven were rightly lauded as a great Irish band; the Revenants received less recognition, but they deserve as much praise. In eight or nine years of the Rollercoaster twelve-date Irish winter tour, I travelled the highways and byways of Ireland and heard maybe about thirty-five bands overall. The Revenants were my favourite of those. They never headlined. By the time the main band started to play, they were more than halfway home, back to Dublin for a few hours sleep before the proper job and the nine-to-five the next day.

You could pick a bunch of tracks from their second and final album *Septober Nowonder* or better still try the first release, *Horse of a Different Colour,* and start at the beginning. 'Let's Get Falling Down' is not a drinking song, but it's a great song about drinking. Listen to Stephen Ryan's voice.

I met a lot of Stephen Ryans on my travels – most, of course, not as talented – singers, guitarists, musicians in general who, through no fault of anything, really, never made it beyond the scene they were involved in but were, of course, often as good and as talented as the very best who did. There were so many memorable gigs in so many different venues from so many different bands. And there still are.

Back on 2FM, I had another encounter with Sinéad O'Connor and I began to understand what Fachtna O'Kelly had meant when he told me she could be a bit volatile. She was fine with me, but by then she had released her debut album, *The Lion and the Cobra*, and enjoyed a massive global hit with the Prince album track 'Nothing Compares 2U'. She had also made a name for herself as being extremely lippy, regularly slagging off two venerable institutions: U2 and the Catholic Church.

Sinéad was incredibly striking with her shaven head and would have looked beautiful wearing a bin bag, but it was clear she could be trouble. Johnnie Walker, a BBC DJ who had never quite lost the subversive edge he had honed on Radio Caroline in the Sixties, told me that he was warned before one live Sinéad interview not to ask her about her shaven head or mention U2. Having agreed in advance, he turned the mike on and greeted her: 'Hi baldy, how's Bono?' Sinéad could not help but laugh, but Johnnie was a braver man than me.

Rocksteady had me travelling up and down Britain and Ireland, and occasionally further afield, for live broadcasts. I was hugely excited by the chance to interview J.J. Cale in the States, as I had been a huge fan of his early Seventies albums such as *Really*, *Okie* and *Naturally*. I'd seen him play the Stadium in Dublin in the punk era but he was fairly publicity-averse and I had never read so much as one interview with him, so the prospect intrigued me.

Cale was playing an early-evening Boston show in a tiny venue and we were to beam a couple of numbers back live to the late-night *Rocksteady* audience in Britain. I strolled down the sunlit Massachusetts street and in through the club doors to find him performing live on a dingy stage. It all went to plan, although he never did the interview for a laudably cussed and independent reason: he didn't want to.

Dave Fanning

While Cale was decades into his illustrious career, Lenny Kravitz was just starting out when I met him for a profile in London. His debut album, *Let Love Rule*, had been launched in a blizzard of hype that saw him compared to Jimi Hendrix, and while this comparison was a little ambitious, the album was still as good as retro rock gets. He also had the looks, the ambition and even the celebrity partner in actress Lisa Bonet, daughter of American comic institution Bill Cosby.

Kravitz had been onstage with Mick Jagger in Paris the night before but was scheduled to play two live songs for *Rocksteady*. Yet something fishy was going on. His escort on the show was Richard Branson, his Virgin Records label boss, and as we chatted before the broadcast, Branson warned us that Kravitz was suffering from 'exhaustion' and might possibly find it difficult to get through the second song.

It all sounded rather suspicious, but Kravitz fired through his first number, a blistering rocker, with no problems whatsoever. Branson had offered to do a short interview to explain Kravitz's place in the rock firmament and why Virgin had so much faith in him, so we quickly shifted the *Rocksteady* schedule around and I sat down in front of the Virgin supremo to chew the cud for a couple of minutes.

Branson and I sat on a balcony overlooking the stage, and the floor manager started to give me the countdown to going live. 'Ten ... nine ... eight ...' Branson asked me if I flew over from Ireland every week to film the show, and I confirmed that I did. 'Seven ... six ... five ...' 'Do you fly Virgin?' he inquired. This seemed odd, as surely he knew Virgin didn't fly that route. No, I told him, British Midland. 'Four ... three ...' 'Right, that's it!'

Branson said, making as if to stand up and unplug his microphone. 'I'm not doing the interview!'

'Two … one … and cue Dave!' Slightly thrown by my celebrity guest's behaviour, I asked the opening question anyway and Branson, the ultimate smooth operator, answered it as if nothing had happened. When we finished our two-minute interview and I cut to Robert Palmer live on the stage below us, Branson was all smiles and apologies and said sorry for trying to wind me up, adding that he was impressed how I had managed to hold it together. It had been quite funny and I really didn't mind.

Later in the show, when Lenny Kravitz came to do his second number, a ballad, he got only halfway through and stormed off, his voice apparently shot. To my eyes, it all looked more than a tad calculated. Sure enough, the next day the newspapers were full of stories of the No. 1 US chart-topper having to cut short a live TV appearance after partying too hard with Mick Jagger in Paris. I guess it did his rock 'n' roll credentials no harm at all.

Guns N' Roses were at their commercial peak when I met them in Dublin at the same time. Slash is always accommodating and we did the interview lying on his four-poster bed in the band's hotel, but Axl Rose was something else entirely. Or, rather, his surreally officious and protective PR people were.

We had hired a room and had a camera set up waiting for Axl, and when he finally emerged from his room to walk down to the interview room with me, the hot-pants-wearing PR girls who surrounded him went into overdrive. Some of them had on wireless headphones, some were talking into their sleeves, and they provided a breathless running commentary as we walked down the hallway: 'Axl's left his shower and is on walkabout,' 'He's at room 204, no, 206, no, 208 ...' 'He's at 212 about to enter interview space on 214!' Despite his reputation, Axl at least had the grace to look mildly embarrassed by it all, and was perfectly charming when we came to talk.

These days, most pop stars have no idea of the damage caused to their name and reputation by overly protective, ignorantly intrusive PR types. The greatest mystique-forming, era-defining iconographic photos of, say, the Beatles or Frank Sinatra in the studio or out on the road were taken without a PR person hanging around. I've seen it more with movie stars than rock stars, but their obsession with their own existence and importance frequently overshadows common sense.

Even when I interviewed chirpy, intelligent 15-year-old Saoirse Ronan for *The Lovely Bones*, I felt the unnecessary, unannounced and uninvited 'minder' was staring me out, daring me to ask a question that shouldn't be asked of a 15-year-old. She really shouldn't bother. Saoirse can look after herself.

Nobody needs to watch over David Bowie, who was hugely engaging when I met him for the second time, in New York to film a career overview. Recording in some dingy little Manhattan studio, he seemed happy to take a few hours out and talk, as ever giving a great quote when he assured me that he couldn't remember a thing about recording *Station to Station* during his cocaine years.

Discussing obscure musicians, at one point Bowie mentioned Harry Partch, the loony whose album I had tracked down in New York all those years ago, and he was dumbfounded that I had not only heard *The World of Harry Partch* but could quote him the entire track-listing. Bowie seemed to feel that was something that nobody should know. Come to think of it, he is probably right.

Yet I must have made some kind of impact on Bowie, because a few weeks later he appeared on my radar in a most unexpected way. Richard Fell from *Rocksteady* had by then become a good friend and had come over with his wife and child to stay with Ursula and me in Dublin. I left them all in the house one morning when I made the short journey over to Foster Avenue to visit my mother.

I was in her outside loo, of all places, when my brother Dermot came and banged on the door and said, 'There's a guy on the phone who says he is David Bowie and he wants to talk to you.' Sensing a Richard prank, I told Dermot, 'Yeah, yeah, tell him I'll call him back.' Dermot left, then returned, explaining, 'He says he IS David Bowie and he really does want to talk to you.' Jesus, I thought, pulling up my trousers, Richard is stretching this joke a bit thin.

Appearing in the house, I grabbed the phone and said, 'Yeah, Richard?' 'No, David,' replied a distinctive drawl, and I knew at once that this *was* Bowie. It turned out that Tin Machine, the band he formed when he temporarily tired of the solo spotlight, were playing a low-profile gig at the Baggot Inn that night. He was rehearsing in a local studio and the people there had given him my number so that he could ask me to plug it on the radio.

That night, I announced on the show, 'There is a surprise gig at the Baggot tonight. It's Tin Machine, and if any of you don't know who Tin Machine's singer is, it's David Bowie.' I had pre-recorded the second half of the show so I could head down to the Baggot myself. The gig was fun, although I don't think that many people would regard Tin Machine as Bowie's finest hour.

The biggest hero of 1990 in Ireland was an Englishman, and his name was Jack Charlton. Jack had managed to pilot the Irish football team to the World Cup finals in Italy. They had got through the group stage unbeaten, including an unforgettable draw with England. With an identical record to the Netherlands, they had squeezed out the Dutch after drawing lots and, for the first time ever, were through to the last sixteen.

The first knockout round saw us drawn against Romania. A tense game finished goalless and went to penalties, and Packie Bonner saved the very last penalty by the east Europeans. The whole of Ireland seemed to erupt. It was one of those moments like: Where were you when Kennedy was shot? Remarkably, Ireland were through to the quarter-finals, where they were to play the host nation and favourites, Italy, in Rome.

I was hosting Gerry Ryan's 2FM show all through the World Cup but there was no way I was missing this game. Ursula and I flew out to Rome with Gerry and Morah, Pat Kenny and Cathy, but the best-laid plans inevitably go astray, and Ursula and I somehow found ourselves in a separate hotel from the other four on the match day with no way of contacting them.

I knew U2 had also flown out for the big match and managed to get in touch with them and Ursula and I accompanied them to the Stadio Olimpico. The whole day seemed somehow surreal. It was all too much: it was oppressively hot, the stadium was so futuristic and sleek it was untrue, the sky looked like a roof. The match didn't seem to have anything in common with any football game I'd seen before. Looking back, it felt like watching a PlayStation, though, of course, those didn't exist at the time.

We were sitting with U2, and the atmosphere was unbelievable, with a few thousand travelling Irish fans trying valiantly to out-sing the fervent home support. Yet Italy were just too strong, and a first-half goal by their wild-eyed forward and cult hero Toto Schillaci finally brought Big Jack's adventure to an end.

After the match U2 were guests of honour at a FIFA-hosted dinner in the grounds of the stadium and they took Ursula and me along. The meal was technically alcohol-free, but let's just say that had anyone drunk a whole bottle of the distinctly vodka-flavoured 'water' on our table, they would have been carried out comatose.

At one stage the Edge wandered off towards the toilet, and out of the bushes at the end of the lawn sprang a gaggle of camera-wielding paparazzi. The FIFA organisers were mortified and apologetic but it was no big deal to U2, who had seen far worse. The next day, Ursula and I managed to track down Gerry and Pat and their partners and regaled them with our adventures.

Ursula and I had by now decided to get married. I had still not managed a big proposal and was probably still dragging my heels a little, like an eternal adolescent, but Ursula got tired of my prevarications, we talked it over and both decided, 'Yeah, OK, let's do it.' When it came down to it, I had no idea what I was afraid of. She was all that I wanted: and, of course, once we'd actually gone ahead and fixed a date, I could not have been any happier.

We married on 24 August 1990. We didn't want an elaborate, massive wedding so we cast around for a location and somehow settled on Rathnew in County Wicklow. We stumbled across a small hotel with about seven or eight rooms run by a very nice, quite eccentric lady and figured it seemed perfect. We put up a marquee in the garden and inevitably, as these things always do, the event started to get bigger and slightly out of hand.

Probably unwisely (though I can hardly say that I regret it), I gave a pre-wedding interview to the *Sunday Independent* in which my inner punk came out and I expressed my scepticism about the whole institution of marriage. I blithely told them: 'I'll give it a bash but I'm not sure if it is human nature to stay with one person your whole life … I'll say "I do" and hope it works out but if it doesn't, that is what divorce is for. Geldof got that one right!' Ursula knew me well enough to laugh it off and not care, but my comments were too much for one of her uncles, who refused to come to the wedding.

As the big day neared, the local press got wind that it was going on and became absurdly over-excited. The *Wicklow People* ran with the headline STARS JETTING IN FOR DJ DAVE'S WEDDING and suggested that U2 would break off from their US tour and postpone dates to head for Rathnew. It would be fair to describe this notion as far-fetched.

The wedding itself was simple but great, all either of us wanted, and the reception was great fun. I had asked the Beatless – a Beatles tribute band that I regularly saw on Grafton Street – to play, but the Rathnew hotel wasn't used to big marquees and bands and the power went off. Luckily, as seasoned buskers they were able to play acoustically by candle-light until order was restored.

The *Wicklow People*'s hyperventilating dreams of rock 'n' roll superstars flocking to Rathnew weren't realised, but Joe Elliott came along as did Elvis Costello and his then wife, Cait O'Riordan from the Pogues. Elvis and Cait were then living in Dublin, and Ursula and I had gone for a meal with them a few months beforehand. They gave us some cool champagne glasses, which we still have.

The exciting news for me was that Jerry Coyle had agreed to come back from LA to be my best man. Because of his troubles with working papers and Green Cards, it was his first time back in Dublin since he had emigrated six years ago, and there was no doubt he was nervous at having to make a speech in front of so many people, a lot of whom he didn't know.

Jerry's speech was pretty ropey but luckily for him I saved him from ignominy by making mine even worse. For some reason I thought I could wing it and didn't bother to prepare anything, which was spectacularly stupid. Rob and Stella, two friends of mine from Penzance and Leeds who now lived in LA, had flown in, and for some reason I fixated on them and just kept repeating like a mantra how good it was that they were there.

It must have been one of the worst wedding speeches of all time. At one point I was struggling so badly that I even told a joke I'd heard that week. I said, 'Have you heard about the one-armed fisherman? He caught one that was that big!' and I held out one arm. It got a laugh but more through sympathy than anything else. Luckily, everybody was having such a good time that nobody cared too much about my public-speaking shortcomings.

A couple of days after the reception, Ursula and I flew to Cyprus for our honeymoon. It was a fantastic sun-and-sea break, if somewhat rushed, but unfortunately we had to bring it to a premature end and fly back early when we learned that flight delays were in danger of making Ursula miss some crucial meeting or other at TV3. It turned out there was nothing important about the meeting at all.

Work rolled on and, back in London, *Rocksteady* came to an end and the Channel 4 producers were keen to find a replacement programme. This was to be *Friday at the Dome*, which was to broadcast live from Kilburn's National Ballroom each week. In contrast to *Rocksteady*, where I had been largely out and about around the country, *Friday at the Dome* was to have me mostly in the National doing interviews and introducing live performances.

My co-presenter, Nicky Horne, did not move across with me from *Rocksteady* to *Friday at the Dome* and so the show's producers cast around for a replacement. The big media buzz at the time was that comedy was the new rock 'n' roll and so they recruited a Scottish comedian, Craig Ferguson.

Craig was not a big music fan and at times, I felt, seemed disinterested in the artists that we were introducing, so the producers gave him a three-minute stand-up slot in the middle of each show. Craig's wife was a jockey, which meant he left a few meetings to watch *Channel 4 Racing*. Things worked out well for him, I'm glad to say: he is now a huge Letterman-style chat-show host in America *and* he voices Gobber the Belcher in *How to Train Your Dragon*.

The live performances from Kilburn were a major part of the programme's appeal but didn't always run smoothly. One week I had to introduce Massive Attack, making their first ever live TV appearance. Their song seemed fine to me, but as I walked over afterwards with a big beam on my face, saying, 'Thanks, that was grand!' their faces were like thunder – their horrified manager had just told them that it had sounded awful on TV.

Manchester band Inspiral Carpets were big at the time, and after we had them on I went for a drink with one of their roadies, a certain Noel Gallagher, and a Cork guy called Mick Lynch, who was moving gear for another band on the show. Mick had been in a quirky art-pop band called Stump; Noel, who was a very entertaining guy, was about to form his own band that would do rather better than Stump.

I occasionally flew to London on non-show days in order to pre-record interviews. Rod Stewart's music had not interested me since the early 1970s but our interview was a blast. The initial signs had not been good. Rod was doing four or five interviews in one day, and when the French hack preceding me started off with the two corniest questions you can ever ask Rod the Mod – 'What was it like being a gravedigger? Oh, and do you think you're sexy?' – he had her kicked out inside a minute.

Knowing Rod was a huge football fan I cannily took a rather different tack and talked about the Scottish national team. Rod warmed to this gambit, and afterwards was perfectly happy to talk me through his long, up-and-down career. He remained charming even when I asked him if he ever said the wrong name in intimate moments. After all, it must be hard to keep track when you've been with all those blondes.

I also met up with Michael Hutchence of INXS, who at the time were big enough to sell out Wembley Stadium as a headline act. Clad in leather, he looked every inch the rock 'n' roller but was a courteous, gentle soul, even if he did leave the room a few times during our interview, only to return each time rather more garrulous and animated.

I have never been the most organised person in the world, and at this point I had so much going on in my working life and was trying to juggle so many balls in the air that I thought it might be a good idea to get a manager. I hired a guy called Eamonn Maguire, who had his own production company called EGM Television, and we began making a show called *Planet Rock Profiles*, which was essentially exactly the same format as *The Fanning Profiles* but also shown by RTÉ.

With my 2FM show, *The Fanning Profiles*, *Planet Rock Profiles* and the weekly *Irish Times* column, not to mention Channel 4, there might have been a danger of spreading myself too thinly. I must certainly have been wearyingly ubiquitous for anyone who didn't like my presentational style: I remember reading a newspaper article in which a columnist basically said, 'Jesus, will Dave Fanning leave something for somebody else to do?'

Yet I never saw things that way and I certainly wasn't mounting a bid for media world domination. It was more that I was having such a good time that I just wanted to do everything that came my way, and I saw it as all part of the same gig anyway: me enthusing over what I love, which is music and movies.

It was in this spirit of wanton eclecticism that in 1991 I decided to audition to host the Irish leg of the Eurovision Song Contest. The truth was that I had a hidden agenda. I had been trying for months to persuade RTÉ to launch a weekly movie programme, and figured that if I could pull off a mainstream show such as Eurovision, it might help to convince them that I wasn't just the rock 'n' roll guy and might have more strings to my bow.

It was a miracle that RTÉ was even holding auditions, because they never normally did that sort of thing. People seemed to just emerge, wander in and start hosting programmes. But I turned up and the audition was a bit of a hoot. The producers seemed to want the presenter just to read the autocue but I ad-libbed a bit, said a few countries' names in a foreign language, and generally behaved like someone who had the freedom to do what he wanted because he didn't actually care if he got the job or not. I didn't, as it happened, but the executives seemed to be impressed with my performance, so maybe it did me some good as regards the way they thought of me.

On a more serious note, my Channel 4 TV stints had got me vaguely noticed in the UK and in 1992 I was asked to be a judge of the inaugural Mercury Music Prize, which was quite a big deal at the time. I and my fellow judges – a team of music pundits, DJs and experts – whittled five hundred contenders for album of the year down to twelve before plumping for Primal Scream's *Screamadelica*, which was effectively an album by its producer, Andy Weatherall.

Also on the shortlist was U2's *Achtung Baby*, an album that had been causing a major stir. Having promised his audience at the Point on New Year's Eve 1989 that U2 were going to 'go away and dream it all up again', Bono had been true to his word – and how. With *Achtung Baby* they had delivered a masterpiece, a work of post-modernist genius that had seen them working with Brian Eno and Daniel Lanois to incorporate electronica and dance pulses into their rock 'n' roll while at the same time hanging on to their emotional heft and swagger. It was a critical and commercial juggernaut: even sophisticates who usually winced at U2's heart-on-sleeve sincerity loved *Achtung Baby*.

U2 were now about to take the album on the road with the Zoo TV tour, a multimedia riot of video screens, William Burroughs-style visual collages, and alter egos (and, as it turned out, crank phone calls). The whole extravaganza was to start in Miami and I flew out for the start-of-tour launch party.

My mission was to present the band with an IRMA Award. That year I was to host the televised predecessor to the Meteors from the Point, and as Zoo TV obviously meant that U2 would not be able to attend, it was my job to present them with their award on camera and get a few words of acceptance from them.

I did not arrive in Miami in the best of shape. I had spent the evening before I flew out in Cork, the night had got out of hand and I had got no sleep at all. It had been a long travel week and I was beyond exhausted as I staggered through US Customs and realised to my surprise and delight that U2's label, Island, had arranged for a stretch limo to ferry me to the venue.

The limo was the full works, with a bar serving both alcoholic and soft drinks and a driver who was a dot on the horizon. When I tried to ask him a question, he couldn't hear me and advised me to use the in-car phone system. Unfortunately, he then decided to appoint himself my tour guide and point out all the buildings of interest between the airport and central Miami. The fact that there was nothing worth talking about save an ugly university did not deter him in the slightest.

The Zoo TV show was beyond spectacular despite a few teething problems in Miami, and I managed to present U2 with their IRMA award by the side of the stage one minute before they walked out. I asked them to ignore the fact that the award was inscribed 'Best Female Vocalist: Sinéad O'Connor'. Sinéad had left it backstage at the Point the previous year, and as the IRMA bosses did not have U2's prize ready by the time I flew out, they asked me to hand over Sinéad's gong: 'Ah, sure, nobody will notice!'

After the show there was a party for about twenty people on the roof of Chris Blackwell's Island Records HQ next to Miami Beach. Michael Hutchence was there but kept himself to himself and brooded quietly in the corner with his supermodel girl-friend, Helena Christensen. By now my exhaustion and jetlag were kicking in big time, and when I found myself chatting with *Vanity Fair* photographer Annie Leibovitz, I had what felt like a brainwave, and enthusiastically and repetitively urged her to park herself in a shopping mall for a day, take photos of members of the public for $10 each and give the money to char-ity. At the time, I could not have been more pleased with the idea. Oddly, she never took me up on it.

Still in America, a few months later Sinéad O'Connor had her own brilliant idea when she decided to rip up a picture of the Pope in front of millions of Americans during a TV interview on *Saturday Night Live*. It was a protest against horrific abuses within the Catholic Church and it took a lot of balls to do it, but I don't think that Sinéad had even begun to imagine the shit-storm that would come pouring down on her head.

Two weeks later she was booed off stage when she tried to sing at a Bob Dylan tribute concert in Madison Square Garden, and shortly afterwards I met up with her in New York. I was feeling apprehensive because she had just released an album of jazz standards, *Am I Not Your Girl?*, which I absolutely could not stand. It was released on 25 September and in the *Irish Times* my pay-off line had been: 'Sinéad should have waited three months to release this album because it's a turkey.'

I was in Sin E, the Manhattan café opened by two Irishmen, Shane Doyle and Karl Geary, sitting with Thin Lizzy's first manager and McGonagles boss Terry O'Neill. Sinéad came to join us and Terry mischievously mentioned my review, but Sinéad pretended it didn't matter, although she was definitely frosty and told me that she still believed in the album. As I left to get a cab to JFK, she even gave me a hug. Or maybe she was just trying to throttle me.

In the same year, 1992, Sinéad had gatecrashed a 2FM outside broadcast I was hosting at Temple Bar. She stormed into the Roadcaster studio uninvited and started ranting about the Irish High Court's barbaric refusal to let a 14-year-old rape victim travel to England for an abortion. Sinéad lambasted the Court and the Catholic Church. It was pure guerrilla radio and I let her go on for a very good reason: she was totally right.

Sinéad might have been a diva-in-training in those days but I was just about to meet the real deal. As 1992 came to an end, I was granted a mini-audience with the cultural icon rivalled only by Princess Diana as the most famous woman in the world: Madonna.

Madonna was in London promoting her *Erotica* album, which was not her strongest, and the accompanying *Sex* book, a huge glossy tome of arty photographs of her naked and in various titillating and provocative poses, including rape fantasies. *Sex* had proved hugely controversial and become THE hot media topic of the day – which, of course, is exactly how Madonna likes it.

2FM had not been deemed worthy of a one-to-one with Madonna so I was to share a twenty-minute chat in a London hotel with three or four other journalists. Leaving an earlier nearby appointment, I got a cab to the West End hotel and was amazed when we got there to find police barriers up and down the street to control the vast crowd of people desperate to get a glimpse of Ms Ciccone.

Seeing the scrum of people, I asked my elderly taxi driver to drop me a little way down the street, saying I would walk the rest of the way, but deaf to my entreaties and seemingly oblivious to the fact that anything whatsoever was going on, he rolled right on up to the hotel door. What followed gave me a small but telling insight into the everyday world of Madonna.

The taxi fare was less then £10 but all I had on me was a £50 note. The old fella driving my cab clearly moved at a glacial pace at the best of times and took an age to extricate my change from his leather bag. Increasingly self-conscious, caught as I was between the paparazzi and a sea of Madonna fans, I even toyed with the idea of saying 'Oh, keep the change!' and giving him a £40 tip, but this seemed unnecessarily profligate.

Eventually, yer man managed to give me my money and I slung my bag over my shoulder and headed for the door. Nobody gave me a second glance … until somebody in the crowd with a rich Dublin accent yelled out, 'Hey, Dave, can ye get Madonna's autograph for us?' and all hell broke loose, with fifty or sixty paparazzi cameras snapping all around me like artillery fire.

Not one of these photographers had the slightest idea who I was or remotely cared, but the fact I was apparently en route to see Madonna and had been recognised by a fan meant there was a slim chance I could be worth photographing. Maybe I was her new boyfriend, or her drugs dealer, or a stud she intended to use to help her promote the book? Whatever: the end result was flashes popping all around me like lightning.

I got into the hotel feeling mildly shaken by this unaccustomed ordeal and feeling sure that meeting Madonna would be a breeze after that. Tabloid hacks and gossip columnists milled around in the bar hoping to find some way to her inner sanctum but they had no chance – a steely, military security operation ensured that you only got anywhere near Madonna if you had a firm media appointment.

Eventually, one of her many PR people led my small gang of four or five hacks upstairs and deposited us in a hotel room that was dominated by a lavish four-poster bed. Madonna was in the next room talking to Jonathan Ross and would be in to us as soon as the interview was done. As I paced around the room, I twitched a closed curtain to look down to the back of the hotel and the second brigade of the massed phalanx of paparazzi again clicked as one. Clearly they knew which was her suite.

Madonna breezed into the room, collecting herself from the TV interview, smoothing herself down and looking for a comb to pull knots from her hair. We all stood around awkwardly, in the presence of pop royalty, and as Madonna fussed around the room and took note of us, she began to berate us for being shy. She was probably right.

We all sat down and my motley collection of fellow hacks, who all seemed to be from different countries, awkwardly introduced themselves. I was the last in line and greeted her with 'Hi, I'm Dave from Dublin', at which she looked me up and down with a smile and said, 'OK, Dave from Dublin. What have you got?'

The ball was clearly in my court so I took a deep breath, fired off a couple of questions, and away we went. The interview was inevitably stilted but that was down to the format. When you are interviewing with a few other journalists it is awkward because you can't always ask a question and then a quick follow-up and get a conversation going; otherwise it looks as if you are hogging the show. Everyone has a job to do and has to have their turn, and when some of the interrogators don't have English as a first language, frustrating pregnant pauses are inevitable.

Madonna was the consummate professional though, feisty and full of confidence bordering on arrogance, every inch the street-smart, no-bullshit ball-breaker you would expect. As I looked at her rattling off her answers, I couldn't help think there was a slight crack in her surface sheen. I thought I detected a hint of the vulnerability we all share that Leonard Cohen so memorably captured in song when he wrote in 'Anthem': 'That's how the light gets in.'

Mostly, I could not help noticing just how bizarre she looked. Madonna conducted the interview still caked in pancake-thick BBC TV makeup that ran from ear-to-ear and gave her a most uncharacteristic moon-faced look. The makeup stopped dead at her chin and, by contrast, her luminously white neck could have belonged to a pensioner. It was not a good look for a 34-year-old.

After our allotted time we were dispatched and caught the lift down, fairly satisfied with what we had gleaned. Or so we thought. As we emerged into the lobby, the tabloid hacks, who all had four or five pages to fill the next day, pounced on us, desperate for any information. I ran the encounter back in my mind and realised that we had come away with no new angles, insights or revelations – nothing at all. Pop's mistress of manipulation had chewed us up and spat us out and given nothing away whatsoever.

As I headed back out into the street, past the paparazzi and the devoted fans, I thought hard about Madonna and what to make of her. It was hard not to admire her intelligence, her iron will, her confidence and her control. But all in all, I thought she was a bit of a wanker.

9

In the early Nineties, my agent at the time, Eamonn Maguire, was working out of an office in the Communication Centre at the top of Booterstown Avenue in central Dublin. This was our base for planning and masterminding the *Planet Rock Profiles* series, and its location was to lead to my broadcasting career taking a very unexpected turn.

The Communication Centre also housed the offices of charity organisation Trocaire, the official overseas development agency of the Catholic Church in Ireland. Trocaire undertook a huge amount of international work aimed at raising awareness of global poverty, and some of the senior officials there asked me if I would be willing to travel to Ethiopia to front a documentary on the state of that troubled nation.

By 1992 it was seven years since Bob Geldof and Live Aid had shown a horrified world the enormity of the famine in Ethiopia and helped at least partly to alleviate that humanitarian crisis. The idea behind the documentary was that it would demonstrate the positive effects that Irish charity money was having on local farmers and how it was benefiting community projects.

I didn't have to think too hard when I was asked. It was going to be a major change from talking to Paul Simon about his new album, sure, but it sounded challenging and rewarding, and it is surely a complete no-brainer that if you can do anything at all to help out in the world's trouble spots and developing nations, you do so. As far as I was concerned, Trocaire was very much the acceptable face of the Catholic Church.

One huge plus point was that Ursula would also be coming out to Ethiopia. Gerry McColgan, the brother of fellow senior RTÉ producer John, was to direct the documentary and asked Ursula to be a researcher and production assistant. Two brothers completed the team: cameraman Declan Emerson and sound engineer Paul.

There is little doubt we were psychologically and emotionally under-prepared for our two-week trip to northwest Africa. No matter how much you might think you know from reading the newspapers or seeing bulletins on TV, having the reality right in front of you is just so stark. The culture shock was severe and at times overwhelming, and it proved a truly powerful experience.

We stayed in the Ethiopian capital, Addis Ababa, but drove out to see refugee camps, some of which had existed since Geldof was there in that nation's most dire time of peril. It was good to see and be able to report on how Irish charity money was being used productively to help local communities help themselves, but there was no doubt that the camps, while efficiently run by magnificent volunteers, were also chronically over-crowded and under-staffed.

One day, we drove in a Jeep over the mountains to neighbouring Eritrea. We were so high up that the clouds actually hung in the air beneath us. The entire production team sat in the back on a swelteringly hot, arid day: Declan Emerson's camera, with its own sun umbrella, needed the front seat all to itself.

As we crossed the mountains, we passed tiny mud-hut villages and stopped to shoot footage and film pieces to camera. We would occasionally pause at food markets besieged by clouds of hovering flies. Every time we left the Jeep, we never had fewer than ten kids flocking around us, beseeching us for change. It was heartbreaking. The price of a cup of coffee in Dublin represented unfathomable wealth to these people – and yet to a man and woman, they were beautiful, stoic, serene people.

We had been warned there was no effective rule of law out in these Eritrean badlands and it was soon easy to see why. As we bumped along the mountain road, we twice turned a corner to find a rudimentary road-block ahead of us, no more than two big Y-shaped sticks holding a plank of wood and manned on each side by teenagers holding guns. Joe, our Trocaire guide, kept calm as he gathered our passports and negotiated with these absurdly young soldiers. It wasn't entirely clear what they wanted and I'd be lying if I said it wasn't a little frightening.

Another day we went to a football stadium in Addis Ababa where some kind of spectacular tribal dance ritual was going on. Declan Emerson hoisted his camera on his shoulder and walked right out into the middle of these flailing guys, sticking his lens in their faces without even asking their permission. I thought he was going to get his head knocked off, but it was an interesting insight into the way hard-nosed news photojournalists function.

Dave Fanning

We flew back from Ethiopia with the feeling of a job well done yet more than a little chastened at what we had seen. I would love to be able to declare that it made me a deeper, better person with a more profound awareness of what truly matters in life, but the truth is that we are fickle creatures and as soon as I was back in Dublin I was immersed back into my normal routine of music, radio and TV. Ethiopia had made a major impact, sure, but before you know it, everyday life has soaked you up again.

Nevertheless, I had no hesitation the following March, 1993, when Trocaire asked me to front up another trip, this time to Cambodia. Ursula would not be on board this time. She had found the African jaunt intensely moving and psychologically overwhelming and wasn't quite ready for another trip yet. There was another, even better reason: she was pregnant.

The two of us had talked over parenthood during the previous months and the dynamic was the same as ever: Ursula with a vision of the future, the big picture, and keen to press ahead, and me nervous of what it might entail, digging in my heels and hesitating. Yet I had come round to the idea the more I thought of it and, let's face it, the Big '4–0' was less than twelve months away. If I was going to be a dad, it was time to get on with it.

So Ursula stayed in Dublin as the Trocaire team headed for the airport to film a report that would be far more political than the humanitarian documentary we had made in Ethiopia. Gerry McColgan was once again the director, with Ken O'Mahony manning the cameras and Carl Merrin on sound. As we left for Dublin airport on the morning of the trip, the *Morning Ireland* headlines on the car radio told of suspected Khmer Rouge members violently killing twenty-eight people less than forty miles from the Cambodian capital, Phnom Penh. My thoughts ran as follows: 'What in God's name am I doing?'

Cambodia was no longer the volatile, murderous land it had been in the time of the Killing Fields that I had read about so avidly in *Rolling Stone* as an impressionable teenager, but nor was it any kind of utopia. In 1993, the king had been restored to the throne, and the country was gearing up for democratic elections, but neither of these developments was universally popular and armed resistance was widespread.

We interviewed suit-attired politicians in their offices and generals in medal-bedecked uniforms sitting at their desks surrounded by flags, and it was hard not to think, 'I don't believe a word you are saying.' Just a few months before, they had been brutal warlords, wreaking mayhem and dispensing injustice as they saw fit, and it was hard to buy their sudden conversion to smooth-talking democracy.

Our driver for the entire trip was a cool local guy who had been a young boy when Nixon had bombed his country back in 1970. He made far more sense when he talked about the forthcoming elections. Whereas Westerners were talking about them in high-flown terms as a chance for Cambodia to usher in a new order and new beginning, he was more realistic, hoping only that his country might take the first tentative steps towards being a less bloody, fairer place. His optimism was very guarded. I guess he had seen it all before.

We filmed at the Killing Fields and at monuments and museums to Pol Pot, the bloodthirsty Khmer Rouge leader who had taken power and slaughtered hundreds of thousands of his countrymen after Nixon and Kissinger had bailed out and left

Cambodia to its fate at the end of the Vietnam War. We also visited the truly beauteous twelfth-century temple complex at Angkor Wat, a sight that I will never forget. Yet the image of Cambodia that stays with me is not of statues and landmarks. It's of the people in the streets and the teeming, insatiable nightlife.

Phnom Penh on first visit is in some ways as memorable and iconic an experience as New York. Whereas Manhattan, with its yellow taxis and steam billowing up from the subway onto sidewalk corners, evokes a million movies, downtown Phnom Penh drops you into one very specific film: *Apocalypse Now*.

The first nightclub we went to looked like a squalid, rundown shopping centre with disco lights and music thumping out across the floor. It had no walls, just three floors of concrete with a disco in the middle. It was not particularly full but that was because the serious action wasn't in the club; it was outside. In the car park, hundreds of pumped-up, shaven-headed American GIs straddled huge motorbikes with wide handlebars and enormous mirrors and toked on joints as skimpily clad local girls and prostitutes clustered around them. There was an air of menace – or, rather, the scene had an electricity that you just did not want to touch.

At the end of the night we made our escape and headed back towards our hotel. We all took individual pedalo taxis – taxi pushbikes where the passenger sits in a huge wicker basket in front of the driver. We stopped off en route at the only building we saw with lights on and empty tables inside. It was a small pizza parlour, and the brightly coloured hoarding proclaimed its name: The U2 Pizza House. There really was no escaping them.

The weather in Phnom Penh could have been from another planet. The heat was vicious, like having pins and needles sticking into your whole body, and a couple of times I had to abandon pieces-to-camera and scamper into the air-conditioned van. Then suddenly a deluge would descend that was so fierce it seemed as if the whole city would be washed away inside ten seconds.

I am loath to parrot the patronising Western line about the people in these benighted lands being preternaturally gracious and serene, but it's another one of those clichés that happens to be absolutely true. Everybody I met seemed self-effacing, charming and interested in what we were doing there – and we saw some scenes that broke our hearts.

One day we went to film a report in a refugee camp where local people who had been displaced by fighting or monsoons could get a small meal; maybe a banana and some clean water. I met a woman who had gone to the wrong camp. She was supposed to walk ten miles east and she had gone ten miles west, and so was twenty miles from her designated camp where she could eat.

The woman sat gracefully and uncomplainingly outside of the camp as she told us her story and I would defy any human being not to want to help her. Trocaire had warned us not to give the kids and other locals money because in the long term it goes against the work the charity is doing and the independence it is trying to instil but, as in Ethiopia, the price of a sandwich in Dublin would feed this woman for a month, and there was no way I was not going to lend her a hand.

When you go to Ethiopia or Cambodia, you may logically know what to expect from research and from the media, but nothing prepares you for the madness and sensory overload of it all. It is the real deal. It explained to me more than ever how Geldof, who has always been impulsive, had to act and instigate Band Aid when he saw Michael Buerk's BBC News report in 1985, and why Bono and Ali went there in the same year and have been quietly, privately returning ever since.

My sole misgiving about going to Cambodia had been leaving Ursula behind. When I left she was eight months' pregnant, and her pregnancy had not been an easy one. She was in pain a lot of the time and suffered from hyperemesis, which is basically chronic morning sickness. Once or twice she had it so bad that she had to be hooked up to a hospital drip.

The birth came both on time and, for some reason, as a total surprise to us. It was a Saturday night and Ursula and I had gone to the cinema in Tallaght to see *Sommersby*, a romantic drama starring Richard Gere and Jodie Foster. Everything was going fine until Ursula leaned across and whispered those words that every man dreads ... sorry, longs to hear: 'I think we have to go to the hospital right now!' Needless to say, we high-tailed it right out of the pictures. I have still never seen the end of that movie.

Our first son, Jack, was born at 7.20 in the morning on 25 April 1993. The birth was straightforward – a relief after the difficult pregnancy – and I was there all the way through. It's strange being at the birth of your child: you're excited and you know it is the most life-altering, seismic thing you will ever be part of, and yet at the same time you are hanging round like a spare part trying not to get in the way of trained professionals as they focus on doing their jobs.

Still. I was now a father and it felt great. Looking down at Jack, and holding him with Ursula, it was impossible not to feel that a corner had been turned in our lives and that, from this point, nothing was ever going to be quite the same. I hate it when people answer questionnaires and invariably, piously say: 'What event most changed my life? The birth of my children,' but I guess it's yet another of those inarguable clichés. Even given the life I have had to date, kids are absolutely the best thing that have ever happened to me.

So, why did we call him Jack? Well, there is a story to that. When I was a kid, growing up on Foster Avenue, the idea of having a pet really appealed to me but we had never had one. My parents had said that the road was too busy and it might get run over and killed. This was a bit rich, given that we played football on the same road all summer long and cars were so rare that when one went by, you wanted to photograph it.

Even so, I had never had a pet until the late Eighties, when my friend Martha thought it would be funny if I had a kitten (on the nights we watched TV until the early hours, I always took in the neighbour's cat) and got me one. I called it Jack.

I loved the name Jack and it seemed to suit the tiny baby that Ursula was cradling in her arms, so Jack it was. If you think it is odd to name your first-born after your domestic pet, I can only heartily agree with you, but there you go. So Ursula, Jack and I went back to Convent Road and family life had truly begun.

The birth came at a good time for Ursula. The TV3 project she had been working on for two years had finally come to grief.

There had been too many obstacles in the path of this valiant attempt to establish a commercial rival to RTÉ, and in my view the useless Minister of Communications, Ray Burke, was one of them. He never seemed to be fully behind the idea, and frankly it was no surprise to me when a tribunal proclaimed him to be corrupt and he later went to jail for tax evasion.

Ursula had instead got a job as a researcher on Gerry Ryan's *Secrets* and later *Ryantown*, then went on to work with Gay Byrne on his last few years on *The Late Late Show*. We juggled work with childcare as I ploughed on with my normal chaotic work routine. At that point, the last thing we needed was for me to find a new job that would involve taking even more flights and being away from home at weekends ... so, obviously, that was exactly what I did.

The offer was too good to refuse. *Rocksteady* and then *Friday Night at the Dome* had made me slightly better known in Britain than previously and gained me a little recognition. I had even squeezed into the *NME*'s Best DJ poll for the last couple of years, the sole non-Brit in there, and they had described me, as usual, as the Irish John Peel.

Richard Branson must have taken note of this, or maybe he just remembered how I had refused to be thrown by his on-air mind games on *Rocksteady* with Lenny Kravitz, because he phoned and offered me a slot on his new London-based network, Virgin Radio. The station was about to launch and he wanted me on board.

My reaction to London work has always been the same: that I will do it as long as it doesn't interfere with my bread-and-butter Monday-to-Friday 2FM show. Branson offered me a

Saturday afternoon programme and I said that I would think it over, talk to Ursula and get back to him.

I was still mulling it over a couple of days later when I got an interesting insight into how Branson worked. By coincidence, he happened to be a guest on Pat Kenny's TV chat show, *Kenny Live*, and Pat mentioned the new radio station. Branson told him, 'Yes, one of your colleagues is going to be on there – Dave Fanning.' This was before I had even given him an answer.

Nevertheless the offer was a good one so we agreed that I would fly over every Saturday morning and do a show from four in the afternoon until eight in the evening. Importantly, there would be no playlist and I would be able to spin whatever I wanted, much as on my 2FM show, and the early-evening finish would give me a fighting chance of getting back to Dublin the same night.

The Virgin Radio launch party at a cinema in Piccadilly was good fun. The launch DJs included Richard Skinner and Tommy Vance, who had jumped ship from BBC Radio 1, Jono Coleman and Russ Williams, who later became a breakfast-show double act, and Kevin Greening. Richard Branson is never shy of a publicity opportunity and was in full flow at the launch party.

So began two years of me flying over to London every Saturday morning for my Virgin show. At this stage, I think I was beginning to suffer from Overhead Bin Syndrome! If I had in some ways failed to give my Channel 4 shows my all, the same was definitely true of Virgin. I never cheated on the programme: I knew my stuff, knew the music inside-out and was as enthusiastic on Virgin as I was on 2FM. But my priority was always getting out of there and home to Dublin as soon as possible.

Dave Fanning

When I got from Heathrow to the Virgin studios at midday every Saturday, Chris Evans was on air. He was hosting a show called The Big Red Mug, which was sponsored by Maxwell House coffee, and at the time was becoming a huge celebrity in Britain because he also presented an anarchic weekday TV morning news and magazine programme, *The Big Breakfast.*

Chris came off air at 1 p.m. and the three hours between his show and my programme were filled by Emperor Rosko, a venerable old Californian veteran of 1970s BBC Radio 1 who broadcast his Virgin show from Los Angeles. While Rosko was on air, Chris and I would go for a coffee and he would bend my ear about my perceived half-hearted attitude towards Virgin.

He was typically funny in the way he did it. Chris worked on *The Big Breakfast* with Zig and Zag from the planet Zog, two over-excitable sock puppets operated by a pair of Irish puppeteers whom I knew well from RTÉ. This pair (the puppeteers, not Zig and Zag) were apparently two homebodies like me who were always trying to get their work done and clear off back to Dublin, and Chris saw this as a shared faulty Irish gene.

'You never give it your best shot!' Chris would complain as he urged me to move to London, or at least come over for two or three days a week. 'You, Zig and Zag are as bad as each other!' I didn't mind his well-intentioned lectures, and had had similar things said to me by Channel 4 people when I declined to fly in for pre-show and production planning meetings, but his idea held no appeal for me. I was married with a few-months-old son and it was important to me that Virgin Radio took up my Saturday but not my entire weekend.

As the months passed and I got more comfortable and confident at Virgin, I devised ever more elaborate ruses to get back to Dublin as quickly as possible. My show finished at 8 p.m., and if I sat there until the bitter end, there was no way that I would make the last flight. The desperate taxi rides from 1 Golden Square to Heathrow airport were an adrenaline kick but they were also exhausting.

I began to revisit some of the harmless cheats that Ian Wilson and I had developed over the years. As I recorded my normal 2FM evening show during the week, I would sometimes say, 'Now, here is the new single from the Lemonheads!,' and as I said it I would click on a mini-disc and record the next forty-five minutes of my show. That forty-five minutes would then become the last three-quarters of an hour of my Virgin programme the next weekend. I would tip the London sound engineer the wink, he would slip the mini-disc in and I would be up, off and on my way home.

Towards the end, occasionally, I would even record the entire four-hour Virgin show in 2FM and stay in Dublin all weekend. I would send the tapes to my partner in crime at Virgin, a girl called Holly Ramos who didn't mind helping me out in these occasional subterfuges. Nobody even knew, because nobody ever listened to both my 2FM and Virgin shows, so I told myself – fairly persuasively – that it was a victimless crime.

Back in those days, I dread to think what my carbon footprint was like, because I was literally taking more planes than buses. By the end of my time at Virgin my prime motivation, my be-all and end-all, was being back in Dublin by Saturday night, ideally in time for last orders in the local.

Dave Fanning

I remember once sitting in a London cab that caught every green light, catching a delayed flight, and being in a Blackrock bar on a Saturday evening when I had no right to be there, feeling happy and satisfied. Conversely, on another night I left Virgin late, knew I had no chance of catching a plane, and ended up getting off the tube at Earl's Court and booking into the nearest dodgy hotel for the night. I felt demoralised and cheated, because I had lost my Saturday night. Of course, I could have stayed up until the early hours in the West End, but I had done enough all-nighters during my Channel 4 days.

The Virgin radio work was a lot of fun and I was grateful to have it, but after a couple of years I knew it was time to pack it in. This wasn't just down to the travel and desire to protect time with Ursula back in Ireland. By then I had another strand of work: one that I absolutely loved and could easily have done forever.

10

If music was my first love, it was not a totally exclusive affair. Ever since I was a kid trying to bunk into the Stella in Mount Merrion, I had been equally mesmerised by the movies. For years I had wondered why RTÉ did not have a weekly TV film programme and I was determined to rectify that omission.

I had not had the chance to turn my love for movies into my life-career, as I had with music, but it was not for want of trying. My affection for cinema had never dimmed. When I went to UCD, the only university club I joined was the Film Society, where I would watch Buñuel and Godard art-house movies via a dodgy flickering projector, and my collection of movie magazines rivalled my stash of music papers.

There had not been an obvious outlet at RTÉ for me to indulge my movie obsession but I had done my best to manufacture one. When Mark Cagney took over the Radio 2 Drivetime show at the end of the Eighties, I became the film reviewer on that, and did the same on Myles Dungan's programme on Radio 1.

Yet I still felt we could do so much more with a specialist, full-on movie show, and the frustration for me was that I knew it would not be expensive to make. The movie companies would value a national show as a promotional outlet and give us clips, trailers and access to the stars. My lobbying at RTÉ gained weight and credibility when my good friend Anita Notaro, the senior producer, added her voice to my nagging campaign.

I guess sometimes you just have to grind people down. Having seemed hostile or, at best, indifferent to the idea of a film show, the RTÉ senior executives suddenly heard the penny drop and had a complete change of heart. As 1993 dawned, Liam Miller, the Director of Television Programmes, called Anita and me out of the blue and said, 'OK, you can do *The Movie Show*. It starts in three weeks.'

Three weeks? That would have been a draconian timetable even if I had nothing else to do, but as well as my usual 2FM duties and trips to London, I had agreed to go the following week on a fun freebie to the US with a drinks company to see how Jack Daniel's was made. It was too late to cancel, so I spent an anxious few days in Lynchburg, Tennessee, gazing at whiskey stills while I worried about how the new programme would take shape.

As soon as RTÉ green-lighted *The Movie Show*, I realised that something would have to go from my cluttered weekly diary, and I settled on the *Irish Times*. I had had a good decade-long innings there, but now that I would be writing lengthy scripts for forty TV shows a year, plus travelling even more, I didn't see how I would have time to continue filing my weekly column.

In truth, I had always found the *Irish Times* hard work. Some things I was naturally confident at – playing music; talking on the radio; interviewing bands – and some I wasn't. When I started on the *Irish Times* in 1982, I had complained to their veteran jazz critic, Ray Comisky, that writing did not come easily to me. He advised me to relax into the role, and said that in six months time the words would be flowing sweet and free.

Well, Ray was wrong, because a decade into my *Irish Times* stint I was still sweating my column, still submitting it at the very last minute, still spending an hour agonising over a single sentence. On 2FM I felt in control, on top of my game, like I knew what it was all about. When it came to writing, I never felt I was as good as I should be.

Looking back, although I never formalised this thought, I wonder if I kept writing for the *Irish Times* for as long as I did as a present to my mother. Annie had always been pleased I was doing OK on the TV and radio, but, as a woman of letters, it was my journalistic work that made her chest swell with pride. It had always been her newspaper of choice and I think she loved my connection to it.

When I flew back from Tennessee, I found RTÉ management had billeted *The Movie Show* in a room the size of a broom cupboard in a prefab office. There was literally room for two people in there at any one time. We eventually managed to agitate for a bigger room, but in terms of facilities we were seldom taken seriously.

So began a period of my life when my travelling levels became utterly surreal. If I'd thought I was notching up the air miles doing my weekly hops back and forth to London, now it was about to get really serious. The London trips didn't drop off, but in addition I was now flying two or three times per month to the two hubs of the American entertainment industry: Los Angeles and New York.

The routines were not the same. I very quickly learned there was a very different dynamic to interviewing a Hollywood movie star than there was talking to a band. The film junkets were strictly organised. The movie companies would fly me in to LA or NY and I would be part of a conveyor belt of interviewers who would get fifteen or, if we were lucky, thirty minutes with a big Hollywood name. Long, rambling, far-ranging chats just did not happen.

This proved less frustrating than it might sound. Unlike the old days when movie stars stuck with one studio, now they follow the movie, not the studio, and so are obliged to make themselves available to plug the film they have just finished. They are great at giving good soundbites, which was perfect for *The Movie Show,* which was to be a thirty-minute, fast-moving review programme broken up with interview inserts and packages.

A typical trip would see me fly via Aer Lingus to the US for two to three days. With the weekly London trips always in business class, you got a small bottle of champagne with breakfast. I arrived home one Friday to find that my collection of over a hundred had dwindled dramatically thanks to Ursula, her friend Rosie and Anita having decided to – as they euphemistically put it – 'take the afternoon off'.

A crucial difference on the flights was whether one sat on the left- or right-hand side of the aisle. The left-hand side had slightly bigger seats, and I must confess I became somewhat obsessed with making sure my seat was located there.

Once in America, we would stay in a fine hotel – compared to record labels, these movie companies had serious heavyweight budgets – where I would work out my questions. There I met

Michael Douglas, Denzel Washington, Lindsay Lohan, Denis Quaid, Richard Gere, Dan Aykroyd, Eddie Murphy, Uma Thurman, Robin Williams, Kate Winslet, Susan Sarandon, Glenn Close, Scarlett Johansson and countless others.

It sounds too good to be true, and in a way, it was. I never quite lost the urge to pinch myself to see if I was having as good a time as it seemed and really had been this lucky. I followed this starry routine for close on ten years and never once took the whole exciting circus for granted.

The London interviews usually took place at the Dorchester Hotel in Park Lane and I'd always ask for the first slot of the day. This meant that I caught the star right at the start when they were still fresh, rather than jaded after ten straight interviews, and more importantly, if the interview was at ten in the morning, I could be back home by mid-afternoon. Shades of Virgin Radio once again.

The Los Angeles encounters normally happened at the Four Seasons on Doheny Drive in Beverly Hills, which is Los Angeles at its most rarefied and La-La Landish. On an early visit I was sitting by the pool with Jerry and Ursula reading a magazine when one of the immaculately groomed attendants who were fussing over sun beds, towels and juice glided over and asked if I'd like any water. When I said, 'Yes please', he reeled off a lengthy list of brand names, including Evian, to which I replied, 'Yeah, Evian would be great.' At which point he picked up a sleek, expensive-looking dispenser and gently sprayed it in my face. Only in LA.

I quickly picked up the dos and don'ts of the conveyor-belt Hollywood interview. Thirty minutes or less was not long to strike up a rapport with a star, so it was important not to bore them. Virtually every interviewer seemed to start with, 'So, what attracted you to this role?', at which point the actor's face would struggle not to glaze over. I soon learned to avoid that opening gambit. The trick was to be interesting and original while still extracting the basic quotes you needed. It wasn't always easy.

The first ever *Movie Show* interview was with Harrison Ford for his 1993 movie *The Fugitive*. He struck me as a guy who had got a few decent breaks and was determined to hang on to them. He knew what he liked and what he didn't. When I interviewed him again a second time a few years down the line for *Air Force One*, he piloted his own plane to Los Angeles from his home in Wyoming. 'I hate LA,' he told me, candidly. 'That's why I like to fly in and then get straight out.'

It was no expense spared for the *Air Force One* junket. The film company had decked out a room at the Four Seasons to the exact interior specifications of a US president's aircraft complete with a presidential seal. An airplane window erected behind's Ford's left shoulder gave the impression we were chatting on a jet. The movie grossed $300m worldwide, so I guess it was money well spent.

The trick in Beverly Hills, and at the Four Seasons particularly, was not to gawp when you chanced upon random A-listers. On one early trip, I was sitting reading on a marble bench by the main entrance when Dustin Hoffman exited the hotel doors with a younger man in thick glasses who was carrying a folder with loose pages hanging out.

Hoffman was talking animatedly with dismissive gestures and had clearly given the guy five minutes to pitch him a movie idea and not been impressed with what he had heard. As he rattled off his objections, he made it fairly clear that he thought he was talking to an absolute moron: 'I wouldn't do that kind of thing, so rewrite it or forget it.' As he hopped into his limo, he landed a final killer blow: 'What's more, Spencer Tracy would never have done that or said that. Never. Goodbye.' The limo sped off, leaving one very dejected Hollywood wannabe who had just got an absolute 'No!' from Dustin Hoffman. I wandered into the bar, where Gerard Depardieu was holding forth to a man with three mid-afternoon Martinis lined up in front of him.

When it comes to star-spotting, of course, there is no better place than the Oscars, and producer Anita Notaro and I managed to get accreditation for the 1994 ceremony just a year or two into *The Movie Show*'s existence. The expense was justified as there was a strong Irish angle that year, with Liam Neeson nominated for Best Actor for his leading role in *Schindler's List* and Jim Sheridan's *In The Name of the Father* up for seven Oscars.

Anita, researcher Gerry McGuinness and I flew in to LA determined to soak up as much Oscars colour, glamour and madness as we could. I hired a tuxedo and a local cameraman called Jim and took up a position on the right-hand side of the red carpet that led into that year's venue, the Los Angeles County Music Center. We were there for four hours, and though we missed Clint Eastwood, Tom Cruise and Nicole Kidman, who ambled up the other side of the carpet, we still managed to snare a bucketful of major names.

Christian Slater stopped in front of me and answered a few career-spanning questions while the questioners either side of me eagerly stuck their microphones in his face. Later, of course, their channels would edit out my questions in favour of dubbing in their own host saying, 'Thank you, Christian!' There's nothing wrong with this. It is just how the game works.

I was standing next to a tall, very voluptuous young woman whose producer, a classic Hollywood asshole, clearly felt she was not aggressive enough in trying to attract the stars and came running over to give her a grade-A rollicking. 'You know why you're here, so show some fire!' he yelled at her, pointing at her ample bosoms that were just contained within her skimpy top. 'Stick 'em out, we got to see more of those!' It turned out the girl's name was Kelly and she was there from a fashion TV show, with a brief purely to talk about designer labels, so she and I worked together from that point. She used her charms as a star magnet and I pitched in with the questions.

Anthony Hopkins wandered over and talked to our group of hacks for nearly ten minutes, clearly wondering why I didn't say a word or even bother to hold my mike up to catch his comments. The truth was, Jim had hit technical problems: eventually, as Hopkins raised his eyebrow at me, I blurted out, 'My mike broke!' He roared with laughter and moved on.

Anita and I had already interviewed Jim Sheridan the day before at the Sunset Marquis, but we wanted to shoot more footage on the red carpet and he amiably agreed and stopped to shoot the breeze on his way into the auditorium. Hardly any of the other interviewers even gave him a glance, presumably because he wasn't Tom Cruise and wasn't wearing Versace.

When the ceremony started, we had passes for the TV inter-view room where the shell-shocked winners were led to give us a few quick quotes. Tom Hanks won Best Actor for *Philadelphia* and took fifteen minutes to answer his first question. He was still talking as his PR minders led him off to his next media appointment.

The Oscars for Best Movie and Best Director went to *Schind-ler's List* and Steven Spielberg, who was gracious and measured in his answers, especially when an East European journalist whose family had survived the Holocaust burst into tears during her question. The *In the Name of the Father* after-show party was rather muted, as the film had picked up none of the seven awards it was nominated for, and at 2.30 a.m. LA time I was bleary-eyed and trying to describe the evening to RTÉ and Ireland on Gay Byrne's radio show.

The Oscars were really too expensive for our relatively meagre *Movie Show* budget and we had to axe our trips there. The same was true of the Cannes Film Festival. Directors, TV cameramen, sound and lighting technicians, flights, parking and accreditation were all expensive and Cannes is not a cheap town. Plus you spent inordinate time on wild goose chases, at the whim of PRs who airily told you they might or might not be able to get you a two-minute one-to-one with Sean Penn or so forth at 4.30 p.m.

At one of the few Cannes we did get to, John Malkovich was promoting *Con Air* and sitting at a table near the top of a cliff, with a perfect blue sky above him and a deep azure sea below. I approached him and placed my coffee and pages of notes for a long day's interviews on the table, at which point a gust of wind caught the sheaf of papers and threw every page into the air and over the edge of the cliff. Malkovich's co-star Nicolas Cage's raucous laughter was the correct response.

Malkovich was entertaining, self-deprecating and yet pompous in an oddly likeable way. His idea of promoting *Con Air* was to tell me that he had never even seen it, adding: 'In fact, I'll probably never see it, unless I come across it by accident some night on cable in a hotel when I can't sleep. I acted in it. That doesn't mean I have to go and see it.'

Without the Oscars and Cannes, *The Movie Show*'s staples were my on-air reviews of new releases and the many interviews we managed to secure via press junkets. It was a simple recipe but a very effective one. When I interviewed Anthony Hopkins concerning a movie called *Surviving Picasso*, he'd clearly forgotten that I was the Irish eedjit on the red carpet whose mike hadn't worked. I must have done better this time, because after our half-hour interview he whisked me off for a convivial lunch where we chewed the fat over everything from the Clintons' Whitewater scandal to the future of Welsh rugby.

The following week, in London again, I spent a fascinating hour with Mick Jagger. Not fascinating in the sense that he had anything groundbreaking or even enlightening to say but – although he seemed totally distracted – he was in no hurry to leave, even though he began the interview by telling me that he might have to cut it short because he needed to get to his daughter's school play. He's not exactly the world's best interviewee. Having led a public life most of his life, he doesn't see any need to explain or justify himself – and he has everything to gain by guarding his privacy. But he was loose and easy, and that's more than a start.

I interviewed Mel Gibson a few times but found him kinda hot and cold. In Barcelona, he yawned as he fed me curt one-liners about *Lethal Weapon III* that were so trite I wondered why I was bothering. On another trip, to New York, he beat a hotel's no-smoking rule by hanging so far out of a forty-third-floor window with his cigarette that his PR people were almost having coronaries as they fussed around him.

Oddly enough, Gibson was charm itself on another occasion when I met him, on the set of his big hit *Braveheart* in County Meath. As I waited while he filmed in a muddy field, he recognised me, sauntered over and, with a swish of his kilt, told me in a perfect Celtic accent, 'Don't worry, now, we'll nail this scene in a minute.' We filmed him that evening looking over the day's rushes and he was still in a cheery, expansive mood.

Frequently, quick interviews on a film set proved to be far more satisfying than anodyne exchanges in a corporate hotel room. The late Dennis Hopper came to Ardmore Studios in County Wicklow to make *Space Truckers* and granted me a hilarious rant about a drunken Hollywood producer that verged on surreal stand-up comedy. At the same location, all that John Hurt wanted to know was how he could get his hands on a copy of my interview with Leonard Cohen.

A future James Bond, Daniel Craig, visited windswept Achill Island and talked to me while bouncing around a few feet above my head on a saddle loosely attached to a feisty horse. He was trying to control his mount and I was trying to avoid being trampled into the sand. The footage looked hilarious, although

I'm not sure the movie, Cathal Black's *Love and Rage*, ever saw the proper light of day.

There was rather more pressure on me when I renewed acquaintance with Madonna, who had just finished playing Eva Peron in *Evita*, the role that was to win her a Golden Globe. The movie was premiering at the Empire in Leicester Square in London and I was in the red-carpet queue broadcasting live to a simultaneous charity performance of the movie at Savoy One in O'Connell Street.

My Oscar red-carpet training clearly came in handy as I squeezed a few nuggets from the attending stars. Louise Nurding of girl band Eternal told me she had no idea that Evita's real name was Eva Peron. England goalkeeper David Seaman stopped to confide that this sort of glitzy night was all a bit weird to a working-class lad from Rotherham.

Evita's handsome male lead, Antonio Banderas, arrived with his wife, Melanie Griffith, and answered a few questions after I told him we were broadcasting live to Dublin. Through politeness, I directed one question at Melanie, who demurred, saying that it was 'Antonio's night'. A few minutes later, as I talked to Tim Rice and Andrew Lloyd-Webber, she came running back, hoping she hadn't been rude when she didn't answer my question. I told her everything was fine and she kissed me on the cheek, waved at the camera and left with a cheery 'Bye, Dublin!' At the same moment, all cameras were turning my way: I found out later that this was the first time Rice and Lloyd-Webber had stood side by side for many years.

Melanie's exchange was topped when Madonna finally arrived in a green Versace dress. As she waved to Dublin, I asked her if *Evita*'s director, Alan Parker, had been angry half-way through shooting when she told him she was preggers. 'Preggers?' she asked me, arching an eyebrow. 'Pregnant!' I blurted out. 'Is preggers some kind of Gaelic word?' she persisted. Hmm. Dissecting the etymology of the word 'Preggers' was not how I had imagined our interview going, but apparently the guests at the Savoy were laughing too much to care.

I was to meet Madonna one more time, around the release of a movie called *The Next Big Thing* in which she co-starred with Rupert Everett. We sat down to do a one-to-one *Movie Show* interview in London but she threw me by demanding to know at once what I thought of the film. I told her the truth, which was that I thought she was good in the movie but didn't like it because the plot and her character were not terribly believable.

This strategy of unvarnished honesty could have gone horribly wrong, but Madonna didn't seem to mind at all, roared with laughter and gave me a great interview. That evening, as I was waiting in the hotel bar to meet a friend for a drink, she tapped me on the shoulder, asking me to tell her some recent movies that I *had* liked, and we chatted for five minutes about Stanley Kubrick's *Eyes Wide Shut*. Maybe she wasn't such a wanker after all.

Will Smith, one of Hollywood's most bankable characters, always enjoyed a laugh and a joke every time I encountered him. Arnold Schwarzenegger was something else entirely. The future governor of California was precious and humourless when I met him around the release of *Batman & Robin*, insisting that he would only discuss that movie and nothing else, and spending twenty minutes talking in tedious detail about what he brought to his daft character, Mr Freeze.

When Schwarzenegger and fellow movie tough guys Sylvester Stallone and Bruce Willis opened their burger-restaurant chain Planet Hollywood in the Nineties, it looked like their big-name endorsement would make the venture a winner. The business has had its ups and downs but seemed to be booming in the mid-Nineties when Arnie came to Ireland to promote the opening of the Dublin branch.

I was the Master of Ceremonies at a so-called 'gala unveiling' of the fast-food joint on a makeshift podium-cum-stage on St Stephen's Green near the top of Grafton Street. There were only around a hundred and fifty people present, most of them looking rather over-muscular and clutching bodybuilder magazines in the hope of getting an autograph, and the event quickly descended into farce.

Schwarzenegger came straight from the airport and announced that he had picked up some knowledge en route. At the end of a very short speech, which was largely unintelligible apart from the words 'Ireland' and 'hamburger', he grinned at the crowd and yelled 'Beidh me arais!' The silence that ensued reflected the fact that nobody had a clue what he was talking about. 'Beidh me arais!' is Irish for 'I'll be back!' but filtered through his impenetrable Austrian-Californian accent to a crowd who probably didn't speak a word of Irish between them, the joke never stood a chance.

Arnie had clearly been busy on that journey from the airport, because it turned out he had asked his driver about the national sport of Ireland and liked the sound of hurling. We dispatched someone to buy a hurley and a sliothar from a nearby sports shop and Schwarzenegger told me to throw the sliothar (the size of a tennis ball, the weight of a small rock) from one side of the stage to the other, where hurley man Arnie would whack it baseball-style across the road. Credit where it is due, he smashed it first time and it vanished into the trees over on St Stephen's Green. All down to the accuracy of my throw, of course.

George Clooney was in *Batman & Robin* with Schwarzenegger, playing Batman, but unlike his co-star, he did not try to pretend that it rivalled *Citizen Kane* in its import. The twinkle in his eye and his roguish grin told me he knew the film was, as one review had put it, 'a crock of shit'. He didn't even bother to talk it up, preferring to show me photos of Max, his pot-bellied pig.

I interviewed Clooney again two years later about *Three Kings*, a satirical war drama about US soldiers trying to track down Kuwaiti bullion stolen by the Iraqi army. He kept saying the word 'bullion' as 'boo yon', which gave me the giggles, and when I explained why I was laughing, he offered to retake the whole interview and change his pronunciation. Clooney is so charming and handsome that you should hate him, but he is such excellent company that it is impossible.

Val Kilmer is a more complex proposition. When I interviewed him for *The Movie Show* about *The Saint*, he asked most of the questions himself and kept talking about the poetry of Seamus Heaney. Kilmer was not to everyone's taste. When I met director Joel Schumacher he said, 'I was told that Val was difficult and wasn't for me. I'm tired of defending overpaid and over-privileged actors. I pray I don't work with them again.'

Ralph Fiennes seemed to share Schumacher's opinion. I was to interview him and Kilmer together after they voiced a Disney animation movie, *Hercules*. The English journalist before me warned that Fiennes and Kilmer had contributed their voice-overs separately, had consequently met for the first time that day, and couldn't stand each other.

As the interview started, I couldn't help but notice that Fiennes and Kilmer were sitting side by side in two chairs but leaning right away from each other. Their body language could not have been more hostile; on the monitor, you could see virtually the whole of the movie poster on the wall behind them. They had no chemistry whatsoever, or at least nothing positive, and even when they picked up on each other's comments, they directed everything they said through me.

My interview with Richard Dreyfuss on the set of the TV movie *Oliver Twist* was not my finest moment. His career had for years not equalled the heights of his golden era in the Seventies and he didn't seem to like being reminded of massive hits such as *Jaws* and *Close Encounters of the Third Kind*. He liked it even less when I asked a dumb-ass question: 'In 1977 you won the Best Actor Oscar for *The Goodbye Girl*. What did that feel like?' 'I won a goddamn Oscar, for Christ's sake!' he exploded at me. 'What do you think it felt like?' I guess he had a point.

Cameron Diaz was as easy as Dreyfuss was difficult. When I talked to her around the release of *A Life Less Ordinary*, a kooky kidnap caper with Ewan McGregor, she appeared to have a separate makeup artist for each cheek and her minders constantly stopped the interview to study monitor shots and angles to justify their own existence. Diaz looked embarrassed by the whole palaver, and when I interviewed her again in London a few years later she was cool and confident with not a PR handler to be seen.

Kristin Scott Thomas was a thornier proposition when I met her in New York to talk about *The Horse Whisperer*. Our interview was delayed by technical problems, so for fifteen minutes she and I sat and shot the breeze about the weather while technicians fiddled with cameras and leads. I thought we were getting along fine, but when we played the tape back in Dublin, I could see more than a little irritation flickering beneath that perfect porcelain skin. I am guessing she does not suffer fools gladly. I also cringed at my clumsy small talk. If all interviews are basically a mild form of chatting up, that day it was clear that my flirting technique needed serious root-and-branch work.

The movie's director and co-star Robert Redford was part of the same junket, and unwittingly provided an insight into the loopy logic of the film PR world. At one point, Redford strolled into the interview space, fixed himself a sandwich from the buffet table and wandered into his own room. His designated minder, a male drama queen in a pair of tiny shorts, sighed at us and squealed: 'Omigod, I *hate* it when the talent goes walkabout!' Jesus Christ, I thought to myself. He only came in for a sandwich!

Also in *The Horse Whisperer* was a 10-year-old Scarlett Johansson, playing Scott Thomas's daughter. She was gauche and endearingly awkward as she sweetly told me how she *loved* to work with such great actors. Six years later, she was rather more confident and worldly-wise when I met her in London to talk about her big breakthrough, *Lost in Translation*.

With two Oscars and seven Golden Globes, Meryl Streep is surely the premier actress of her generation, and when she came to Ireland to film *Dancing at Lughnana*, there was no way *The Movie Show* was going to miss out on an interview. She came to a famous Dublin hotel and for some reason they put us in a tiny anteroom that was soon like a sauna due to the burning heat of the camera lights in such a restricted space. The fact that Meryl kept talking and stayed serene as the beads of sweat formed on her top lip confirmed to me just what a talent and trouper she is.

Oprah Winfrey is obviously better known as a chat-show host than an actress or movie producer but she acquitted herself well with *Beloved*, the adaptation of Toni Morrison's Pulitzer Prize-winning novel that was directed by Jonathan Demme, whose Talking Heads movie *Stop Making Sense* had so transfixed me a decade earlier. It is not an easy movie to like, but Oprah was gracious when we met in London and later sent me a note thanking me for 'our time together and stimulating conversation'.

After the interview in the Dorchester I had one of those bizarre encounters that seem like a game of real-life Consequences. As I came to leave, I got in the lift and bumped into Pierce Brosnan, whom I had interviewed previously concerning the Bond film *Tomorrow Never Dies*. We got out on the ground floor just as Oprah and her movie entourage exited the next lift. She smiled at me and I said, 'Oprah, this is Pierce Brosnan!'

Having introduced the most powerful woman in America to James Bond, I wandered out and trudged through the rain to Hyde Park tube station.

Keanu Reeves has always been a spectacularly limited actor but was always fairly engaging whenever I happened across him. He had ranted against racism and discrimination when I interviewed him for *The Devil's Advocate*, and before that his *Johnny Mnemonic* had been typically silly but harmless fun.

When I met him in Hamburg to talk about *The Matrix*, the film had been out in the States for a few weeks and had begun to explode, and it was clear that this was far more than a movie to Keanu. He spent five minutes staring moodily out of the window at the German traffic before we began the interview with co-star Carrie-Ann Moss. There were rumours the pair of them were an item and I certainly felt like a gooseberry as they stared intently at each other as they spoke. Keanu looked enthralled and grateful as I struggled manfully with the film's copious levels of meaning and symbolism, and the black-clad German camera crew didn't exactly lighten the mood either. As interviews go, it was a tad light on chuckles.

There are those who say that when it comes to acting, Keanu looks like Laurence Olivier compared to Stephen Seagal, but whatever Seagal's thespian failings, the veteran tough guy is not short of confidence and attitude. At the Dorchester, Seagal barrelled into the room wearing what looked like a leather kaftan, annexed the interview and launched into an irate tirade about the many failings of his movie company. When he left, I was not even sure which conglomerate he had been slagging off, but it was spectacularly entertaining nonetheless.

On a rather more elevated plane, Robert de Niro is a genius and consummate actor, but his dislike of the interview process is legendary. Given the opportunity in Paris to grill him and co-star Billy Crystal around the release of *Analyze This*, I went in excited and determined, but, like so many interviewers before me, came away defeated.

To lighten the mood, I had strategically tossed the first few questions towards Crystal, who was as upbeat and cheery as I have always found him, but de Niro was not interested. A few of his half-hearted answers were at least coherent, but mostly he limited himself to disinterested grunts and deeply expressive withering looks. Thankfully, some kind editing made Bob look far more forthcoming than he deserved.

Out in Los Angeles, Tom Hanks and Tim Allen were a far more willing double act and spent the whole time trying to out-joke each other as we discussed *Toy Story 2*. Despite voicing the clean-cut Woody in the film, Hanks was sporting a considerable beard during the interview, as he was filming *Castaway* at the time, but ultimately his and Allen's tomfoolery was every bit as evasive and uninformative for viewers as had been de Niro's taciturnity.

In 1999 I stayed in New York for a fortnight during one of the hottest summers the city has ever known. Unlike in 1974, I wasn't slumming it this time with a rucksack. I stayed in a couple of nice hotels and stacked up some interviews.

I can't remember if it was the Ashley Judd interview for *Double Jeopardy* or Sarah Michelle Geller, Ryan Phillipe and Reece Witherspoon for *Cruel Intentions*, but somewhere along the way, in my bag of promotional swag (usually tacky) which the movie companies hand out to journalists, I had been given a tube of fake tan – a new-at-that-time, cancer-free way to get a tan from a tube. It sat there for a week. I can't say I even knew it was there. I was due to fly home from JFK on a Sunday night. During that day, interviews were set up across town with the stars of the Hugh Grant mafia-comedy movie, *Mickey Blue Eyes*.

I wasn't particularly looking for a tan, but the bottle was there, so on the Saturday – without checking any instructions – I used half of it. By 'used', I mean 'splashed it on'. By Sunday morning there was a freak in my mirror. I used the rest of the bottle to try to make the white bits match up with the yellow and orange bits, packed my bags, checked out and dashed over to the interview hotel.

Hot, sweaty and multi-coloured, I managed somehow to get through the first few interviews. James Caan (who had played Sonny in the *real* mafia movie, *The Godfather*) was delighted to talk to an Irish guy. He didn't say an awful lot about *Mickey Blue Eyes*. He was too busy regaling me with stories of drinking sessions in various hostelries across the south of Ireland.

By the time I got to the movie's producer, Liz Hurley … let's just say, at the very least, I looked seriously jaundiced. She didn't push her seat back and I'm not going to use the word 'recoiled' but there was a definite look of discomfort on her face as I sat down a couple of feet in front of her. She feigned concern (she was definitely more worried that she might catch it herself, whatever 'it' was). 'Are you OK?' she asked, adding: 'Can we get you a glass of water?'

As I stumbled through some nonchalantly, dismissive response, anxious to get the interview started and, more importantly, finished, she came right out and said it: 'What on earth's happened to you?' Now everyone was curious, with the PR people donning their 'Is there a problem?' face. 'It's cool, it's a fake tan experiment that didn't work. Not contagious. I'm fine!' I stuttered. The interview happened, the cameraman smirked sympathetically as he handed me my tapes, and I left. I can't imagine the conversation that took place after I shut the door.

Liz Hurley may have thought I was a twenty-four-carat nutter but Julia Roberts was far more well-disposed towards me. When I met her to discuss *Notting Hill,* she let out a squeal of delight and leapt up to kiss my cheek, not because I was particularly irresistible that day but because I was Irish. While many Hollywood stars feign, I feel, a deep affection for Ireland, her love was genuine. Back in 1991, when her engagement to Kiefer Sutherland was called off, she had hidden out with actor Jason Patric away from the press in Dublin, always appreciative of the minding she got from Mick Devine, well known in Dublin as the driver for the stars.

Nicolas Cage is another star with a soft spot for Ireland. When I interviewed him in Athens, where he was filming *Captain Corelli's Mandolin,* he raved about a recent holiday in my homeland with his dad. 'We landed in Dublin and drove all the way over to the west coast. It was an amazing trip,' he reminisced, as though he had ridden Route 66. I gently pointed out that you could easily drive from coast to coast in Ireland inside three hours. 'I know, but we didn't,' he replied, before grilling me on the best place to buy a castle in Ireland.

On the same trip to Greece, I hooked up with Angelina Jolie, who was promoting *Gone in Sixty Seconds.* It was a fairly turgid movie, so despite being warned against it by her PR, I chanced my arm and asked how things were going on her next project, *Tomb Raider*. Angelina immediately became far more animated and held forth at length on everything about the film, from her rigorous exercise regime to the enhanced-breast expectations of the movie's potentially huge male audience of computer gamers.

I probably interviewed Sandra Bullock more often than any other female Hollywood A-lister. She was always welcoming and giving, always remembered our previous meetings, and had come to realise that romantic comedies were her forte. When I chatted to her with Hugh Grant for *Two Weeks Notice*, they traded affectionate insults as Sandra stressed just what an under-rated comedian her co-star is.

Jennifer Lopez was rather less grounded, and our chat got off to a somewhat shaky start. I was J-Lo's first interview of the day when she arrived in London to promote *Maid in Manhattan*, and as she settled into her seat in the Dorchester I decided to test her diva reputation. In the film, J-Lo stars as a hard-working, conscientious, intelligent single mother who dreams of a better life. While struggling as a maid she falls for a rising politician, who mistakenly assumes she's a socialite who's staying at the hotel. A large part of the film centres on how well or how badly the hotel staff are treated.

I asked her when she had arrived and she said she had checked into the hotel two hours earlier. 'You must have met some of the staff. Were you nice to them?' I teased. It must have been a bit too early in the day for such mischief-making because on TV her response looked awkward and irritated.

It's another of those well-grounded clichés, but Hollywood can be cruel to women of a certain age. Meg Ryan was America's golden girl in movies such as *When Harry Met Sally* and *Sleepless in Seattle*, but as she passed forty and the romantic leads fell away, the roles dried up. When I met her, she had taken a distinct left-turn to star in *In the Cut*, a charged psychodrama by *The Piano* director Jane Campion.

I thought the movie was ambitious but quite boring and a bit of a mess, and while Campion spiritedly tried to change my mind, it was noticeable that there was a real air of resignation to Meg's soft-sell of the film. Or maybe she was in another mental place entirely: later that same day she filmed a now-notorious BBC interview with British chat-show host Michael Parkinson in which she appeared befuddled and distinctly unfocused.

Senior studio executives can arbitrarily end the careers of stars like Meg Ryan by deciding they are past it, and I interviewed two such creatures on *The Movie Show*. They were really horrible. The two execs sat having their hair trimmed as we set up our cameras and were arrogant beyond belief. They slagged off one huge Hollywood name after another: 'He is a fucking wanker'; 'I could kill him.' They got off on themselves and could not have cared less that the hair stylist was in the room, as was I: we were the little people, and were nothing to them. As a rare glimpse behind the Hollywood machine at the people who pull the levers, it was deeply depressing.

The biggest compliment I ever got paid with regard to *The Movie Show* was when a critic said I was now like John Peel and Barry Norman rolled into one. You can't get much better than that. I don't think RTÉ ever quite treated the show properly. We got constantly shifted around the schedules, from time slot to time slot and even from channel to channel, and when it was suddenly yanked off air in 2001 I felt it still had another five years or more in it. But I couldn't really complain. What a long, brilliant, truly unforgettable experience it had been.

11

Launching *The Movie Show* in the early Nineties had not led to any falling-off in my music work. The 2FM show was my main priority, as ever, and Channel 4 and Virgin Radio were making sure that I knew every inch of the route from Dublin to London as viewed from a small round window at 35,000 feet. Luckily, it was a very exciting time for music.

I liked the grunge explosion that came out of Seattle in the first part of the decade as much as I had liked the Madchester scene a couple of years previously. I played a lot of the tracks on 2FM but I can't claim that Mother Love Bone, Soundgarden, Stone Temple Pilots or Alice in Chains particularly over-excited me. I figured, good luck to it, but it wasn't the greatest music I'd ever heard.

Nevertheless, Kurt Cobain's suicide was obviously a huge story and difficult to take in. On the night it happened I was preparing for my 2FM show at about twenty to eight and took a call from a contact on a Dublin newspaper. He said, 'Dave, a body has been found in Kurt Cobain's house and it looks like it is his. We are not sure but it looks like suicide.'

The RTÉ news at the start of my show at 8 p.m. didn't have the story, either because they didn't know about it or figured that it wasn't important enough. When my programme started, my guests were US college rockers Buffalo Tom, and I greeted them and said, 'It looks like Kurt Cobain is dead.' We talked about Cobain for a lot of the evening and I played Nirvana tracks throughout the show.

At the time, I didn't think I was being particularly offhand in the way I relayed the news, but years later *Hot Press* ran a Nirvana retrospective and asked its readers where they were when they heard that Cobain had died. At least half of them said, 'I heard it on Dave Fanning's show and couldn't believe it when he said it – I thought he must be joking.' Not that it would have been a particularly funny joke.

It made me realise that, for that generation, Cobain's suicide was a really major, culturally important event. In America, and to a lesser degree in Europe, there were shrines, candlelit vigils and kids crying in the street, and I guess they were feeling the exact same pain that had gripped me fifteen years earlier when Mark Chapman shot John Lennon.

Maybe because it was closer to home and more culturally resonant for me, I found the Britpop bands that followed and took the media spotlight away from grunge far more exciting. Suede were probably the progenitors of it all, and when I was on the Mercury Music Prize panel that gave their debut album the accolade in 1993, it genuinely felt like the start of something. On the night, they narrowly pipped another group of Britpop tyros, the Auteurs. Their singer was a very sharp guy named Luke Haines and they never quite got the success they deserved.

I interviewed many of the major Britpop progenitors and also followed the Blur v Oasis spats avidly from across the water, although it all seemed to me rather a pat, diluted version of the Beatles v the Stones. After I'd met Noel Gallagher in his days lugging flight cases around for Inspiral Carpets, we'd struck up a good relationship that has lasted to this day.

It always seemed to be Noel rather than Liam who came in to do the Oasis interviews, and having met them both I would say that was very much the right decision. Noel and Bonehead came in to 2FM and did a couple of live acoustic numbers just as their debut album, *Definitely Maybe*, came out.

Noel always had an answer for everything and to me is one of the best interviewees around. He's unpredictable and a very clever man behind that bluff, jokey Northern façade. I have only ever thrown him once on air and that was when he rhetorically asked me to name a better debut album from rock history than *Definitely Maybe* and I said the debut Roxy Music album. After a surprised pause, he wriggled out of it by saying it was 'before his time'.

Another Britpop-era band that I loved from the start were Radiohead. I thought that *Pablo Honey* was a good rather than great debut album, but it had some fantastic songs on it and I played 'Creep' and 'Anyone Can Play Guitar' to death. The band came in to 2FM on their first trip to Dublin and have made many repeat visits over the years.

In the Cool Britannia mid-Nineties, Britpop seemed to rule the musical airwaves, yet while this is not something that I tend to boast about, I was arguably responsible for one of its setbacks in its early years. In my final year as a Mercury Music Prize judge, in 1994, I had helped to whittle the initial longlist down to twelve finalists that included Blur's *Parklife*, the Prodigy's *Music for the Jilted Generation*, Pulp's *His 'n' Hers* ... and

Dave Fanning

judges towards a wide and eclectic short list and with the two previous Mercury Prizes having been won by Primal Scream and Suede, I guess he was desperate to avoid it becoming seen as an indie music prize. He has certainly succeeded in that aim, as has been proved by later wins for Roni Size, Talvin Singh, Ms Dynamite and Speech Debelle.

In May 1994 I spent a very enjoyable evening at the Point in Dublin watching Peter Gabriel, who had planted a tree in the middle of the venue. I spent the gig with Terry O'Neill and a friend of his, who seemed amiable enough but kept his duffle-coat hood up all night. It wasn't until the encore as we ambled over to the bar that Terry formally introduced us and I realised I had spent the evening with Johnny Depp. He was a big Pogues fan, and went on to star in one of their videos.

Outside of 2FM and *The Movie Show*, *Fanning Profiles* and *Planet Rock Profiles* were still keeping me busy. US art-rock band Smashing Pumpkins had always gone down well with 2FM night-time listeners, and their single 'Bullet with Butterfly Wings' even dislodged U2 from the top of Fanning's Fab 50.

I had interviewed them three or four times before, but when I met them in Amsterdam around the release of their ambitious double album *Mellon Collie and the Infinite Sadness*, they were, as Americans like to say, not in a good place. Billy Corgan and his fellow band members seemed to have stopped liking each other and were making no attempt to hide the fact, and by the end of the fraught TV interview I felt more like a shrink than a journalist. The band didn't last too much longer.

Lou Reed was no easier when he came to Dublin. The legendary former Velvet Underground singer is a notoriously abrasive

240

Elegant Slumming by Manchester acid house po[
People.

I had by then started *The Movie Show*, and my comi
to that meant I could not make the Mercury awards
London, which understandably did not go down terr
with the organisers. Things took a turn for the wors
night when the head judge, Professor Simon Frith, ph
to say the panel could not decide between Pulp and M
albums and I had the casting vote.

Instinctively, this was an easy decision. The acid hous
music explosion sounded great but much of it just fe
reheated disco. I had absolutely no interest in M P
whereas I was constantly playing Pulp on my 2FM s
explained to Frith that Pulp were my thing whereas M
were not, but this was not what the professor wanted to

Frith asked me if I remembered the list that we judges had
given at the start of the process, itemising the criteria f
award: stuff such as was the album truly consistent and ori
and did it in some way reflect the year? I asked him if he was
to tell me to choose M People, and he said he wasn't trying to
me do anything, merely reminding me of the task in hand.

I commented that the Pulp album had a few filler track
that I felt their best record was still to come, we talked a
more, and suddenly I seemed to have come down in favou
People. The decision was not a popular one, with media p
and music magazines queuing up to proclaim that Pulp –
come to that, Blur and Prodigy – had been robbed.

With hindsight, I think Professor Frith was keen to m
political statement that year. He was always trying to pu

soul and can be curmudgeonly around journalists, but when I got the chance to film an interview with him at the Pink Elephant, I hit on a strategy I was sure would have him eating out of my hand. The strategy was simple: flatter him.

Reed turned up twenty minutes late for our scheduled forty-minute slot but I stuck to my interview plan. Opening with questions about his college education and tremendous literacy, I complimented the depth of his material, compared him to James Joyce, and I think even threw in W.B. Yeats. Reed was purring and clearly enjoying having his ego stroked.

Fifteen minutes into the interview, I turned to *Songs for Drella*, the concept album he had made in 1990 with former Velvet Underground colleague John Cale in homage to their former friend and mentor Andy Warhol. Telling him I loved the album, I hazarded a few guesses as to the meanings of some of the songs, only to be met with a typical Reed rebuff: 'I wrote the fucking songs! Unlike you, I know what they are about!'

Never mind. That would look good on TV, and in any case, having spent the first half of the interview buttering Reed up, I was about to switch to bad cop mode and challenge him on the many stories about him that tend to imply he is not a very nice guy. I opened my mouth to begin my *J'accuse* litany of unsavoury incidents in which he had allegedly been involved, and in walked his manager: 'OK, time's up!'

My protests were in vain. The fact that Lou Reed had turned up twenty minutes late for that forty-minute appointment did not mean he was inclined to hang around for even one second beyond the scheduled departure time. I was left with a short and rather too fawning interview that we managed to make into a surprisingly decent TV programme. Years later, Thom Yorke phoned up and told me he had seen the interview and thought it was hilarious.

I was expecting a rather easier time when Bryan Adams came to town but was sadly mistaken. The Canadian soft rocker was big news after his 'Everything I Do (I Do It for You)' had topped charts around the world for months, and he had a reputation as an easygoing guy-next-door, but I found him to be anything but. We talked on the roof of U2's Clarence Hotel and he alternated smart-ass comments with giving the impression that he really did not want to be there. I don't always see the end version of programmes that I make, and that was one I have never bothered to watch, although a few people over the years who have seen it told me that Adams came over as very brusque and unfriendly.

I definitely warmed rather more to Alanis Morissette, whom I interviewed in London around her massive breakthrough album, *Jagged Little Pill*. The album was full of spikey psychological insights and autobiographical tales of relationships gone wrong but, despite her record's colossal sales, she came over as quite serene, with the kind of relaxed persona that must be hard work to maintain. I could take or leave the music but I liked her a lot.

At home, Jack was two by now and Ursula and I had decided that we didn't want him to be an only child. Having fallen pregnant again in the autumn of 1994, she gave birth to our second son, Robert, on 14 May 1995. Like Jack, who had come along in the early hours of a Sunday morning, Robert also arrived on the Sabbath, just after six o'clock in the evening.

We didn't go for a domestic-pet name this time (I'm not sure Fido or Rover works for a boy) and in fact for eight weeks he didn't have a name at all. In July we went to a Page and Plant gig at the Point and Ursula, having grown up with Led Zeppelin and finding Mr Plant pretty cool on the night, settled on Robert. She loved the name and also wanted to see, as an experiment, if it was possible for him to go through life without having it short-ened to Robbie, Rob or Bob. The experiment has had mixed results: most of his friends just call him Fanning, with the occa-sional Rob thrown in every so often.

The Page and Plant gig was also an ingredient in my latest adventure with Sinéad O'Connor. A few days earlier, I had bumped into her at a gig at the Tivoli. I was filming more *Planet Rock Profiles* and felt she would be a fascinating subject, so I asked her if she would consider doing an interview. Sinéad asked me to send her the questions in advance.

This surprised me, as nobody else had ever made this request, but I acceded and sent her a list of the topics I wanted to talk about. She was very prone to talking in public about her mother and her childhood; so much so that her brother, Joseph, had recently passed a comment in which he essentially said, 'Sinéad has been washing our dirty linen in public for years – can she not shut up and let us get on with our lives?' I asked her for her reaction to this.

A few nights later, while Ursula and I were at the Page and Plant gig at the Point, we had left a friend, Dolores, babysitting Jack and Robert. When we got home, Dolores said that a woman had turned up at midnight, banging on the door and saying, 'This is Sinéad O'Connor and I need to see Dave – now!' A fan of

Dickie Rock and Val Doonican, Dolores had no idea who Sinéad O'Connor was and asked her to repeat her name, which had feasibly not gone down terribly well. Sinéad handed Dolores a sheet of paper and left.

On the paper were my original questions to Sinéad with the answers written alongside, and the singer had clearly not been in a good mood when she supplied them. They were bizarre and often malicious, telling both me and her brother to fuck off, and I decided on the spot that I would not be pursuing that interview opportunity. Yet I interviewed Sinéad six months later in London and she was grand. I like her a lot – you just never know which version will show up on any given day.

Another great Irish star is Van Morrison and I've met him a few times over the years while never really getting to know him. Once I went to some opening or launch in Dublin and bumped into his partner, Michelle Rocha, who dragged me over to say hello to Van. He said: 'I remember you. You interviewed me in a church in Bristol for some programme on Channel 4.' 'What a memory!' I thought. 'You see, Dave,' added Michelle, her tongue firmly in her cheek, 'he's not just a pretty face.'

I had indeed interviewed Van in 1991 at the altar of a Bristol church. We had invited Mose Allison along to duet with him – one of the reasons the interview turned out so well. Put Van with one of his heroes and he's as jovial as the next rock star. Well, almost.

Van doesn't suffer fools easily: in fact, he doesn't suffer many people at all. His reputation for being stubborn, idiosyncratic and sublime is well founded. Musically, over the years he has excelled in numerous different fields, from rock, blues, R&B and folk to blue-eyed soul, jazz, country, Celtic rock and, I'm sure, a few other genres besides. In a six-year period between 1968 and 1974 he released seven classic albums and since then has been on an often wayward but always fascinating transcendental journey.

A mid-Nineties trip to the Fleadh gave me an interesting encounter with Nick Cave. I have always admired Cave, and Ursula absolutely loves him, even his noisily attitudinal early albums with the Birthday Party, but he and I had a bit of history. Interviewing him live on 2FM a few years earlier, I had asked him about spending time in rehab for drug-related problems. 'Who the hell told you that?' he had snarled as he leapt from his chair and aimed a punch at me across the desk. He may or may not have been joking, it was hard to tell, and all I could do was duck and point at my source for this information: his own record company's press release.

He was in a better mood at the Fleadh as I took advantage of a break from stage-announcing duties to change Robert's nappy backstage. Cave strolled past, then paused to admire my efforts: 'You're good at that, Fanning. I'm impressed!' We have now locked horns in interviews four or five times, and while he can be curt and impatient, he is always erudite and intelligent.

Back home, it was time for the Fanning clan to move on. With our family now expanding, Ursula and I had decided to leave the house in Convent Road and bought a bigger place just a few hundred yards from the one we were vacating. We had lived in Convent Road for five glorious years and had nothing but good times – really good times – and it was a very upsetting moment for me when we drove away for the very last time.

Having sold our place, we had to be out by the end of August, but the new house needed a lot of work and would not be ready for habitation until the end of the year, so Gerry Ryan and Morah offered to let us doss down at their place in Clontarf. It was a fun few months. Between Jack, Robert, Gerry and Morah's three kids, visiting parents and nannies, Gerry doing his breakfast show, and me going back and forth to London between my 2FM shows, there was drama and excitement every day. By now Ursula was working as a researcher on *Gay Byrne's Late Late Show*, a job she loved, so we all brought something to the party and every day the house seemed to be full of gossip, drama and excitement. Gerry and I hatched a plan to get it sponsored by Pampers. Oddly, it never came to anything.

I was once again doing a long commute into work; one of my pet hates. The only consolation was that it was a pretty drive down the coast, and that short spell in my life will for me forever be associated with 'Miss Sarajevo' by U2 side-project the Passengers, which I loved and was playing to death on the car stereo system.

So was all the upheaval worthwhile? There is an easy answer to that question. Fifteen years after Ursula and I moved into our new home, we are still happily ensconced there. I don't think I would mind if I never live anywhere else. It also proved to be a good base from which to begin yet another of the deeply eclectic experiences that have defined my career ...

12

People have sometimes asked me if I am a workaholic and I guess in some ways I must be but, to be honest, I've never seen it that way. It's certainly not a case of being money-driven; none of the Fannings ever were. My philosophy has always been that if I have enough money for petrol and a bag of chips, that is all I need. Ursula has frequently despaired of this attitude, especially on the occasion she had to ask me why my RTÉ salary had not been paid into our account for four months. The errant cheques turned up tucked into an album sleeve in the RTÉ library.

You only need to look at me to realise that I don't spend my money on clothes. My only obsessions are music and movies, which I am mostly lucky enough to get for nothing. If it might seem bizarre to many people that I have frequently had four or even five jobs on the go simultaneously, the explanation is actually simple: I love what I do so much that, most of the time, it doesn't even feel like work at all. Anyhow, it's not five jobs; it's all the same one with a few different faces.

Throughout the Nineties and into this new century I filled in each summer on Gerry Ryan's morning talk show. Once, David Beckham was scheduled to make a personal appearance in

Eason's bookshop to promote and sign copies of his autobiography. His plane was delayed so his PR people decided to let him make his own quick apology, assuring his fans that he'd be a few hours late but that he would be here. We were told 'two minutes'; we got half-an-hour. And that bit from the tabloids about wearing Victoria's underwear while he does the washing-up? Not true, it seems.

Back in 1995, when 2FM and *The Movie Show* were eating up my time five days a week and I was still flying to London on Saturdays, the only completely work-free day that I had each week was Sunday. So when RTÉ offered me the chance to host a new Sunday morning TV show, I naturally grabbed it with both hands.

The show was called *2TV* and was to air on RTÉ2 for two hours every Sunday morning. It was a music programme, but this was a long way from my staple diet of late-night too-cool-for-school indie rock and guitar bands on 2FM. *2TV* was to be all about chart pop and was aimed firmly at the school kids, pre-teens and tweenies who powered boy bands and airbrushed-R&B stars to the top of the weekly chart. That was the reason I wanted to do the show.

Maybe a leather-jacketed rock 'n' roll guy was not the obvious host for this show – or maybe that was the whole point. In any case, I quickly decided to give it a go. It sounded like fun. The basic format was to involve me playing the latest videos and interviewing visiting pop poppets, which I knew I could handle even if the music was not to my taste. Basically, I would be doing the same as I always had, except that it would be goodbye Radiohead, hello B*Witched.

I did have one strong stipulation before agreeing to do the show. With two young kids and my ever-demanding existing work and travel commitments, my time was already too tight to mention. I told the *2TV* producers that I would not be able to attend any midweek planning or pre-production meetings but I was happy to turn up on the day and present the programme.

They seemed entirely happy with this situation and I stuck to my word so rigidly that I did not visit the *2TV* office for nearly two years. When I finally did have cause to call in, I discovered Ray D'Arcy, who sat next to *2TV* because he hosted a kids' show called *The Den*, roaring with laughter. Ray pointed out that *2TV* had broadcast more than a hundred shows before its presenter finally managed to make it in to the office.

2TV went on air at 11 o'clock on Sunday mornings and I usually rolled into the studio at 10.45. The set-up was me sitting on a couch on the left-hand side of the screen while the latest chart popster or group sat on the sofa opposite. Between us lay a plate of croissants and bananas, which I had normally demolished by the time the programme was over.

The producers were completely cool with me saying whatever I wanted about the abominations against music that I was forced to present, which gave *2TV* a nicely subversive edge. I would like to think the show developed a cult following, because kids would tune in eager to see Britney or Take That's latest poptastic video, and students would fall out of bed and watch in order to see the piss being taken out of them.

The running joke was that I would mercilessly slag off some sickly slice of plastic pop, then the next week its makers would come in for an interview and I would fawn over them. 'That dreadful old nonsense was by Eternal,' I would inform the viewers. 'They will be here next week, and obviously I will be telling them how great they are!' Everybody was in on the joke and it was all part of the game.

Occasionally we veered away from bland chart-pop to invite more interesting guests. Damon Albarn co-presented an entire show with me. Green Day plastered their band stickers all over the set, the cameras and my forehead. Remarkably, legendary Beatles producer George Martin came in to discuss the Fabs (we had to swap seats because he is deaf in one ear). God knows what the pop kids made of that one.

Bizarrely, we also once made the curious decision to have Shane MacGowan on 2TV. Wisely, we decided to pre-record the interview rather than broadcast it live. A bottle of wine replaced the usual coffee-table croissants and bananas; consequently, the interview was not a great success. We decided not to use it.

These credible guests were exceptions, though, and the bread-and-butter of 2TV was relentless pop pap. The majority of the artists didn't take themselves at all seriously and were happy to join in having a laugh at their expense. German dance band Scooter were a prime example. Boy bands I could just about understand, but the appeal of groups like Scooter and their tacky, almost illegally cheesy club bleep-music passed me by completely.

When Scooter came in, I told them I was flabbergasted they had sold more than 30 million albums and regularly sold out arenas, as I absolutely couldn't stand their music. They nodded thoughtfully as though they were taking my point on board. 'My brother gets a headache at the very mention of our name,' one of them divulged. 'Unfortunately, that means he has a constant headache!' They knew they had many detractors but they loved what they did and they stuck to it, which was cool.

2TV was a very loose and informal show, both on the screen and in the studio. The production team and camera crew always seemed to be falling about laughing as we sailed by the seat of our pants. Frequently, a producer or floor manager would be saying to me, 'Phwoargh, look at the arse on that!' just as the camera was cutting back to me so that I could say, 'Great, that was All Saints!' It wasn't this cavalier approach that led me to make a gaffe that triggered quite a little media storm but, although completely out of my control, I made one anyway.

The Corrs, the Irish family band whose soft rock had conquered the world, had come in for a live chat. Our interview segued into the news and then the first airing of a new video by Boyzone, who had just enjoyed a major hit with 'Love Me for a Reason' and seen their debut album top the Irish and UK charts.

The Corrs had just come back from a world tour, so, while they had heard of Boyzone, they didn't know a lot about them and asked me to fill them in. As the video played and Irish teenage girls' latest heartthrobs pouted moodily in a desert, I happily informed the Corrs off-camera that Boyzone were rubbish. The lead singer, Ronan Keating, could sing a bit, I told them, but frankly, 'the rest of them have as much talent as my big toe'.

We might have been off-camera but unfortunately we were not completely off-air. Unknown to me, the sound man a couple of doors down had not turned my microphone down, and so my comprehensive dissing of Boyzone's (lack of) talents was heard loud and clear by every *2TV* viewer.

By the time the song had ended, the switchboard had lit up and the fun had begun. Ursula had been watching the show at home and rang RTÉ in a panic, imploring them 'Tell Dave to turn his mike off!' When the cameras came back to me, it never struck me as being too big a deal and we pressed on to the end of the show, but it was too late. The genie was out of the bottle and was not going back. Sensing the furore that would ensue, the Corrs' manager, John Hughes, came in to listen back to the tape and discovered to his relief that his band had said nothing untoward. 'Good, we are not implicated in anything here,' he told me, laughing. 'You're on your own on this one, Dave!'

As soon as I was off the air, journalists from all of the major Irish papers were calling RTÉ to ask to speak to me in order to get, as they diplomatically put it, 'clarification' of what had gone on. I was convinced that none of them had actually been sitting watching Sunday morning kids' TV. I was equally sure that I knew who would have been, and who would have alerted them to what had happened: Boyzone's manager, Louis Walsh.

Louis and I went back a long way. I had known him in the Seventies when he was working at Tommy Hayden Enterprises, a Dublin artist management company that specialised in old-school showbands. We had always got on well, partly because Louis had never tried to push the showbands or Eurovision-style acts such as Johnny Logan on me because he knew they didn't belong on a late-night alternative-music radio show.

Although Boyzone and their ilk were anathema to me, I liked Louis and admired what he had done. Before he came along, mainstream international Irish pop successes were limited to Val Doonican, the Bachelors, the Nolan Sisters, and, at a push, Gilbert O'Sullivan. Louis had come up with the idea of an Irish boy band to rival New Kids on the Block and Take That, and he had made it happen.

It hadn't all been plain sailing. With his partner, John Reynolds, Louis had held auditions for Boyzone and picked a whole bunch of people who didn't have a clue what they were doing. Their first TV debut, an under-rehearsed, appallingly choreographed, bare-chested dance routine on a 1993 edition of *The Late Late Show,* was such a disaster and so unintentionally hilarious that it is still a bloopers show and YouTube favourite nearly twenty years on.

Louis had persevered and worked his magic and, with Boyzone and Westlife, had created not one but two boy bands that had managed to do the impossible and out-sell Take That in Britain. It had been quite miraculous and, even now, I take my hat off to him. In 1995, when I was on the panel for the IRMA Awards, I proposed Louis as a fitting recipient for the Industry Award. Ursula had urged Gay Byrne to interview him on *The Late Late Show* when she was working there as a researcher. There was no bad feeling between us at all.

This didn't mean he wouldn't go in for the kill over the *2TV* fiasco. Louis liked to get a Boyzone story in the tabloids every day and wasn't too fussed what they were as long as they got the band's name right. He intuitively knew that he would get at least a week's worth from this incident and he was going to milk it for all it was worth.

Dave Fanning

On the Monday morning, four Irish newspapers ran FANNING DISSES BOYZONE stories on their front pages. In truth, the headlines promised more than the stories delivered. When you read them closely, all I had really said was I thought Boyzone were rubbish. I was just relieved the mike hadn't caught me saying far worse about them, or swearing my head off. Either one could easily have happened.

Morning Ireland phoned me up for an interview, as did Gerry Ryan and Pat Kenny. I went on Pat's show and tried to laugh it all off. Ronan Keating was also on the programme and played his hand immaculately, talking of his 'major disappointment' like a jilted lover: 'We can't believe it ... we thought Dave liked us. We thought he was our friend.'

The day was utter madness. Every single radio station called to 'give me the chance to put my side of the story', as they disingenuously put it. One network mounted a two-hour discussion programme under the title 'Was Dave Fanning right?' 'Are Boyzone crap, or is Dave Fanning just a rock snob?' asked the DJ. In my opinion, the answer to both of those questions was very definitely yes.

The death of Ireland's most famous sports commentator, the voice of the GAA, Michael O'Hehir, was banished to the back pages of the papers as Fanninggate raged. Louis toured the TV and radio shows and played a blinder. 'Fanning is a decent guy but he should stick with those awful bands he plays on the radio every night that nobody buys,' he declared. 'In the words of Bob Dylan: "Don't criticise what you don't understand."'

That afternoon I called Louis, not sure and not really caring what his reaction might be, and found he was totally unfazed by the whole business. 'Look, Dave, it's all grist to the mill,' he freely admitted. 'I'm sorry and all that, but you put your foot in it and we are going to make sure we get all the publicity we can out of it.' It was all a big joke; a big scam. I couldn't blame him, and in fact I found myself thinking: 'Good luck to him!'

The next few days I had to roll with the punches and make the best of it. I was Public Enemy No. 1 with Dublin's school-girls, and crossed the road if I saw any of them coming towards me. The schoolboys mostly gave me the thumbs up, while a few people congratulated me as if I had been waging a campaign of some sort: 'It was about time somebody said they were crap – well done for putting them in their place.'

The tabloids wrote about the whole scandal as if I should have been mortified at being caught dissing Boyzone, but the truth is I loved the whole episode. I had a blast. Once it became clear to me that nobody was genuinely offended and we were all just playing a media game, I decided to enjoy the ride. The incident did me no harm whatsoever. I was supposed to be the late-night, leather-jacketed, rock 'n' roll guy: it would probably have been far more damaging if I had been caught confiding that I actually adored Boyzone.

Underpinning it all was the irony that I had nothing against the group. Louis was cool. I had met Ronan many times by then and really liked him. Keith Duffy is a great guy and I always had a laugh with him if I met him out for a drink. As for the music ... No, nothing has changed there. The music IS rubbish. You'll probably hear me on the radio defending this viewpoint when this book comes out. I look forward to it.

Dave Fanning

In 1996 I was a guest on *The Late Late Show*. Ursula was working on the show at the time but had no hand in my participation. Gay Byrne is a true legend of Irish broadcasting and I guess in some small, silly way, it made me feel as if I had arrived. It was a true rite of passage.

I had been on the show a couple of times in the early Eighties: once with a bunch of colleagues from Radio 2 and once as a guinea-pig for one of the programme's lighter items. The John Travolta movie *Urban Cowboy* had briefly popularised the plug-in, buckin'-bronco mechanical bull and the programme invited a few of us on to test it out. Gerry Ryan, Dave Heffernan, myself and Phil Lynott were invited down to open the show, none of us, of course, having ever seen one of these contraptions up close, let alone 'ridden' one.

When we got to RTÉ we were told the item had been bumped from the start of the show to the end. So the four of us popped down to Madigans in Donnybrook for a couple of hours. Four pints of Guinness later, I was in no fit state to be in charge of a mechanically propelled anything, least of all a bull. I was last on. The other three wisely mounted the bull, acted silly for less than a minute and fell off. My first problem was getting on the damn thing. Even though the varispeed was down at minimum, I couldn't coordinate or negotiate, so I'd already made more of a fool of myself than the other three combined. But when I finally got onto it, I lasted longer than any of the others. It wasn't a question of skill. It was more a case of being too stupid and stupefied. I hung on for dear life in the mistaken belief that this was somehow nobler than throwing in the towel, an exercise infinitely more sensible than throwing up the Guinness. I didn't deserve to, but I got away with it.

In 1996 members of the studio audience also asked some of the questions and one guy asked me, 'Dave, you have done so many different TV and radio programmes, are you some kind of Renaissance Man?' I don't know how I kept a straight face on that one. I told him that if he knew me, he'd know that I was pretty lazy. Maybe I should have said pretty lucky.

My fellow studio guest was Lauren Bacall, who is a Hollywood legend but not remotely as legendary as she thinks she is. She will always have a certain status because of films such as *The Big Sleep* and *Dark Passage*, both also starring her husband Humphrey Bogart, but her career later waned until she was making movies like *Murder on the Orient Express* and appearing on *The Rockford Files*. She was rude and kind of dismissive on *The Late Late Show* and I regret that I didn't have the balls to take the piss a little bit.

Boyzone's Keith Duffy is clearly a very forgiving soul because he came to work with me on *2TV*, conducting funny, irreverent interviews with his fellow pop stars. He was to talk to Robbie Williams in 1998 when Robbie headlined Slane Castle. Robbie had also played there the previous year, as support to the Verve, but 1998 was very much his show.

Having initially not been taken all that seriously when he left Take That, Robbie was now at his absolute superstar peak and it was impossible to go for more than an hour in any given day without hearing 'Angels' blasting from a radio or car window. I was still sceptical but had to confess that his Slane headline set was pretty spectacular, everything you could hope for from a stadium pop show. I wandered down to the heart of the crowd for some of the set and it was one giant love-fest on a beautiful summer's night.

Keith interviewed Robbie just before the gig. Afterwards we travelled back to the Merrion Hotel in a convoy of cars. Keith and I went up to Robbie's room, where he was hanging out down the corridor from where his mother and various band members were staying. Robbie had just played the gig of a lifetime in front of 100,000 adoring fans and yet he seemed unfazed, calm and even detached.

Keith told Robbie how much he admired him for leaving a boy band and going on to do his own thing. I was about to leave them to it but Robbie said, 'No, stay here, it's fine', after which he gave me another beer and the three of us sat for an hour putting the world to rights. Robbie was courteous and deadpan yet it amazed me that of all those who'd been at Slane, he seemed the least excited about the gig he had just played.

When I was first offered 2TV, I had figured I would probably only present the show for a year or two as an ironic sideline and then move on. I never expected to enjoy it as much as I did. It soon became a very valued element of my weekly routine, and to my surprise I found I could have as good a craic talking to the Sugababes or Eternal as chatting with Blur. Different strokes, and all that. It may even have slightly cured my endemic rock snobbery. Only slightly, mind you. By this stage, the beautiful Bianca Lyux was a welcome co-host and we were enjoying the haphazardness of it all.

I was hugely disappointed then when the RTÉ management pulled the show off the air after five years. I thought it had at least another two years in it yet. That's how it works at RTÉ. The station bosses know the network is still the only game in town so can do whatever they want, depending on their political agenda of the day.

Television executives are like gods, and while the RTÉ top dogs are decent and not remotely as bad as the awful Hollywood executives that I interviewed for *The Movie Show,* some of the same principles hold. The other week, a newspaper article listed ten attractive women who had on-screen presenting jobs on RTÉ while they were in their twenties. Having hit their thirties, none of them have a gig today.

I felt that RTÉ pulled both *2TV* and *The Movie Show* before they had run their course but that is the nature of TV. It can be a cut-throat business. There is no point in running to the newspapers with your complaints if you lose a show because they will print every word, it makes you look like a whinger, and ultimately it achieves nothing.

Instead you play the game, you say the programme had come to the end of its natural life, and you wish whoever takes over the replacement show the best of luck, even though, human nature being what it is, you might just want to kill them.

It is important to hang on to the big picture – and the reality for me is that in the range, depth and variety of TV and radio shows I have been invited to present, I have been, and still am, very, very lucky. Long may it continue.

13

Into even the luckiest, most charmed life, tragedy must fall. In 1998 we were hit by a devastating hammer blow that logically we knew would have to come one day, but emotionally we still were not remotely ready for or insulated against.

My mother had survived and even prospered for fifteen years since my father had died. She was still the family matriarch and, even as she headed into her late eighties, she had an indomitable spirit. It helped, of course, that she had a large family, and she loved nothing more than her kids and grand-kids piling round to Foster Avenue to visit her every week.

Annie was never a great traveller but in the early Nineties she had flown over to Toronto to stay with my brother Peter and his wife Ruth. Peter was a teacher there and Annie had a great time in Canada, becoming very close to Steve and Clare, Peter and Ruth's kids. Typical of my mum's waste-not-want-not Dublin spirit, when she got back she proudly showed us how she had saved her spare sugar lumps from the flight for future use at home.

Early in 1997 we had suffered a family tragedy that hit all of us but hit my mother particularly hard. Clare was 17, her school prom was coming up, and Ruth had been to Seattle to buy her the exact dress she wanted. Clare was never to wear it. On St Patrick's Day, she was knocked down by a drunken driver and killed instantly.

Annie had been through plenty of hardships and disappointments in her life, including the premature loss of her husband and the death of her second child, and had always survived them, but the granddaughter she loved so much being taken away in such a cruel and pointless fashion seemed too much for her to bear. Her health deteriorated significantly during the second half of 1997. She suffered various falls and, with great reluctance and on medical advice, we all decided to find her nursing-home care until she became stronger.

Her faith never deserted her and we got her a taxi twice a week to go to the Clarendon Street church she had been worshipping at for more than fifty years. The taxi drivers all knew that she was Dave Fanning's mum and looked after her, and the steady stream of visitors to the house never abated as she continued to hold forth in the kitchen and dispense her legendary, delicious biscuits. She spent the rest of her time visiting the few friends of her own vintage who were still alive.

We talked of hiring a nurse to look after her in Foster Avenue, but Annie was not well disposed towards this scheme, even when she grew weaker and had to go back into the nursing home. By now she was 88, and although her willpower was strong enough for her to go home yet again, even a fighter like my mother couldn't cheat time forever and by early 1998 she was in the institution for a third time.

On 11 March 1998, I went to visit her with Robert, who was then nearly three. She seemed subdued and was sitting in a day room, where other old people who looked much more enfeebled than her were drooling over their plates and being helped to eat their evening meals. She looked great, was sitting up straight and had no interest in eating. She put on a brave face, as ever, but she had a look in her eye. She'd lived enough and this environment was not for her. Maybe she was finally giving up. She perked up when she saw the two of us and we went back to her room for an hour or so to chat.

The next morning the residential home phoned all of her children. Annie was unconscious when we got there but we were all around her bedside when she died. It was not like my father's death, where he dropped dead out of the blue, but even so, I was not prepared for it. I genuinely had thought she would come out of the home, because in the kitchen at Foster Avenue, at the centre of her own world, she had always seemed indestructible.

There are no words or formulae to cope with the death of a mother, but I was just so pleased that we had always enjoyed such a wonderful relationship. My mother had invariably been immensely proud and supportive of me, and never judgemental, even after UCD when I was living under her roof, doing my best to avoid respectable work, lying in bed until lunchtime and then charging round Dublin all night playing rock 'n' roll on illegal radio stations. It wasn't her thing, this arty woman of letters and literature, but she knew I was passionate about what I was doing and that was good enough for her.

The funeral was moving, emotional and, yes, cathartic. Annie had had a full and happy life, so everybody was sad but relaxed on the day. I remember in the cortege on the way to the church, my brother John asked the driver if he knew the latest football scores, and it wasn't inappropriate or disrespectful. In fact, to borrow that much-abused but yet again truthful cliché, it was just the sort of banter that Annie would have wanted and expected.

Having been born in 1909, my mother so nearly made it right to the end of the century. We thought of her on Millennium Night, when Ursula and I went to a big party in Stepaside hosted by Ursula's cousin, Noel Smyth. It was a fancy-dress bash. I went as Paul McCartney in his *Sgt. Pepper* outfit and, oddly, Ursula's brother Kevin went in the exact same costume. We had no idea about the duplication until we arrived.

Back at work, RTÉ might have pulled the plug on *2TV* and *The Movie Show* but they still seemed to be coming to me with new programme ideas. Early in 2000, they offered me the chance to do something I had never done before: host a chat show. Back in the 1980s, the network had launched *Saturday Live* with a series of guest presenters, including ex-footballer and pundit Eamon Dunphy, the singer Brian Kennedy and the Reverend Ian Paisley's daughter Rhonda Paisley. I wasn't particularly nervous about doing it, although it was a serious step outside of my comfort zone, but so had many things been over the years, from *Jobsuss* to *2TV*, so I decided to give it a go. My first guest was bestselling author Cathy Kelly, after which I spoke to former middleweight boxing champion Nigel Benn, and my own recent sparring partner, Louis Walsh.

My final guest was the *pièce de résistance*. It was quite a coup but in a deliberately casual, offhand manner, I said, 'Now, here is the singer from a local Dublin band ...' and out came Bono. The interview went great, because it was around the time Bono had been doing a lot of major-league charity and lobbying work and had given the Pope his sunglasses, so I gently took the piss out of him about that. After all that, RTÉ couldn't get the budget together so the idea of bringing back *Saturday Live* was quietly dropped, but I watched that show for the first time quite recently and was pleasantly surprised that it was halfway decent.

Ursula and I had been trying for a third child and, to our delight, as the new millennium got underway she fell pregnant. She was not too perturbed by repeated bouts of morning sickness, as she was accustomed to them now: both of her previous pregnancies had been difficult. However, a few weeks into this pregnancy, she suffered a miscarriage.

This is a devastating occurrence for any woman and it hit Ursula hard. If I am honest, I am not sure I showed her the empathy I should have done. Whereas my brother Peter and his wife Ruth had lost a teenage daughter they had raised and loved, we had never even known our child: I guess, for me at least, he or she had never existed. I wasn't blasé about the miscarriage, and I hope that I was understanding and supportive, but part of me suspects that I could have done or said more. Actually, now that I think about it, maybe I *was* blasé.

With my movie and kids' TV programmes off the air, my work was all about rock 'n' roll again, and I got the chance to re-meet a long-time hero. Joe Strummer had long left the Clash and was fronting a feisty band called the Mescaleros when he arrived in Dublin to play a festival at the Olympia. As I talked to him backstage, he raved about the venue and wondered why he had never heard of it before: 'Where have you been hiding this one, Dave?' He seemed so full of life and fire, which is why it was such a shock when he was dead little more than a year later.

There was something a little dead in Brian Wilson when the legendary former Beach Boy called in to 2FM. I had heard from Ursula's sister Deirdre that the excesses of the Sixties had taken their toll on the man who created one of the most peerless back catalogues in pop history, but I hadn't realised quite how much damage had been done until we started talking. Wilson was willing, but had trouble grasping even straightforward questions, and it was one of the few interviews I have ever called a halt to before the allotted time was up, even though I liked him.

Around this time, I also finally got to meet my all-time musical hero: Bob Dylan. Admittedly, the circumstances were far from ideal. Dylan was releasing his thirty-first studio album, *Love and Theft*, and his record label was ferrying a few selected European journalists to Rome for a handful of brief round-robin interviews with the great man. When the opportunity arose, I offered the story to the *Irish Times*, who asked me to write a cover feature for their Saturday magazine.

My experience with Madonna had given me a profound distaste for these cattle-class interviews where a slew of journalists cluster around the star at a table for a stop-start, unsatisfying conversation. There were not many people I would go through this ignominy for but Bob is Bob, and any chance to genuflect before a man I had worshipped for more than thirty years was not to be missed.

As I had expected, the experience was simultaneously uplifting and frustrating. Just being in the same room as Dylan was a buzz, and although our interview was somewhat dominated by a pushy Scandinavian journalist, Bob was reasonably engaged and didn't adopt the evasive, smart-assed persona that he donned to coast through most of his Sixties media encounters.

Dylan didn't open up and give us loads of never-before-heard autobiographical detail: nobody expected that. He placed a few questions carefully to one side, expertly parried a few others, and hit the more inane enquiries out of the ground. Yet by his guarded standards he was relatively open and mellow; and the best thing of all was that he was still really, really cool. It was an honour and a privilege to be there.

It was from the sublime to the ridiculous a few weeks later when I set off to Sweden to interview Eminem. Hip-hop generally has never been my thing and the whole hardcore gangsta-and-bling music and lifestyle leaves me cold, but as a white boy who had risen to the top of that world and then crossed over to be a genuine superstar and celebrity, Eminem was a fascinating one-off.

The Swedish trip was a disaster. Eminem had four interviews lined up before his arena show and I don't think he did any of them. Instead, he holed up in his dressing room as his daft entourage of protégés, DJs and wannabe gangstas strutted around the place. A few hours before the show, his PR had to apologise and tentatively suggest rescheduling our meeting for his show in Manchester two weeks later.

Backstage at Manchester's Manchester Evening News Arena, Eminem a.k.a. Slim Shady a.k.a. Marshall Mathers III finally sat down for a chat. His two twenty-stone minders who sat in on the interview were a tad disconcerting, but once I got past Eminem's skinny-shouldered swagger and attitude, he was an attentive and intelligent interviewee. I actually thought he was a nice guy.

The live show was something else. Eminem pranced around in dungarees and a silly face mask brandishing a chainsaw while a DJ mixed a few twelve-inch singles behind him, despite the fact that all the sound appeared to be coming from a pre-recorded mini-disc. It was a bit like a kids' party where the parents had splashed out on a clown, albeit a very grumpy one with a chainsaw. Or maybe it was a pantomime, although a rather unusual one in which the largely early-teenage audience were encouraged to shout out 'Look be-fuckin'-hind you!' at regular intervals.

Back in Dublin, Fleetwood Mac's Lindsey Buckingham and Mick Fleetwood could not have been more different characters when I interrogated them together: the extremely American Buckingham with his ear for commercial rock, and the very English Fleetwood steeped in the British blues tradition. If ever a band was ripe for a fly-on-the-wall reality show years before the genre was invented, it was Fleetwood Mac.

In 2002, U2 were out on the road again, touring the *All That You Can't Leave Behind* album, and producer Jim Lockhart and I received a very exciting offer. Representatives from Grupo Radio Centro, the largest radio network in Mexico, visited Dublin and invited us to go to their country and broadcast on their Mexico City station as part of a two-week 'U2 excursion'.

U2 had boycotted Mexico on their previous world tour after an unsavoury incident when a bodyguard looking after the Mexican president's son, Emiliano Zedillo, had allegedly beaten Adam Clayton's security guard unconscious after an altercation. Grupo Radio Centro had reached out to U2 and run a major campaign beseeching the band to let bygones be bygones and put their nation back on their touring agenda, and it had worked.

What followed was a distinctly surreal fortnight down Mexico way. Jim and I knew we had a bizarre time in store as soon as we got in a taxi at Mexico City airport. The cab radio kept repeating an absurdly long promo consisting of three-second bursts of what sounded like every guitar riff, run and frill the Edge had ever recorded, followed by a DJ gabbling like a Spanish Wolfman Jack and ending by yelling: *'El gruppo, U2! El hombro, Dave Fanning!'*

The trip got off to a bit of a damp-squib start. Excited, jetlagged and full of tequila, Jim and I took our places near the front row at a Peter Gabriel concert that our Mexican hosts had kindly got us tickets for. Gabriel spent a large part of the evening bouncing around the stage in a giant inflatable ball, the show turning out to be so boring it put a bit of a dampener on our mood.

Thankfully, that was the only down note of the entire trip. As well as having fun stuff lined up for us every day, *El hombro, Dave Fanning!* was live on Grupo Radio Centro every day, hosted a question-and-answer session at the local university, undertook an online chat with U2 fans and seemed to have a concert or a party to go to every night.

We stayed at a city-centre hotel called the Camino Real, which is the establishment that Pierce Brosnan drunkenly walked through wearing only his underwear and cowboy boots in the film *The Matador*. It was plush and the bedrooms were the size of football fields. Every floor had an armed guard, and each night an ultra-cheesy cabaret band murdered the same handful of easy-listening standards in the lobby.

Whenever we finished a radio broadcast, Jim and I would leave the studio to find people waiting for us. Some were band members and musicians keen to give us demos. One guy who introduced himself was Steve Skaith, who was living in Mexico City but had previously sung in a London band called Latin Quarter. They had had a single called 'Radio Africa' which I had played to death on Radio 2 in the mid-Eighties.

However, most of the people politely waiting around to meet us were fervent U2 fans who wanted to talk and hear stories about the band and asked us if we could get records and photographs autographed by them. For some inexplicable reason, a lot of these fans appeared to possess ultra-rare, perfectly preserved seven-inch vinyl copies of the very earliest five or six U2 singles.

Mostly we hung out in the sprawling and chaotic metropolis of Mexico City but one Tuesday afternoon we visited a picturesque cobblestoned village about fifty miles from the city. Our guides took us to the local church for what they said was just a normal afternoon mass. I have to say, it looked anything but normal to me. The church was crammed with both elderly and younger worshippers, some of whom were shouting out, others speaking in tongues, all simultaneously praying and venting their hopes and dreams. To me it simply looked sinister and did nothing to challenge my well-established horror of organised religion.

In June 1977, when Queen Elizabeth II celebrated her Silver Jubilee in Britain, the Sex Pistols put a safety pin through her nose and rocketed up the chart with a song that proclaimed her a moron and a potential H-bomb. A quarter of a century on, the music world gathered respectfully at her home to celebrate her fifty years on the throne. How times change.

RTÉ dispatched me to London to cover the Golden Jubilee Party at the Palace, held in front of Buckingham Palace before around ten thousand excited royalists and music fans who had won their tickets in a lottery. The event got off to a faintly ridiculous start as Brian May from Queen strode across the palace's roof with his guitar playing the main riff from 'God Save the Queen' (the national anthem, not the Pistols' version). Tony Blair and Princes Harry and William were among the VIPs looking on beside us.

The TV and radio journalists were billeted in temporary studios to the side of the courtyard. For a large part of the afternoon I had to endure being in the next studio to Sharon Osbourne, a woman always happy to appear on reality TV dispensing words of wisdom on things she knows nothing about. She was loud and vulgar, which I guess is what the radio station wanted.

The bill was surreally eclectic, with kiddie bands such as Blue, Atomic Kitten, S Club 7 and Mis-Teeq rubbing shoulders with long-established stars like Elton John, Cliff Richard, Brian Wilson, Rod Stewart and Ray Davies and even a few people that Her Maj might have liked, such as Tom Jones and Dame Shirley Bassey. I provided a running commentary for RTÉ between the acts, to the backdrop of Sharon Osbourne's screeching.

As evening fell, Paul McCartney materialised on a smaller stage nearer the crowd to play 'Blackbird' and then Prince Charles invited the Queen up on to the main stage with the priceless words: 'Your Majesty ... Mummy!' HRH looked distinctly bemused as compared to amused as she stood there for the grand sing-a-long finale flanked by the Corrs looking radiant on one side and Ozzy Osbourne looking out-to-lunch on the other. I'm not sure what the inner punk in me made of it all but it certainly made for a unique spectacle.

As a Beatles fan, and a man whose first ever album purchase was *Sgt. Pepper's Lonely Hearts Club Band*, it's always a huge thrill to see McCartney play. It's true I always tell people that for me John Lennon was the great interview that got away, the hero I never got a chance to talk to, but McCartney is just as much a stellar talent and I have always found him a delight to deal with.

Lennon might have been the cool Beatle because he was angry and political and a rebel but he also had a well-documented nasty streak. The critics have never been so kind to McCartney because he is that very un-rock 'n' roll thing, a nice guy, but it's surely no surprise that, post-Beatles, when Paul threw himself into music and family, he had more success in both areas than the other three Beatles put together. The biggest touring band of the Seventies wasn't Led Zeppelin. It was Wings.

Dave Fanning

Despite all he has achieved, McCartney remains an extremely positive and enthusiastic guy, and those traits were both to the fore in 2003 when I went to London with producer Jim Lockhart to interview him. In his office, he talked of how his 9/11 flight out of New York had been held on the runway and then grounded as US airspace was shut down. He used his extra days in NY to visit firefighters who lost colleagues when the Twin Towers came down. Their courage reminded him of his own father, who was a fireman in Liverpool during the Second World War.

When it came to talking about the Beatles, I concentrated on his relationship with Lennon. Paul was fairly forthcoming but neatly swerved my question about whether Lennon and he had missed writing songs together and found it more difficult after the split. He was happier fondly remembering long phone calls between the two in John's last few years, when they had chatted about domestic stuff from kids to bread recipes.

McCartney may not top the charts any more but he has never stopped making great music, and early in the twenty-first century he got together for the third time with dance-music producer Youth, as the Fireman, to make an album called *Electric Arguments*. It's a great record and I have to admire the way Paul keeps trying new things and reinventing himself when he really does not need to, either financially or reputation-wise.

I must confess it is not exactly the same thrill to talk to Ringo Starr, but a Beatle is a Beatle and when he came through Dublin it was good nonetheless to get a long talk with him before cameras upstairs at the Point. We went through the motions of discussing his new album, but Ringo is no fool and knew I was itching to talk about the Beatles, just like everyone else he meets. He was very droll on the subject of how absurd it was having Yoko Ono – and her bed! – in the recording studio at the end of the Beatles, when they were recording *Let It Be*.

I've seen footage of those sessions, with George Harrison telling Paul through gritted teeth: 'I'll play any fucking chords you want me to as long as I can get out of here!' Ringo said a lot of the bad blood was because it was so preposterous to have Yoko sitting in the corner of the studio, in bed, knitting. There is no doubt John was in love with her, but frankly, I have always thought that she's more of a charlatan than anything else, as the bed-in-studio event might indicate.

After our interview, Ringo and his All-Star Band played at the Point. The All-Stars in question included Gary Brooker from Procol Harum and Jack Bruce from Cream, but the show was distinctly ropey. They played their own songs, some Beatles tracks, the odd one by Procol Harum and Cream, and it all seemed vaguely pointless, like watching a tribute or wedding band.

The gig may have been mediocre but I still indulged myself and got a real thrill at the Point that night. While the band played, I stood with Point owner Harry Crosbie at the back of the stage, hidden from view, and looked at the gig as Ringo saw it. OK, these guys weren't John, Paul and George, but this must have been how actual Beatles gigs looked to Ringo. A bit sad, I know, but it was a special moment.

The Beatles may be forty years dead but the Stones are still rolling on, and I saw them also at the Point on their *Licks* tour in 2003. In some ways, they are now also their own tribute band. Their record label held a meet-and-greet before the gig for seven or eight of us, at which the Stones were to be presented with a gold disc, and beforehand the company's representatives warned us earnestly to smile at all times, as the band would only have one photograph taken at each side of the room.

Ursula and I waited with the other assembled liggers, including my old 2FM colleague Ian Dempsey, for half an hour and then the Stones loped in, looking ridiculously skinny for men nearing pensionable age. They lined up for the photo op and what followed was a fantastic master class in self-parody.

'Don't smile too much, lads,' warned Ronnie Wood. 'It makes the age lines look bigger in the photos.'

'Mine aren't age lines,' claimed Mick Jagger. 'They're laughter lines.'

'Nothing is that fucking funny!' muttered the ever-droll Charlie Watts. Meanwhile, Keith Richards wandered over to our group. Noting that Ursula was the sole female there, he draped himself over her.

'Right, I'll take this fine chick!' he declared. 'Flash away, Mr Photo Man!' I got the impression they had done this routine, or various versions of it, a million times before, but that didn't make it any less hilarious.

I also encountered Jagger at the Point when his daughter, Elizabeth, was modelling at a *Late Late Show* fashion extravaganza. Mick was relaxed, engaging and aloof all at the same time as we discussed U2, Manic Street Preachers' missing guitarist Richey James, and the fact that Keef apparently needs loud music playing in his hotel room every minute of the day and night when the Stones are on tour. Seeing I had downed my pint, Mick asked me what I wanted, and got me a lager and himself a vodka and tonic before strolling off.

Seeing Eddie Jordan staring at me, I wandered over. 'That's a decent claim to fame!' I gloated. 'Mick Jagger bought me a drink!' 'No he didn't,' replied the ever-laconic Jordan. 'It's a free bar.'

Another of my heroes, Neil Young, passed through Dublin in 2003 playing songs from his new concept album, *Greendale*. It wasn't an album about Postman Pat, although it might as well have been – a fairly wretched show not really salvaged by the handful of classics he fired out at the end of the gig. No matter: he has always been hit-and-miss, and there is no way I could miss a Dublin Neil Young show, especially in a venue as perfect and intimate as Vicar Street.

At home, Ursula's miscarriage in 2000 hadn't put us off trying for a third child. If anything, it had made us keener. She had fallen pregnant again in the middle of 2002. The pregnancy was difficult, as usual, with a lot of illness and morning sickness, and the added shock and danger provided by a fall down a short flight of stairs. Five days before the birth I was down in Blackrock village with Jack and Robert. On the mobile phone Ursula's faint voice was telling us that something was very wrong. Nine months' pregnant and now with a broken arm, she had somehow managed to crawl to a phone. The worst part was the ambulance drive through the hospital grounds. The driver ignored the ramps, each one adding to the excruciating pain. A few days later, on 13 March 2003, Ursula gave birth to our first daughter.

We were absolutely stunned to have a girl. Having Jack and Robert, we had just assumed that boys were our lot, and while

275

another son would have been fine, it was fantastic to have a daughter. Her birth was memorable, not just because of the broken arm and the difficulty it posed in the nursing of the baby, but because it was the start of St Patrick's week and Dublin was staging its traditional Skyfest, which meant that there were fireworks lighting up the sky outside the hospital window.

We talked of calling her Annie or Anna, as both my mother and Ursula's had been called Anne, but decided against it. We mulled over Molly but it didn't quite seem to fit. The hospital gave all of its parents a list of baby names to help them and we flicked through it. Every name seemed to have some long, complex etymology ('Helen: derived from Greek mythology, the beauteous daughter of Zeus', etc.) except for Hayley, which merely said: 'As in the actress, Hayley Mills'. A nurse walked into the room and asked what we were going to call her, and I said 'Hayley'. It was as random and simple as that. Sometimes, thankfully, the biggest decisions in life just make themselves.

14

If I had a euro for every time in my career I have been described as the Irish John Peel, I could pay off the national debt. Every time my name gets mentioned in a British magazine, it appears to be a compulsory qualification. The comparison, of course, isn't valid – John Peel was John Peel, for God's sake – and the only real similarity is that we both made our names playing alternative music on late-night radio programmes. However, when Peel died, I was in a highly inappropriate place.

Gerry Ryan phoned me while he was live on air in October 2004 to talk about the legendary BBC DJ, who had died of a heart attack while on a working holiday in Peru. I paid him a heartfelt tribute as a genuine fan of real music that means something, at which point Gerry asked me where I was. I had to confess that I was in Kerry being a judge on *You're a Star* – a talent contest to select Ireland's Eurovision Song Contest entry.

Gerry had a laugh about this and it didn't really sound great in the context of Peel's death, but when I had been asked to do it, I had simply thought, why not? Eurovision is shite, everybody knows that, but I thought it would be a laugh. Larry Gogan later told me that he had only ever met John Peel once and that was at a Eurovision Song Contest final. Larry had asked him why he was there, and Peel had said, 'I like music. All kinds of music.'

Shortly after Peel's death, I was invited to Patrick Guilbaud's restaurant in the Merrion Hotel, which is probably the most expensive eatery in Ireland. Paul McGuinness had hired the place out because U2 were releasing *How to Dismantle an Atomic Bomb* and Jo Whiley from BBC Radio 1 was over to record the band doing four numbers in their rehearsal space live on her show.

McGuinness made a speech, as did Bono, as did Whiley, then someone whispered to me that I should say something if I felt like it. I was just about to rise and make a toast to John Peel when I remembered that Peel had disliked U2 right from the word go and had made a point of never playing any of their records. I made a wise decision and stayed in my seat.

In July 2005, Bob Geldof marked the twenty-fifth anniversary of Live Aid by staging Live 8 concerts across the world. The shows preceded a G8 conference in Scotland and were intended to put pressure on world leaders to ease the pressure on penniless African nations struggling to repay crippling 'debts' to the West. The slick slogan was 'Make Poverty History'.

RTÉ sent me over to cover the London show, which attracted more than two hundred thousand people to Hyde Park. High points included U2 and Paul McCartney opening the day with 'Sgt. Pepper's Lonely Heart's Club Band', and Geldof making an impetuous, spontaneous decision to sing 'I Don't Like Mondays'. The low point was probably Pete Doherty, who looked like he had no idea what his name was or what day it was when he joined Elton John to sing T. Rex's 'Children of the Revolution'.

As night fell, the classic line-up of Pink Floyd reunited for the first time in nearly twenty-five years to play a headline set. By now I had left my broadcast booth to head down by the stage, and Laura Woods, my younger RTÉ co-presenter, asked me: 'What's so special about Pink Floyd anyway?' It was hard to explain – but thankfully, they did it for me.

The Floyd played five songs in the summer gloaming and for some of those who had been crammed against the crush barriers all day long waiting for this moment it was clearly close to a religious experience. The band played all the right things from *Dark Side of the Moon* and at one point Roger Waters glanced over towards David Gilmour, from whom he had been estranged for years, and told the crowd what a privilege it was to be up on stage with these people who meant so much to him. At that point you would have bet your house on a full-on Pink Floyd reunion and tour, but the enmity between Gilmour and Waters ran too deep, and the death three years later of keyboardist Rick Wright confirmed that it was not to be.

The Live 8 gig got a very mixed reaction in the media, with a lot of commentators calling it misguided and questioning Bob Geldof's motivations for staging the event. I must say, the cynicism that regularly raises its head, both in Ireland and Britain, towards Geldof and Bono over their charitable initiatives irritates me beyond belief. They have gone out to Africa, they have seen the problems and they have tried to make a difference. They have done a lot more than me, or you, or just about anyone outside of major NGOs – but still they get so much stick. It seems to me Geldof and Bono are two sincere individuals who take on a huge amount of demanding, time-consuming extra-curricular charity projects that they could easily ignore, and yet still they get regularly slagged off.

It is so much easier for people to sneer and criticise Geldof for living in a big house, or U2 for taking their tax affairs out of Ireland: has it not occurred to these same people that the band *earned* 99.999 per cent of their income outside of Ireland? They say Ireland is a nation of begrudgers, and while I love my homeland, in some ways it's true.

With the demise of *The Movie Show* and with my Channel 4 projects long gone, I was doing less international work in the new millennium, but that changed somewhat in 2005. A US company called Rave TV had seen tapes of a few of my TV shows such as *Fanning Profiles* and *Planet Rock Profiles* and invited me to New York to meet them. They had an intriguing proposition: they wanted me to host an interview show on the channel called *Talks with Dave Fanning*.

I gave the Rave TV channel bosses a fairly idiosyncratic list of possible interview subjects, they made their choices, and off we went. I flew to Cincinnati to meet Peter Frampton, who had been the Face of 1968 in Britain and flirted with superstardom in the US. I found a contented, relaxed guy who was philosophical about his ups and down in the Herd and Humble Pie and had somehow preserved his looks despite years ploughing around the globe playing hard-ass rock 'n' roll.

From Cincinnati I got an internal flight to Los Angeles to hook up again with Lindsey Buckingham, whom I had met in Dublin all those years ago. Buckingham had just released his first solo album in fifteen years and it had critics foaming at the mouth. Sadly, the five-star reviews did not translate into sales for the former Fleetwood Mac man.

Initially, I flew to the States to film all the *Talks with Dave Fanning* interviews but this soon struck me as a crazy and expensive way of doing things. I pointed out to the Rave TV bosses that rather than taking constant transatlantic flights and hiring costly local camera crews in the States, I could save money on the budget by catching the subjects when they visited Ireland or Britain. They happily acquiesced.

Rave TV had surprisingly agreed to a profile of Paul Weller, despite the fact neither the Jam nor his solo records have ever really done that well in America. Weller's reputation precedes him and, despite being a fan of his music, I was braced for a bad-tempered curmudgeon when we met to undertake a career overview. To my relief, he was an absolute gentleman.

Brandon Flowers of the Killers was not. I had interviewed him before for 2FM backstage at Ireland's Oxegen festival and he was fairly monosyllabic. I'd generously assumed he was having a bad day, but when we met again, in Blackpool of all places, to film a Rave TV special, I began to wonder if it really had been a one-off.

Flowers was filming five or six TV interviews during the day, and I witnessed first-hand the interviewer before me – a young Canadian woman – struggle through her questions while getting nothing worthwhile back from the singer. My session was a little better but still had a pulling-teeth quality to it and my overriding impression was of a self-absorbed man rather too keen to play the enigmatic rock star.

Dave Fanning

Ryan Adams was not trying to be difficult when I met him at the Clarence Hotel in Dublin, but nor was he a walk in the park. A ball of nerves, Adams seemed to treat the interview as a session on a psychoanalyst's couch and had enough neuroses to put Woody Allen to shame. With ten albums to his credit in about the same number of years, you might imagine him to be in a happy place and creatively satisfied, but clearly he was anything but.

Bruce Springsteen agreed to be interviewed backstage at the Point. His only stipulation was that I had to make sure that I watched the whole gig. This was hardly a chore. It was his solo *Devils and Dust* tour, and afterwards producer Jim Lockhart and I had a couple of beers with the Boss. He was completely genuine and relaxed, even though some of his responses to my questions were disarmingly ingenuous.

The nature of Rave TV also meant that I met up with a string of supposedly difficult pop divas. I had arranged to talk to Christina Aguilera in London when she was promoting her jazzy *Back to Basics* album. She was filming a few interviews in a hotel, and as Rave TV only used high-definition footage, I arranged with her record label that we would hire the room next to the interview room and set up our equipment there. Christina would only be required to walk from one room to the one next door.

The night before the interview, I had a call from Christina's manager who wanted to know what we had planned. I explained the arrangement and she very calmly said, 'I am sorry, but this cannot happen. Christina does not change rooms. It just is not possible.' I tried to persuade her but although she remained sweetly polite throughout the conversation, the lady was not for turning and I had to abandon the Rave TV interview and talk to her for RTÉ instead. When I met Christina, she was as sweet as can be. The stars normally are. It's the people around them that develop the attitude problems.

Cher was totally in control and happily ordered her assistants around the place non-stop, although it must be said that she didn't do it in a particularly nasty way. She checked all of the monitor shots herself and repositioned the lights and cameras before she was happy to begin. Before the interview we walked down a very long marble corridor together and she has had so many nips, tucks and cosmetic surgery operations – as well as bone repositioning, if rumours are to be believed – that I wondered if she would rattle if I nudged her. Gossip magazines were reporting that she had spent $2m on surgery, but seeing her close up, it looked like money well spent.

In my forty-five minutes with Beyoncé she was friendly, attentive and gave absolutely nothing away, choosing instead to thank God, her father, God, her mother, God, Kelly Rowland and God for her blessed success. While clearly an extraordinarily beautiful woman, a bad hair day made her look surprisingly ordinary for our cameras.

I also talked to Pet Shop Boys, PJ Harvey, Beck and Flaming Lips for *Talks with Dave Fanning*, and when I was stuck for an interview, a few old contacts helped me out. Oasis had played a gig in Belfast, Rave really wanted an A-list subject, and when I sent out an SOS, Noel Gallagher postponed his flight back to England and drove to Dublin to bail me out. The interview was our usual piss-take sparring session and it made for great TV, assuming the Americans could understand banter between a fast-talking Dubliner and a drawling Manc.

Radiohead had allowed me to interview them around every single album since *Pablo Honey,* and Thom Yorke and Ed O'Brien came to Dublin and sat down in the Shelbourne Hotel with me for an exhaustive run-through of their career. Even after all these years, it never fails to surprise me how serious they are about their music and how much recording their albums takes out of them.

Rave TV were delighted when I managed to secure R.E.M. for an interview, but less so when Michael Stipe was forced to cry off, meaning that the tape featured only Peter Buck and Mike Mills. Those two have been in the band right from the start and Buck in particular is a fantastic talker and raconteur, but Rave would not agree to a profile of the band without input from their singer and I received an earnest call from New York: 'Dave, we need the bald guy!'

Maybe this is where I got my karmic payback for choosing R.E.M.'s debut single as my soundtrack on *Youngline* all those years ago, because I got in touch with Stipe and, despite a pressing schedule, he agreed to do it. He asked if we could meet in downtown Manhattan but, when that proved impossible, came all the way uptown to Rave TV's HQ next to Madison Square Garden, which caused no little excitement in the office. Stipe was reliably courteous, declining only to talk about his friendship with the actor Heath Ledger, who had died a few weeks previously.

By the time of the second and much better Rave series, *The Dave Fanning Interview,* it was also possible for Ursula to work on the show with me, handling legal matters and most of the production duties. While in TV3 at the start of the Nineties, and all through her time in RTÉ working on Gerry Ryan's shows and *The Late Late Show*, Ursula was studying law. In 1997 she look leave of absence from RTÉ and, instead of going back, she became a lawyer with her own practice, specialising in the field of licensing, covering anything from late-night club extensions to Ireland's big one-day and three-day festivals. She does that to this day.

Rave TV were basically good guys and I got on well with their editorial and management team of Sal La Curto, Donna Wolfe and Dana Perri, but they could be very onerous to work with. As a high-definition TV channel, their production standards were necessarily so much higher than we were used to and their attention to detail was staggering.

I am no technical expert but I could handle the occasional email telling me that the EQ or the 5.1 surround was wrong in certain shots and needed tweaking. It got a bit much though when they were complaining that there wasn't enough makeup under my left eye and my shirt collar was awry during one question. They never seemed to twig that we didn't get five or six hours with these superstars to shoot to our hearts' content and it was more like guerrilla interviewing, snatching twenty minutes with them and filming on the hoof. Still, it was enjoyable, they were great people to work with, and I was sorry to see it go when the big cheese behind Rave sold the channel. Luckily, Ursula and I went on to form a good relationship with the Sky Arts channel in London.

The years roll by and while new bands and artists still excite me, and always will, sometimes you just go back to the heroes you worshipped of old. In 2008 two seminal figures in my musical development came to Dublin. Mel and I went to the Tripod to see Steve Winwood, whom I had loved when he was in Traffic – in my view, one of the greatest British bands of all time.

Winwood played three or four Traffic songs during a fine show and I decided on the spot that we HAD to go backstage and meet him and get a photo to mark this momentous night. Unfortunately, as I reached for my phone, complete with its camera, to explain the plan to Mel, I dropped it into my pint of Guinness, instantly rendering it totally useless, so we had to venture backstage armed only with Mel's phone. He had never used it as a camera and we had no idea how it worked.

Steve Winwood was very receptive and agreed to a photo after a short chat. I put my arm around the singer and Mel pointed the camera at us and, as far as I am aware, sent a text. He certainly didn't make anything flash. We swapped over, Mel put his arm around Steve and I pointed the phone ... and probably opened the draft-message folder. No photographic souvenirs for us, then.

The real big news came when Leonard Cohen came out of retirement to do a world tour. Cynics were calling it the Bankruptcy Tour because, after Cohen had gone up Mount Baldy in California to be a monk for five years, his accountant had been busy siphoning his money into his own account, leaving the ageing star no choice but to go back on the road.

Every cloud has a silver lining, because although I wouldn't wish embezzlement on anyone, it did mean Cohen was taking his peerless catalogue of songs on the road one more time. His show at Royal Kilmainham Hospital was just stunning and I loved it, which was pretty amazing because he didn't play even one of my Top 20 Leonard Cohen songs. Admittedly my favourites are all from his first three albums and he was concentrating on more recent material, but it's a testament to his genius that I went home on an absolute high and not feeling cheated.

I met an even bigger name than Cohen – arguably – in 2008 when Ursula and I were asked by the 3Ts (Turn the Tide on Suicide) – an Irish suicide awareness/prevention charity – to organise a musical interlude during a tenth anniversary dinner at Dublin Castle to honour some of the main players in Northern Ireland's Good Friday peace agreement. Geldof was bending my ear, and that of the British ambassador, with some rant or other when in walked Bertie Ahern together with Paul McGuinness, Bono and Tony Blair.

McGuinness introduced me to Blair, explaining to him who I was and finishing with a question aimed towards me: 'Did you know that Tony was once in a rock band?' I had indeed known that Blair had sung in a band at university, and even that they had taken their name from a phrase deliberately hidden on a Grateful Dead album sleeve, but this name temporarily escaped me.

'They were called Ugly Rumours,' said McGuinness, 'and Mark Ellen was in the band.' Ellen was a veteran British music journalist who, over the years, had presented the BBC's *Old Grey Whistle Test* and founded magazines including *Smash Hits*, *Q*, *Mojo* and *The Word*.

'Yes, Mark was my bass player,' confirmed Tony Blair. I had never met Ellen, but this was too good an opportunity to miss. 'Really?' I said, mock-surprised. 'He told me that you were his singer!' Blair laughed along, and also took it in good part when I told him that I had heard he had modelled his stage style on Mick Jagger.

'I did copy Jagger,' he freely confessed. 'I actually took the band really seriously. The problem was, I was the only one who did, so I always ended up humping all the gear before and after the gigs ...'

So there I stood, benignly watched by the Taoiseach, happily chatting away with the former British Prime Minister about rock bands. Life takes you to some very strange places. I couldn't help feeling that if Annie had had the chance to see me now, my mother would have got a good laugh out of this one – even though I can't imagine that she would have had the time of day for someone like Tony Blair.

15

In my thirty years at RTÉ, I have only once been profoundly disappointed by the broadcasting authorities' response to my work. This anomaly occurred in 2007, when an incident occurred which, to me, showed that while Ireland may be a thrusting, twenty-first-century democracy, one particular dominant strain – or should that be stain – in its society should have been left behind in the Middle Ages.

Ever since the mid-Noughties, I have reviewed TV programmes and movies on Marian Finucane's hugely popular weekend radio show on Radio 1. On April Fools Day 2007, fittingly, I went on Marian's programme to talk about *Deliver Us from Evil*, Amy Berg's searing, powerful documentary about Father Oliver O'Grady, a paedophile priest whose rapes of dozens of children in America in the Seventies were covered up by the Catholic Church. The Church had instead simply moved him from parish to parish, allowing O'Grady to continue his sick assaults.

When you see *Deliver Us from Evil*, the double standards of the Catholic Church are frightening. They not only knew about the priest's predilections; they actively protected him and in effect delivered unto him one bunch of vulnerable pre-teen victims after another. Watching the film, it was hard not to conclude that there was evil incarnate in the Church's actions, and in the very institution itself.

In my review of the documentary I really went to town, leaving Marian, I think, utterly taken aback. I laid into the profound corruption of the Church that this story had exposed, and didn't imagine for a moment that anybody could take issue with what I was saying. My review and my outrage came from the heart as I lambasted an organisation that, frankly, seemed to care only for its own self-preservation. I had prepared assiduously for my impassioned but measured outburst and I was proud of it. Naturally, I also mentioned that, over the years, I had met many wonderful Catholic priests, all of whom were let down not just by the despicable behaviour shown in *Deliver Us from Evil* but also by the horror that resides at the very core of the institution itself.

My review did not initially provoke too much reaction, and I am sure most people listening to Radio 1 on that Sunday lunchtime would have nodded in agreement. However, there were two complaints about my comments, one by a Catholic priest, Father Terry Toner, who objected to my use of the phrase 'evil incarnate' and further accused me of issuing slanderous statements and 'promoting hate for the Catholic Church'.

Peter Feeney, the head of information at RTÉ, was resolute in my defence when the Broadcasting Complaints Commission (BCC) asked for the station's response. He said that when I had used the phrase 'Hell is the Catholic Church' I was referring to the hell that O'Grady's victims were put through and the

Church's failure to address the situation, and argued that I was an established film reviewer who had given a powerful response to a very powerful movie.

Nevertheless, the BCC upheld the complaints. The standards body acknowledged that I had been shocked by *Deliver Us from Evil*, but went on to conclude:

> *However, having heard the broadcast item, the Commission is of the view that the opinions expressed by Mr. Fanning went beyond the bounds of his brief, namely the reviewing of a film. He made generalised comments and statements about the Catholic Church and the Pope in the course of the discussion which went largely unchallenged by the presenter. In the opinion of the Commission, Mr. Fanning was permitted to air opinion outside of his remit as a film reviewer and was not sufficiently challenged on this occasion. The broadcast treated the subject matter unfairly.*

I could only wonder if anybody on the Commission had actually seen the documentary. A week later, when I was at the Oxegen festival watching Muse and Snow Patrol, RTÉ read out an apology for my review. The station had its hands tied by the BCC ruling and was legally bound to do so, but it still rankled enormously with me and it does to this day. I just wonder if the BCC would have taken the same standpoint if it had known what has since come out about paedophile priests within the Catholic Church.

In 2009, the Ryan Report found that beatings, rape and sexual molestation were endemic for decades at as many as two hundred and fifty Catholic-run Irish schools and orphanages. More than thirty thousand orphans and other at-risk children were delivered to possible abuse by a significant number of predatory priests and clergy. In the light of this, does the phrase 'evil incarnate' really sound so extreme and unfounded?

Even outside of the paedophile scandals, the influence that the Catholic Church continues to hold over so many people in their day-to-day lives in my country baffles me. Thankfully, things are not as bad as they were. As I was growing up in the Sixties, THE paramount and controlling influence in Ireland was religion, and the Church's tentacles extended through every inch of society in this devout so-called Land of Saints and Scholars.

In school we were all taught about a vengeful God, seemingly bereft of love, who would chuck his fiery wrath down upon our heads were we to question any of his deeds or commandments. At least those days are gone. Jack, Robert and Hayley have not – unlike me – had to learn the Catechism by rote in junior school. They have not been caned if they innocently got confused and harmlessly transposed two words.

Obviously, I know that religion can be a crutch for some people in times of need. Her faith helped my mother to come through the loss of my father and lead a happy and productive life for more than fifteen years after his death, and I respect that. It was for Annie that Ursula and I had Jack and Robert baptised while she was alive.

Yet, to be frank, the more I think about organised religion as a concept in the modern world, the more preposterous it seems. I don't try and force my atheism down my children's throats, it is entirely up to them what they decide to believe, but when I see people such as George W. Bush invoking God to justify his invasion of Iraq, it merely increases my antipathy.

Religious people who take issue with me ask: so how do you explain life? Well, Charles Darwin did a pretty thorough job on that one. Here is what I think: we don't go to Heaven after we die; there is no afterlife; there is no God. Genuinely, I would no more believe in God than I would in the existence of James Stewart's six-foot-tall phantom rabbit best friend in the 1950 film *Harvey*. Decent movie, by the way.

It is inexplicable to me that as we head into the second decade of the twenty-first century, people are still living their lives by the Bible, a collection of myths and superstitions that were assembled in the days before science and reason. In 2008, our Minister for Justice, Dermot Ahern (ironically, the same man who claimed that he came to my house as a student to listen to Pink Floyd!) decided that in the midst of a global recession, and the collapse of the Celtic Tiger economy, the pressing priority for Ireland was to rewrite the blasphemy laws. It seems he had no choice. Successive governments had been advised to reform the law on blasphemy, the only alternative to legislation would be a referendum – which, of course, no one wanted. The 1961 Defamation Act provides that a person can be both fined and imprisoned for a maximum of seven years for the crime of blasphemous libel. To me it all sounded like 1608, not 2008.

Even my mother, a truly intelligent and devout woman, knew that the clergymen were often flawed. She once told me tales of priests on a mission in Carlow when she was a young girl who tried it on with some relation of hers. Annie was not in denial, but she never allowed these men's human failings to interfere with her belief in God. I am glad that Catholicism helped her through her dark days, and I still talk to her in my head sometimes. This doesn't mean that I believe in any kind of afterlife: it is just a comfort for me to remember the woman that I loved. I know she is no longer there and I don't need a 'God' to act as a conduit to her.

There was a time when Annie would have loved one of her children to become a priest, but none of us showed the slightest interest. Yet – and, I promise, here endeth my sermon – she would be pleased that we all live according to the basic, decent tenet that undercuts all religions: do unto others as you would have them do unto you. If you follow that rule every day, you won't go too far wrong.

I didn't embrace my mother's religion but I hope I inherited a lot of my parents' values. As the father of three children, every day I do my best to be a good dad to them. When they are first growing up, you have this urge to wrap them in cotton wool, but then you realise you have to let them find their own way. You have to let them grow and hope for the best.

It's always tempting to spoil your kids and I know at times we have been as guilty as anybody else. There was one Christmas in the Celtic Tigers years where Ursula and I sat trying to work out what presents we should buy, and we realised the problem was that they already had every electronic toy we could think of. If you have a little money, it's hard not to indulge them.

There is a saying – yet another of these true clichés! – that we all turn into our parents eventually. In my case, I don't think that would be a bad thing. I remember seeing some cheesy medical ad on American TV where a guy was watching his father play with his kid, and he said, 'I never thought I would turn into my father – now I aspire to be like him.' In truth, I never aspired to be like my father, but I really liked him.

The men of my generation are typically much more involved with their kids than in the previous generation. Barney was incredibly laid-back and left us to do whatever we wanted, within reason. Maybe that is the best way. All you can do is try to keep your kids on the straight and narrow and help them along. And at least Jack, Robert and Hayley will never have to beg me to let them watch *Christmas Top of the Pops*!

None of my children seem to have inherited my total obsession with music. Hayley likes the Beatles and Michael Jackson. Jack and Robert have iPods, but though they use them regularly they are not glued to them in the way I was surgically attached to the record player in Foster Avenue when I was their age. My music gene has not been passed on, although Jack is a movie fanatic.

The important thing is that they are three cool kids and all seem happy. Jack and Robert are at the age where they want to be seriously independent and, particularly in the summer, are happier doing their own thing most of the time. That's OK: it's just all part of growing up. Hayley is still at the age where she loves being with Mum and Dad, and hanging out with her is brilliant. We make the most of it. And when we're both working, the world's greatest nanny, Karen Coyle from Four Roads in Roscommon, has kept it all together for over a decade.

Work-wise, my life is good. There is, though, a sense of existential horror attached to being an ageing DJ, a whispering voice in your head that asks if it's dignified to be making your living playing rock 'n' roll records when you're just half a decade away from being 60. Nobody ever tells an estate agent or a banker they should have grown out of their job, but in my line of work, it's different.

I guess there is a little nagging voice that asks, when did I get to be the old guy? Has there been some kind of mistake? For more than ten years on my 2FM show Jim Lockhart was the producer, and one day I said to him, about some band or other, 'Jeez, they're a lot younger than us.' He laughed and said, 'Dave – everyone is younger than us!'

These days I work with younger producers but Ian Wilson still sits at the same desk, still producing, still booking bands for sessions and recording festival performances. Turning 50 was a sobering moment, no doubt about it. Nobody likes getting old, especially in a calling like mine that is all based around youth culture. Having said that, most daily radio shows that I've presented since the Millennium have been 'talk radio' rather than music-based.

In truth, I don't worry about age all that much, partly because there's no point, but mainly because I am having such a good time. My job would be ridiculous if I were just going through the motions and had lost my love for new music, but it is still a thrill to open my post and get new releases. If that ever goes, I will call it a day, but it is showing no signs of fading so far.

Some people might think I have had a charmed life, and I can see why. I got my lucky break, when *Scene* and Radio Dublin came calling back in the punk days, by being in the right place at the right time, and since then I've hung in there by working hard and being crazily enthusiastic. I haven't dropped the ball and it's been more of a buzz than any job has the right to be.

In more than thirty years, I have never missed a day at work just because I couldn't face going in. When it comes to my job, I feel like I've won the Lotto and have kept on winning it. It worries me sometimes that my kids might see how much I love what I do and assume that the world of work will be the same for them. I feel like saying, no, your dad has just been very lucky.

Of course, the music world has changed hugely in recent years. Today, all music is instantly available at the click of a button. This is a good thing in a way, but part of me fears that when something comes that quickly and easily it loses, if not some of its power, then some of its lustre. When I was a kid I had to really search and fight to hear the music I loved, and that made it seem even more important. And except for the radio, none of it was free.

As well as my 2FM programme, for the first decade of this century I have presented a late-night TV show called *The Eleventh Hour* (previously *The Last Broadcast*), a magazine show with a wide brief that could easily feature Bob Dylan, Kylie Minogue and Eminem on the same edition. It's pretty varied and I'm the glue that holds it together: my kind of show. It's the twenty-fifth year in a row that I have done a TV programme for RTÉ, and that seems pretty good to me.

Nothing goes on forever and even the brightest career in the public eye can be extinguished quickly. I was shaken to the core by the tragic death of Gerry Ryan – a man who had been by my side all through my career, whom I had holidayed and lived with, who always seemed so much larger than life. He did a lot to carry this country's media kicking and screaming into the twenty-first century and, like many people, I will never forget him.

Gerry, a friend and ally from the first day I met him on the Big D, was a rogue, and if you think that sounds like a euphemism for anything and everything, you're right. He never acted as though he was to the manor born, as the saying goes, but if an opportunity arose to take things to the next level, he always took it. When Gerry, Morah, Ursula and I holidayed in Disneyland in Florida with our kids, Gerry pointed to a gigantic towering hotel. 'Donald Trump stays there,' he said. 'That's where we'll stay next year.'

Total mischief and massive intelligence were always in the mix. He told great stories and bluffed his way through a thousand supposedly true tales that were so entertaining that you never felt like correcting or interrupting him. Anyway, you were too busy laughing. It's another of those clichés to call Gerry Ryan larger than life, but he certainly was.

I'm incredibly proud that my two best friends in the world are still the same two people I used to hang out with in my schooldays. In 2008, Mel, Jerry and I hooked up and did a short road trip from Los Angeles to Las Vegas. I had been there two months earlier for a TV travel show (where at one stage I had to report from the Grand Canyon Skywalk, which sits 4,000 feet above the Colorado River) and went back to see Cirque de Soleil's Beatles-based *Love* show at the Mirage Hotel.

Jerry lives out in the wilds of Oregon now and has a big pickup, so he did all the driving. It was a great trip because in a way none of us have changed. Mel is maybe a tad more cynical and Jerry has gone a bit New Age, but our banter hasn't changed and in some ways it was just the same as it used to be when we were hanging out in Foster Avenue. Well, except for the bikini-clad women in Vegas bringing us exotic drinks by the pool. We never used to have that.

I guess to many people my career has been partly defined by my escapades with U2, and the band's promotional circus was up and running again in 2009 for the release of the *No Line on the Horizon* album. Ever since I asked Radio 2 listeners to choose U2's first ever single back in 1979, Paul McGuinness has always insisted that I get the worldwide preview of all of the band's singles, and this was to be no exception.

The first single off the album was to be 'Get on Your Boots' and I could play it at ten past eight in the morning, with the rest of the world getting it at 8.30 on the dot. Radio 1's *Morning Ireland* programme wanted to broadcast the song, but their producer correctly pointed out that if a major news story happened to explode at precisely 8.10 they could hardly ignore it while they played a rock record, so we played the single on Colm and Jim's breakfast show on 2FM instead.

Shortly afterwards, U2 went to Washington to play at President Obama's inauguration along with Springsteen, Stevie Wonder and Beyoncé. I watched it on TV, and just as Obama was putting his hand on the Bible, I got a phone call from U2's office inviting me to a playback of the album with the band and a few other people at Bono's house a few days later.

It was nice to get the invitation but the date clashed with a party I was going to for our friend Caroline Henry, who

Dónde está el baño
Gracias

worked with the Corrs, so I said I'd have to decline. With the excitement of the Obama inauguration I guess the message never got passed on, because the following Saturday I was at Caroline's party when the phone calls started coming in from Bono.

Apparently Edge and Bono, Jim Sheridan, Neil Jordan and a few others were all at the house and Bono was refusing to start the playback until the band's lucky charm, Fanning, was there. When the Edge called me to insist, I figured I had better head up there, and Ursula and I got a taxi for the mile-and-a-half journey.

When we got there we sat at the top of the table with Bono as he blasted *No Line on the Horizon* so loud that we could only just hear each other speak. It had been a long, long time since we had sat listening to 'Out of Control' in 1979 and we took a trip down memory lane. We reminisced about the band's first two albums, both of which they had played to me as they were being recorded in Windmill Lane.

We remembered *War*, U2's third album, and how my first listen had been on a small tour bus as we travelled for five gigs from Cork to Galway to Belfast before finishing with two at Dublin's SFX. Then there had been *The Unforgettable Fire*, which Paul McGuinness had sent me some months before its release, and *The Joshua Tree*, for which I had interviewed them on the video set for 'With or Without You'.

For *Rattle and Hum*, of course, I had sat with Adam as he drove through the Hollywood Hills en route to the Vietnamese restaurant, and they had played me Achtung Baby in two halves in Dublin. *Zooropa*? Well, I had met Edge by chance as we both stopped at traffic lights at 1 a.m. and he had invited me back to his house to listen.

We recalled how Ursula, Ali, Adam and I had sat in Bono's house twelve years earlier as Bono sang along to *Pop*, explained each track and showed us the ambitious plans for the Popmart tour. I had seen the big yellow arches and told him they'd get sued by McDonald's. Now, here we were again, back in the same spot, as Bono sang along with himself and tried to decide which tracks would make it onto the 360° tour. Yes, it had been a long, long time since 'Out of Control', but the principle and the main question hadn't changed: here is our new music; do you like it?

The band I am most closely associated with will always be U2, and the first band I ever loved and still love the most is the Beatles, but when it comes to a solo artist, it is all about Bob Dylan. When my brother Peter used to insist on playing him on the family record player when I was a boy, I didn't think I liked his music, but with hindsight I think Bob got under my skin then and has been there ever since.

I have never met him outside of that round-robin interview a few years ago, but every time Dylan has played in Dublin, I have been to see him. It would be rude not to. I don't always like the way he deconstructs the songs and tears them to bits until they are hardly recognisable, but I go, more in hope than expectation, because it is still Dylan up there.

In 2009 he came to play the O2, and I took Jack along because I figured since he'd seen Paul McCartney when he was eight or nine, it was time he came to see another musician who has excited and fascinated his dad for the best part of forty years.

Bono, Ali and their friend Guggi were sitting a few rows in front of us, but didn't spot us until towards the end of the concert.

As they made their way up the stairs towards the exit, Bono saw us in the dark and came to say hello. He asked me if I wanted to go with them, I presumed to get something to eat, but I told him I was with Jack and that, since we were recording the Champions League semi-final at home between Chelsea and Barcelona, we would give it a miss.

When Jack and I got home, we found that one of the worst referees in the history of football had ensured Chelsea were robbed of a place in the final. To make matters worse, the next time I saw Guggi, he told me that Bono and Ali had been inviting me that night to go backstage with them, where they had arranged to meet Dylan. He said Bob had been in tremendous form, and they had talked and laughed into the night.

The Thing Is ... that is probably the biggest regret to date of my life spent living for music. Thankfully, there have been very, very few.